THE UNITED STATES AND
SIX ATLANTIC OUTPOSTS

Kennikat Press
National University Publications
Series in American Studies

EDWARD W. CHESTER

THE UNITED STATES AND SIX ATLANTIC OUTPOSTS
The Military and Economic Considerations

National University Publications
KENNIKAT PRESS // 1980
Port Washington, N. Y. // London

0885858

110304

Manufactured in the United States of America

Published by
Kennikat Press Corp.
Port Washington, N.Y. // London

Library of Congress Cataloging in Publication Data

Chester, Edward W
    The United States and six Atlantic outposts.

    (National university publications)
    Bibliography: p.
    Includes index.
    1. United States—Relations (military) with foreign
countries. 2. United States—Foreign economic relations.
3. Islands of the Atlantic—History. I. Title.
E744.C467   355.03'30182'1   79-12046
ISBN 0-8046-9236-X

CONTENTS

ACKNOWLEDGMENTS vii

PREFACE ix

1. INTRODUCTION: The Destroyers for Bases Deal 3

2. THE BAHAMAS: Columbus's Splendid Discovery 14

3. JAMAICA: Land of Wood and Water 48

4. BERMUDA: Prospero's Magic Island 85

5. ICELAND: Land of Ice and Fire 120

6. THE AZORES: The Hesperides' Golden Apples 154

7. GREENLAND: The Home of the Weather 184

8. CONCLUSION: A Pattern of Diversity 216

NOTES 227

BIBLIOGRAPHICAL ESSAY 246

INDEX 254

ACKNOWLEDGMENTS

Among those individuals to whom the author is the most indebted are those who have read critically various chapters of this manuscript, although he assumes full responsibility for the final version. These are: for the Azores—J. K. Sweeney, Leo Pap, Ronald H. Chilcote, Charles R. Halstead, and R. J. Houk; for the Bahamas—Harry Kline, Peter J. Barratt, Zoé C. Durrell, and D. Gail Saunders; for Bermuda—Sister Jean Kennedy and Frank Vandiver; for Greenland—H. Peter Krosby and Finn Gad; for Iceland—Franklin D. Scott and Donald E. Nuechterlein; for Jamaica—Wendell Bell, Ransford Palmer, and Gisela Eisner; conclusion—David DeBoe. The Portuguese and Iceland embassies also have checked portions of the manuscript for errors, while Harold J. Sutphen has most graciously consented to the quoting of several passages from his doctoral dissertation.

Other persons have contributed to this work in a number of different ways, including bibliographical assistance, personal contacts, personal recollections, and the furnishing of material. Of these the most helpful have been:

for the Azores—Hyman Bloom, Angelo Cerchione, Francis M. Rogers, Carlos Lameiro, Douglas L. Wheeler, John B. Jensen, Steven S. Ussach, Álvaro Monjardino, James Duffy, Henry H. Keith, Pamela McNulty, Manuel Coelho Baptista de Lima, Joao Afonso, and the Portuguese Continental Union

for Greenland—Angier Biddle Duke, William McC. Blair, Jr., Katherine E. White, Robert Coe, Harrison M. Ward, Jr., William T. Crocker, Carlo Christensen, Ingrid Baklev, Donald V. Eversoll, and Inge Winkelmann;

for Iceland—Luther I. Replogle, Tyler Thompson, Marshall F. Thayer, Hördur Helgason, Benedikt Gröndal, Dave Zinkoff, D. R. Aggers, George E. McGrath, C. Robert Dickermann, and the Central Bank of Iceland

for Greenland and Iceland—H. G. R. King. A. G. Ronhovde, Gene G. Gage, and Peter V. Curl

for the British West Indies—Marcus A. McCorison, R. R. Mellor, Woodville K. Marshall, Cedric Joseph, F. A. Baptiste

for the Bahamas—A. L. Cambridge, Robert A. Fliegel, Public Record Office/Archives Section/Ministry of Education and Culture

for Bermuda—Carol Tully, Sue K. Smith, Donald B. McCue, Hans W. Hannau, Cecelia A. Latimer, F. Van Wyck Mason, Kenneth L. Geitz, David L. White, Mrs. Terry Tucker, Mrs. Hugh Skeffington, Roger Willock

for Jamaica—Walter N. Tobriner, William P. Kelly, Richard S. Eisley, Ainsley Elliot, Cynthia Humes, Rosalie Williams, Steve H. Evans, Martin Mordecai, Olive Senior, James C. Palmer, Carol S. Holzberg, Mrs. D. A. Jones, Mrs. Joyce L. Robinson, Ministry of Labour and Employment, Jamaica Industrial Development Corporation.

In addition, the following research collections have made their facilities available: the Naval History Division at the Navy Yard in Washington, D.C. (D. C. Allard); the Naval Aviation Office in Arlington, Virginia; the Maxwell Air Force Base in Montgomery, Alabama (Gloria L. Atkinson); the National Archives and Records Service in Washington, D.C. (Milton O. Gustafson). Among the other military personnel who have assisted the author are George S. Pappas, Fred Souk, Anna C. Urband, and John B. Taylor. Portions of this manuscript also have been read at the second annual meeting of the Caribbean Studies Association at St. Lucia (1976), the first Conference on War and Diplomacy at the Citadel in Charleston, South Carolina (1976), the twentieth annual meeting of the Missouri Valley History Conference at Omaha (1977), the eighteenth annual convention of the International Studies Association at St. Louis (1977), the eighth annual meeting of the Society for Spanish and Portuguese Historical Studies at Lexington, Kentucky (1977), the nineteenth annual conference of the Western Social Science Association at Denver (1977), and the first Third World Conference at Omaha (1977).

PREFACE

In his novel *The Bridge of San Luis Rey* Thornton Wilder tells how a bridge in Peru collapsed in 1714, sending five travellers to their death. This quite unexpected tragedy led one Brother Juniper to make an inquiry into whether there was some pattern in the lives of these quite dissimilar individuals which may have brought them to a common fate. Similarly, in the case of Greenland, Iceland, the Azores, Bermuda, Jamaica, and the Bahamas, each island or island group had a shared experience during and after World War 2: the American military presence, once directed against the Nazis, now set up as a defense against the Communists. But unlike Wilder's travellers, none of whom perhaps had ever crossed that bridge previously, these six Atlantic island states had entered into a wide variety of relations with the United States in the past, and have continued to do so since World War 2, with the economic contacts being as worthy of study as the military ones.

Although the Bahamas, Jamaica, and Bermuda have been parts of the British colonial system rather than of the American one, economic realities if allowed to prevail would have dictated the latter linkage. Americans long have played a key role in the tourist industry of both the Bahamas and Bermuda, the main source of income to each island state. In addition, the United States has shown a continuing interest in Jamaican exports over the years, whether these have been bananas or bauxite. The American economic presence has been perhaps less obvious in the case of the three non-British islands, but the United States has been a leading importer of cryolite from Greenland and fish from Iceland. In the case of the Azores, the most pronounced American economic impact has been through the military base, the counterparts of which have likewise stimulated the economies of the other five nations. It is true that in terms of total dollars and cents the United States contributes more to the economy of a major power like Japan than it does to that of such island states as the Bahamas and Bermuda, but this should not obscure the fact that relatively speaking the American economic impact on the latter has been of far greater consequence.

In attempting to trace these military and economic relations, the author not only has examined the pertinent books and articles, both contemporary and retrospective, but has also delved into the *New York Times, The Times* of London, the National Archives, naval and air force archives, the *Foreign Relations* series, other published governmental documents, and the *Congressional Record.* He also has been in correspondence with approximately one hundred individuals both here and abroad, who have furnished him with a wide variety of information relative to this project. The result of his labors is an extensive narrative which necessarily touches on several areas other than the economic and military, but which does not cover the activities of island immigrants in the United States. (Other writers have already analyzed the latter topic at considerable length.)

In this volume the author will first examine the three British nations as a group after analyzing the destroyers-for-bases deal in the introduction, and then will survey the three non-British countries as a unit. The treatment will be chronological, but at times there will be a topical approach which it is hoped will result in a clearer exposition of the data. Rather than divide the material comprising each chapter into broad pre–World War 2, World War 2, and post–World War 2 groupings, the author will employ smaller but more cohesive units, numbered up to fifteen per chapter. In the case of each nation, he will set the stage with some background data and then refer to the history of the island intermittently where appropriate, since few if any readers have an in-depth knowledge of all six countries.

The point of departure for this work, of course, is the series of bases which the United States set up in certain colonies during World War 2 in the aftermath of the destroyers deal. Nevertheless, the mass of information which the author has assembled relative to American relations in general with Greenland, Iceland, the Azores, Bermuda, Jamaica, and the Bahamas over the entire course of U.S. history enables one also to make an attempt at judging the validity of the so-called "cocacolization" thesis. Did or did not the growing American military and economic presence throughout the years literally overwhelm this group of a half-dozen nations, causing them to become nearly identical satellites of an at times imperialistic United States? To the author, the correct answer is probably no, as he will attempt to explain in the conclusion.

THE UNITED STATES AND SIX ATLANTIC OUTPOSTS

ABOUT THE AUTHOR

Dr. Edward W. Chester is an Associate Professor of History at the University of Texas at Arlington. He has been the recipient of several grants and has read many papers at scholarly conventions. His special interest in the field of diplomatic history has been U. S. relations with the Third World. Aside from the present volume, he published a book on American relations with Africa in 1974, and is currently writing the most comprehensive study of U. S. oil policy and diplomacy during the Twentieth Century.

1

INTRODUCTION
The Destroyers for Bases Deal

The islands of the North Atlantic, stretching from Greenland near the North Pole to the Lesser Antilles close to the equator, have long attracted the attention of the American government and of private U.S. individuals and groups: fishermen, merchants, investors, tourists, scientists, and others. Prior to the American Civil War the slaveholding South cast a covetous eye on the Spanish colony of Cuba, but looked with scorn and even fear upon the black republic of Haiti. Following the termination of that conflict Secretary of State William Henry Seward undertook an abortive campaign to get the United States to annex the Dominican Republic and the Danish West Indies (Virgin Islands). Although Congress purchased Alaska from Russia at this time, the American public was rather lukewarm to Seward's expansionist designs; the U.S. military was much more enthusiastic about the possibility of acquiring these Atlantic islands.

Unlike the United States, during the nineteenth century Great Britain enjoyed territorial footholds in the Caribbean and the West Indies, as well as maintained the largest navy in the entire world. The legal focal point of Anglo-American relations in the Caribbean was the Clayton-Bulwer Treaty of 1850, which defused transit concessions across the Central American isthmus as a possible cause of war. The British (as well as the French) had designs on Cuba prior to the American Civil War, but never obtained either this island, Texas, or the Yucatan Peninsula. Great Britain, however, was in a position to evade the Monroe Doctrine because of its superior navy, and it did seize the Falkland Islands off Argentina, as well as expand in the Belize area of Central America.

3

With the Suez Canal now a reality, in 1878 Ferdinand de Lesseps and his French company obtained a concession from Colombia to build a canal across Panama. The reaction of President Rutherford Hayes was to call for a canal under American control, and President James Garfield later followed suit. Garfield's secretary of state, James G. Blaine, sought a modification of the Clayton-Bulwer Treaty; then, with Chester A. Arthur president, Secretary of State Frederick Frelinghuysen negotiated a treaty with Nicaragua granting canal rights to the United States. (This was withdrawn from senatorial consideration after the inauguration of Grover Cleveland as president.) The French company proceeded with its operations in Panama, only to collapse in 1888.

By the end of the nineteenth century the United States was confronted with a choice: either construct a two-ocean navy of the first rank or build an isthmian canal. (The construction of the modern American navy had begun under President Arthur.) During the 1890s Alfred T. Mahan pointed out that the United States would have to assume a dominant naval role in the eastern Pacific and the Caribbean Basin to safeguard such a canal; to build such an isthmian waterway prior to enlarging its navy would be to court disaster.

During the presidency of Benjamin Harrison the United States unsuccessfully sought naval bases at Môle St. Nicholas in Haiti and at Samana Bay in Santo Domingo. But when the Danish government proposed to sell St. Thomas and St. John to the Americans, Secretary Blaine—who minimized their strategic importance—was unenthusiastic about their immediate acquisition. His successor, John Foster, expressed more interest in purchasing the Danish Virgin Islands, but by this time the Harrison presidency was nearing its close, so that no action was taken. While there were some prominent Americans—Carl Schurz is one example—who opposed United States expansion into the Caribbean, the acquisition of islands and bases there was favored by Theodore Roosevelt, Henry Cabot Lodge, and Mahan. The latter regarded Cuba, Samana Bay, and St. Thomas as being of great strategic importance.

Although the United States wished to build up its navy to the point where it would be competitive with that of Great Britain, by the turn of the twentieth century Americans were beginning also to manifest an increasing unease at the possible role which the German navy might play in the Caribbean. There already had been friction between the two nations over faraway Samoa in the Pacific. It is true that German and Swedish interests in the Danish West Indies did attempt to develop Charlotte Amalie into a commercial coaling port, but the Germans had no colonies either in the Caribbean Basin or on the mainland of Latin

America. The fears of President Theodore Roosevelt and others were nevertheless magnified by the additional American burden of defending the Panama Canal, built between 1907 and 1914 after Panama had obtained its independence from Colombia with the blessing of T.R.

As a result of the Spanish-American War, the United States acquired Puerto Rico from Spain. Eighteen years later, in 1916, the United States signed a treaty with Denmark transferring the present-day Virgin Islands to America. Cuba was not annexed in 1898, but it was made a quasi-protectorate of the United States under the Platt Amendment from 1901 to 1934. In fact, there was an American military occupation of Cuba between 1898 and 1902, and between 1906 and 1909; the United States landed troops in Haiti in 1915 (where they remained until 1934), and in the Dominican Republic in 1916 (where they stayed until 1924). Earlier, under the so-called Roosevelt Corollary to the Monroe Doctrine, President Theodore Roosevelt had taken over the revenue-producing customs houses of the Dominican Republic in 1904 to prevent the possible intervention of impatient European creditors, thus establishing an important precedent.

Less publicized has been the attention paid by the United States to the major British North Atlantic island possessions—Bermuda, the Bahamas, and Jamaica—and the various British holdings in the Lesser Antilles, among them Trinidad, St. Lucia, and Antigua. One of the first Americans to express an interest in the annexation of some or all of these British colonies was General George McClellan, who retrospectively observed in *Harper's* magazine in 1886 with respect to the Civil War that "if Bermuda and Nassau had been in our possession, the contest would have been shortened some two years, for blockade running would have been well-nigh impossible."[1] A dozen years later, at the time of the Spanish-American War, expansionist Republican Senator Henry Cabot Lodge of Massachusetts suggested that the United States might swap the Philippines (possibly minus Luzon) to Great Britain for the Bahamas and Jamaica. Then in 1917 Rear Admiral A. P. Niblack, the commander of the U.S. Atlantic Fleet, came out for the American government acquiring Jamaica, the Bahamas, and Bermuda, and the General Board followed suit in January 1918.

It was not until after 1918, however, that American interest in acquiring the British islands of the North Atlantic became more widespread. At this time there was a growing impatience in the United States at the failure of Great Britain to pay off its World War 1 debt more speedily; some Americans favored payment via the transfer of certain British colonies. Among the senatorial advocates of the latter approach was Democratic Senator James Reed of Missouri, who recommended that America obtain Bermuda and the British West Indies (including Trinidad).

Other members of Congress aside from Reed who were annexationists included Republican Senator Frank Willis of Ohio, who literally wished to grab up everything in sight, and Republican senators Albert J. Beveridge of Indiana and William Kenyon of Iowa, who focused their attention on Bermuda.[2] Still another prominent American to support the acquisition of the entire British West Indies was former Secretary of the Treasury William Gibbs McAdoo. But the sentiment in favor of a transfer of these colonial possessions of Great Britain was by no means universal. Thus, the London *Daily Telegraph* commented on March 8, 1920, that "we believe this suggestion was first made in a London newspaper, but without receiving the slightest support in this country, while the reception given to it in the West Indies themselves was hostile in the highest degree."[3] It was at Port-of-Spain, Trinidad, moreover, that the Prince of Wales made a speech the same year in which he observed that British subjects were not for sale. Back in the United States, on February 15, 1921, the *New York Times* pointed out that in contrast to a hundred or even fifty years ago, it was now necessary to ask the people of the islands themselves whether they would consent to such a transfer. "We have an idea," observed the *Times,* "that the people of these islands might prefer to remain Britons. . . ."[4]

During the inter-war decades the question of the American acquisition of the British West Indies seems to have been a continual obsession of the Kingston, Jamaica *Daily Gleaner.* Thus, on July 10, 1933, in an editorial entitled "Not for Sale" this newspaper sarcastically observed: "The British West Indies prefer to remain within the Empire [rather] than to share the fate of the Virgin Islands, whose inhabitants are in the welter of poverty."[5] Nevertheless, the *Daily Gleaner* harangues to the contrary, the American consul, William W. Corcoran, was by no means convinced that the inhabitants of the island felt the same way. To quote Corcoran, "There is a decided feeling among certain elements of the Jamaican population, especially among persons high in the island's commercial and professional life, favoring American acquisition."[6] The absence of scientific polls of the Gallup type at this time unfortunately made any measurement of public opinion a highly speculative process, in either Jamaica or any other of the British Atlantic island possessions.

Shortly after the outbreak of World War 2 in Europe, there was set up in the United States an organization known as the Make Europe Pay War Debts Committee, of which Farmer-Labor Senator Ernest Lundeen of Minnesota was chairman; its objective was the acquisition of the

British and French West Indies in partial payment. The vice chairmen included Democratic Representatives Martin Sweeney of Ohio and Jennings Randolph of West Virginia, Republican Senator Smith Brookhart of Iowa, and Democratic Governor Edward Carville of Nevada. Among the other members were Mayor Thomas Holling of Buffalo, General Smedley Butler, ex-Consul General T. St. John Gaffney, and editor Michael O'Reilly of the *Gaelic American.* All parties and ideologies thus participated in this grand coalition of Democrats, Republicans, Farmer-Laborites, Non-Partisan Leaguers, and independents.

As the war in Europe grew to epic proportions, hemispheric defense became an increasing concern to America, and the payment of the war debts a matter of lesser importance. Although the British desired more military equipment with which to defend their besieged island, the government in London also was concerned with the backward condition of the West Indies islands at this time. Shortly after the outbreak of hostilities in Europe, the West India Royal Commission released a report in which it proposed a program for upgrading living conditions there, at a total estimated cost of £1 million annually for twenty years; among other things, this document advocated new directions for agriculture, improved labor conditions, slum clearance, land resettlement, more schools, and improved health services. In this connection, *U.S. News* observed on January 24, 1941, that "if the territories became possessions of the United States, these problems would be transferred from London to Washington. Prospects are that they also would add to domestic problems."[7] This magazine article then went on to compare the backward state of the British West Indies with that of the American Virgin Islands and Puerto Rico.

Significantly, President Franklin D. Roosevelt was well acquainted with the British island possessions of the Atlantic. To quote Cordell Hull, ". . . he had an amazing personal knowledge of almost all of them. He had either cruised, swum, or fished in those harbors. He knew how many feet deep and wide they were and how many ships they would take. He also knew the penurious condition of the native populations of most of the islands, and consequently did not want to assume the burden of administering those populations."[8] It was this intimate knowledge that turned F.D.R. away from his original desire to purchase these islands outright; instead, he proceeded with the destroyers-for-bases deal.

On May 14, 1940, Paul Reynaud, the French premier, suggested that the United States might sell or loan his government some of its destroyers, while Winston Churchill, his British counterpart, made a similar inquiry on the following day. Later that month the British ambassador to the United States, Lord Lothian, recommended that Great Britain lease base areas in Bermuda, Newfoundland, and Trinidad to the American government, but the British cabinet rejected this proposal, complaining that the United States had yet to turn some of its destroyers over to the British navy. But conditions on the Continent from the military standpoint were worsening; on June 22, 1940, a defeated France signed an armistice with Hitlerian Germany. It was only six days later that Congress passed the administration-backed National Defense Act, which made possible the sale to foreign governments of naval and military equipment which was not essential to national defense, provided that the transfer had the approval of either the chief of Naval Operations or the chief of staff of the Army.

With the way now cleared for action, the New York branch of the Committee to Defend America by Aiding the Allies, known as the Century Group, proposed a destroyers-for-bases transfer. By late July the British cabinet had reversed its earlier position, thanks in part to German military victories on the Continent, and was now willing to offer base rights to America without any quid pro quo; on July 31 Prime Minister Churchill issued a personal plea to President Roosevelt for fifty or sixty destroyers. At a U.S. cabinet meeting held on August 2, the main concern appears to have been that in the event of defeat the British navy would not fall into the hands of the Germans. Legal objections were raised by Green H. Hackworth of the State Department, who pointed out that section 33, title 18, of the United States Code "provides that during a war in which the United States is neutral it shall be unlawful to send any vessel built, armed, and equipped as a vessel of war . . . with reasonable cause to believe that the said vessel shall or will be employed in the service of any . . . belligerent nation after its departure from the jurisdiction of the United States."[9]

Such objections to the contrary, Franklin Roosevelt wrote Winston Churchill on August 13, informing the latter that America would make available to England at least fifty destroyers. On this occasion he demanded that these never would be turned over to the Germans or sunk, and that Great Britain in return would authorize the use by the United States as naval and air bases of eight colonies stretching from Newfoundland in the North to British Guiana in the South. Two days later Churchill accepted F.D.R.'s proposals, on the condition that the destroyers be delivered immediately; as for the British fleet, he proclaimed: "We intend to fight this out here to the end and none of us would ever buy peace by surrendering or scuttling (it)."[10]

On August 20, though, the British Prime Minister made a speech in which he offered the outright gift of bases to the United States without even mentioning the destroyers, since he had come around to the position that the American and British publics would receive a mutual exchange of presents with greater enthusiasm than a quid pro quo. Two days later Churchill, moreover, informed the President that the British cabinet had already decided to make a gift of the Atlantic naval and air facilities to the United States with no strings attached,[11] but on August 25 he declared: "We should not however be justified in the circumstances if we gave a blank cheque on the whole of our transatlantic possessions merely to bridge this gap through which anyhow we hope to make our way through with added risk and suffering."[12] Almost totally critical was Lord Beaverbrook, the British minister for aircraft production, who looked upon the destroyers-for-bases deal as a bad bargain.

Although the ambassador to Great Britain, Joseph Kennedy, had written F.D.R. on August 15 that he was still worried about the fate of the British fleet in light of the French experience, negotiations with Great Britain nevertheless proceeded to a successful conclusion. On August 26 the Department of State suggested that the transfer of Newfoundland and Bermuda sites take the form of gifts, while the Caribbean ones go in exchange for the destroyers; Green H. Hackworth had earlier made such a proposal to Secretary of State Cordell Hull. Antigua was now added to the list of Caribbean bases by Churchill himself voluntarily, and the general locations for the various base sites were spelled out.[13] Attorney General Robert Jackson by this time had placed his stamp of approval upon the destroyers-for-bases transaction, on the grounds that the President acting in his capacity as commander in chief of the armed forces had the legal authority to sell the destroyers to England. Jackson, though, expressly announced that the United States was not undertaking the defense of the possessions of any country.

On September 2 British and American officials exchanged the appropriate notes with respect to the destroyers-for-bases deal, and on the following day the President transmitted these notes to the U.S. Congress. The sites of the eight bases were to be Newfoundland, Bermuda, the Bahamas, Jamaica, Antigua, St. Lucia, Trinidad, and British Guiana. Comparing the deal to the Louisiana Purchase, F.D.R. told the press that he personally regarded it as a good trade. Public opinion polls revealed that six Americans out of ten were favorably disposed to the transaction, while *Newsweek* captioned its story: "Swap of Destroyers for Bases Makes U.S. Dream Come True; Nation's Eastern Flank Thus Made Almost Impregnable."

The American press as a whole was favorable, while Democratic Senator Robert Wagner of New York called the deal one of the great achievements of all time.

Perhaps the most formidable critic of this transaction was Republican presidential candidate Wendell Willkie, who was by no means a hard-core isolationist. Cordell Hull had written in a memorandum dated August 4 to the President that "Mr. Willkie agrees in principle on these and other methods of aiding Great Britain,"[14] but on September 3 Willkie complained that "the people have a right to know of such important commitments prior to and not after being made." Two days later he speculated that F.D.R. might trade off the Philippines without consulting Congress, and then on September 6 he openly blasted the destroyers-for-bases deal as "the most arbitrary and dictatorial action ever taken by any President in the history of the United States."[15] Willkie, it should be noted, was more critical of Roosevelt's handling of the deal than of the deal itself.

Other nay-sayers included anti-Roosevelt author John T. Flynn, who called for Roosevelt's impeachment, and publisher Joseph Pulitzer, Jr., of the St. Louis *Post-Dispatch,* who labelled F.D.R. as America's first dictator. Professor Edwin Borchard opined that ". . . there is no possibility of reconciling the destroyer deal with neutrality, with the United States statutes, or with international law."[16] Writing retrospectively in 1952, revisionist diplomatic historian Charles Callan Tansill charged that Roosevelt and Jackson had ignored certain provisions of the 1871 Anglo-American Treaty of Washington and Article 8 of the Hague Convention 13 of 1907; the latter provided that a neutral government must take steps to prevent the departure from its shores of vessels prepared for war within its jurisdiction which intended to engage in belligerent operations elsewhere.[17] In a broader perspective, though, the destroyers-for-bases deal was simply one step in the evolution of growing presidential authority in the foreign relations field, a trend which was not reversed until the closing days of the Indochina War a generation later.

Largely ignored at the time that the exchange of notes was made public early in September was the fact that the U.S. navy already was enjoying limited access to the base facilities at Bermuda, St. Lucia, and Trinidad, and thus was not in desperate need of additional ones. Nevertheless, by December 3 President Roosevelt had allocated $75 million in emergency defense funds for various types of construction at the eight sites. A month later, on January 6, 1941, a board with Rear Admiral John W. Greenslade as its senior member made its report. Since this document became the key blueprint for the setting up of U.S. military bases in both the North Atlantic and the Caribbean, it will play a leading role in this narrative.

While the actual construction of the bases progressed, thorny diplomatic questions remained. As early as September 26 the British ambassador, Lord Lothian, raised the point with Secretary of State Cordell Hull that according to a press release dated September 7 "The resulting facilities at these bases will, of course, be made available alike to all American Republics on the fullest cooperative basis for the common defense of the hemisphere and in entire harmony with the spirit of the pronouncements made and the understandings reached at the conferences of Lima, Panama, and Havana." In this connection Lothian wanted to know whether British ships and aircraft in the leased areas would enjoy equal privileges in using the facilities.[18] Hull's delayed reply, dated December 30, was in the negative, since Great Britain was a belligerent rather than a neutral, and geographically was not a part of the Western Hemisphere. The British also had made inquiries as early as August 8 about their use of air facilities on British soil which Pan American Airways was planning to develop on behalf of the War Department; by the end of the year Pan American had abandoned its original plans, aside from seaplane facilities at Port-of-Spain, Trinidad, so that this became a dead issue. In a conversation with Under Secretary of State Sumner Welles on January 4, 1941, Chargé Butler complained that Hull's late December reply had placed the British government in a position of inferiority with respect to the Latin American republics, but Welles remained firm in the U.S. decision to grant the latter preferential status.

By March negotiations in London with respect to a final agreement on the bases had reached their final stage, with the most local friction occurring in Newfoundland and Bermuda.[19] The President's Base Lease Commission, which arrived on January 26, was confronted by the British with a lengthy agenda consisting of twenty-three items. As late as March 8 the articles dealing with rights, defense, and customs had yet to be consummated. According to the ambassador to Great Britain, John Winant, "The Prime Minister indicated that our requests in some respects went beyond the intent of the exchange of notes of September 2, 1940, but that he had no desire to restrict our necessary military requirements and that in view of the general situation he was prepared to accept our views. He considered, however, that the concessions given represent the maximum which the British could give."[20]

The points at dispute resolved, representatives of the United States, Great Britain, and Canada signed the Base Lease Agreement on March 27, implementing the agreement concluded on September 2 of the previous year. Among the diverse topics dealt with in the thirty articles were necessary rights, special emergency powers, ground transportation, shipping and aviation, immigration laws, and customs and other duties. In evaluating the agreement Ambassador Winant observed: "The rights and powers it conveys are far-reaching, probably more far-reaching than any the British Government has ever given anyone over British Territory before. They are not used to giving such concessions and on certain points they have fought every inch of the way."[21] But the American military presence was soon to extend to other islands of the Atlantic as well. In April the United States occupied Greenland, then a Danish possession, to forestall a possible German takeover, and then in July it announced plans to move into Iceland, now independent of Denmark, replacing the British forces which were temporarily occupying the island.[22]

In his outstanding study of those British islands which the United States occupied militarily during World War 2, Harold John Sutphen concluded in 1967 that the construction, development, and operation of the United States bases had a major impact on the social and economic life of the colonies in which they were situated. In the social area the primary impact of the bases was the introduction of modern life and modern techniques of construction and management to the colonies. Traditional patterns of life at the isolated island sites were forced to adjust to the twentieth century's increasingly rapid tempo. All the sites required some degree of "Americanization." They also acquired daily air and radio communications with the rest of the world, reducing both their geographic and their intellectual isolation. These changes had long-term implications for almost every aspect of local life. Modernization was accompanied by the problem of rising expectations among the population; it spawned nationalistic sentiments that boded ill for the future of colonial relations in some cases and for the continued occupation of the bases in others. An irreversible process of accelerated change was begun.[23]

Individual sites were affected in different ways by the bases. In many cases, the bases were accompanied by an improvement in the health of the local population. The bases had their most significant impact in the economic field. The United States benefited primarily in a military sense through the development of a strong outer line of defense. Britain benefited militarily to a small degree from the services of the old destroyers, but her main benefits were political. Perhaps the most lasting impact of the bases will be produced by the physical facilities which were established at the base sites.[24]

Since World War 2 the Base Lease Agreement with Great Britain has been modified on several occasions. Thus, in an exchange of notes in 1948 American civil aircraft obtained access to the airfields at Bermuda, Antigua, St. Lucia, and British Guiana on a carefully controlled basis, while in the case of bad weather at these locations pilots were allowed to use Trinidad and Jamaica as alternate fields. Two years later, in 1950, the American and British governments approved new jurisdiction provisions of a highly complex nature superseding Articles 4 and 6 of the original agreement; these applied to every leased area except Newfoundland, which had become an integral part of Canada in 1949. (By 1967 only the naval base at Argentia remained operational.) In 1961 the Defense Areas Agreement replaced the Base Lease Agreement at the West Indies sites. Aside from these more universal modifications, the American and British governments also have exchanged a series of notes dealing with individual colonies, the majority of which have focused on the conversion of decommissioned base areas to agricultural development.

Thanks to the post-World War 2 cold war between the United States and the Soviet Union—which has thawed somewhat in recent years—the various Atlantic islands, British and non-British alike, remain of military and strategic importance to America today. Speaking of Iceland, Newfoundland, the Azores, and Bermuda on the floor of the House on June 16, 1964, Republican Representative Charles Mathias of Maryland concluded that "when we consider recorded history these four islands have always been absolutely vital to mainland North America."[25] Thus, in the age of the intercontinental ballistic missile the pattern of American involvement around the North Atlantic fringe remains as variegated as it was a century or more ago, when clipper ships and whaling vessels rode its waves.

2

THE BAHAMAS
Columbus's Splendid Discovery

According to tradition, Christopher Columbus discovered San Salvador Island (later renamed Watling Island) in the Bahamas during his momentous voyage to the New World in 1492. Upon his arrival Columbus encountered the Arawak Indians, whom he called Lucayans; the Spanish deported up to forty thousand of these to neighboring Hispaniola (Haiti and the Dominican Republic) to work in the mines there between 1492 and 1508. Since the Spanish made no attempt to settle these islands themselves, they remained deserted for over one hundred years before the British began to colonize them midway through the seventeenth century.

When the Bahamas were finally settled in 1648, it was the result of a joint endeavor involving the Company of Eleutherian Adventurers, which had been formed in London, and former governor William Sayle of Bermuda, who sought a new home for a group of religious dissidents. At this time Governor Winthrop of Massachusetts sent the latter a gift of eighty pounds; in return the colony on Eleuthera sent the Harvard College Endowment Fund ten tons of brazilietto, a valuable dye-wood.

Despite this dual effort, the Bahamian settlement did not prosper, and some of the Bermudians returned home as early as 1650, with Sayle departing in 1657. In 1670 King Charles II granted the islands to the duke of Albemarle and five other individuals, but the new owners in the long run displayed little more interest than their predecessors. To complicate matters further, the Spanish began a series of attacks on New Providence in 1680, and a combined French and Spanish force almost decimated the British settlement in 1703.

Given the inability of the Bahamian government to defend the islands against these foreign incursions, it is perhaps not surprising that there would be an accompanying breakdown of internal law and order leading to piracy. Perhaps the most famous of these pirates was Edward Teach, alias Blackbeard. A generation later the besieged proprietors threw up their hands in despair, and surrendered the government of the islands to King George I, who in turn appointed Captain Woodes Rogers as the first royal governor. Rogers brought order to chaos, hanging eight unrepentant pirates after a thousand others had surrendered and received the king's pardon; by 1728 the colony was able to adopt the motto *Expulsis piratis restituta commercia.* The following year Rogers set up a representative assembly, and island affairs proceeded in a somewhat more tranquil fashion in the half-century that remained before the outbreak of the American Revolution.

The first U.S. contacts with the Bahamas are lost in the mists of history, but by 1700 a strong commercial link had developed between the islands and Charleston, South Carolina. During the early eighteenth century there also were mercantile relations between New York City and the Bahamas, although the statistics which are available with respect to the islands' trade with New York City reveal a rather limited commerce in comparison with the Bahamas' trade with Charleston. By 1768 ships from the islands also were visiting such American ports as Boston and Philadelphia on a regular basis. Whether the fluctuations that occurred in this commerce over a period of years were the result of chance or of a more tangible factor is difficult to ascertain from the bare statistics which are available, since these unfortunately do not give breakdowns by type of cargo.

THE AMERICAN REVOLUTION

Thus, as the American Revolution approached, merchant vessels from the Thirteen Colonies were hardly strangers to the Bahamas. Naval ships, however, were decidedly a novelty; it was in the islands that the first encounter between American and British sea forces took place in Marsh 1776. In the opinion of John McCusker, "The amphibious assault against Nassau was the first and most ambitious American challenge to the colonial empire of Great Britain during the Revolution." When the British reacted to this and later maneuvers of the American fleet by dispatching most of their fighting ships to the Western Hemisphere, it enabled the French to sail their fleet from Toulon without British interference. Although the English navy was the finest in the world at this time, its division made it far more difficult for it to humble its lesser French counterpart in European waters.

The hero of this March 1776 Bahamian assault was one Esek Hopkins, an individual whose revolutionary war reputation is far less formidable than that of such well-known figures as John Paul Jones. In favorably contrasting his campaign with Benedict Arnold's abortive onslaught against Quebec, Edgar Maclay has concluded that, had he been given the chance, Hopkins on sea might have rivalled George Washington on land.[1] Anchored with his fleet of eight ships at Philadelphia at the beginning of 1776, Hopkins received instructions from the Naval Committee to proceed with his fleet to Chesapeake Bay. There he was to attack Lord Dunmore's ships, after which he was to rout the British forces off the Carolinas and then proceed to Rhode Island.

The icy condition of Delaware Bay, though, delayed Hopkins's departure for six weeks, until February 17. By this time reinforcements for Lord Dunmore's mosquito fleet had arrived, and there was a growing need for gunpowder on the part of the American military. Commodore Hopkins thus took advantage of the conclusion to his orders, which stated that he might plot his own course in the event of bad winds or stormy weather, or any other unforeseen accident or disaster, and accordingly proceeded to the Bahamian island of Great Abaco. (This maneuver proved to be the first cruise of an American naval fleet). In Nassau on New Providence, only 50 miles distant, there supposedly existed a large cache of gunpowder.

Whether there was advance collusion in this invasion between the American naval forces and residents of the islands remains an unsettled question even today. Months after the episode had occurred, Governor Montfort Browne of the Bahamas wrote officials in London that the Speaker of the Assembly, James Gould, has assisted the Americans, but the Governor failed to offer convincing proof of Browne's complicity. Replying from London two months later, Lord George Germain concluded that "there can be little doubt from the whole behaviour of the generality of the Inhabitants of the Bahamas, that the Rebels were invited to undertake the Enterprise they formed against those Islands. . . ."[2] If there indeed was preliminary intrigue between certain Bahamians and the invading American forces, however, it paled into insignificance compared with the explicit invitation by a group of Bermudians the previous August for the Continental navy to come there and help itself to the military supplies.

Despite the fact that Governor Browne was aware that the American fleet had held a rendezvous off Great Abaco, and was then proceeding towards Nassau, that official did nothing to stop it at sea. He had ample opportunity to transfer the gunpowder to an adjacent island before the Americans landed, but failed to do so; he moreover did not even attempt to foil the first amphibious assault in U.S. marine corps history upon New Providence. It was only after the American invaders had landed, and had rather stupidly delayed until the following day their seizure of the gunpowder, that Governor Browne smuggled most of the cache out of the harbor early on the morning of March 4. Enraged upon finding most of the gunpowder gone, Commodore Hopkins took Browne back with him to the United States as a hostage. Prior to this the Americans had spent two weeks loading the available military stores on U.S. ships; among the munitions they captured were 88 cannon, 15 brass mortars, 5,458 shells, 11,077 round shot, and 24 casks of powder. The Continental navy's experiences on this return voyage were by no means without incident, since during an encounter off Block Island it crippled the British vessel *Glasgow,* but allowed the latter to escape.[3]

During the course of this voyage to the Bahamas and back, the "Don't Tread on Me" flag flew over an American fleet for the first and only time. This consisted of a yellow silk rectangle bearing what was described at the time as a lively representation of a rattlesnake. As for the Bahamian invasion flag, it was probably either the "Don't Tread on Me" one or the Grand Union (Great Union, Striped Union, or Cambridge) flag, which resembles its present-day American counterpart in that apart from the upper left hand corner it consists of horizontal stripes.

The loading of the military stores aside, Commodore Hopkins did keep his pledge that there would be no injury to private property. By fulfilling this promise he raised his stature in the eyes of the Nassauvians. Nevertheless, in the opinion of McCusker, "the descent of the Americans destroyed effective government and thus left New Providence prey to external harassment and internal dissension throughout the war."[4] The result was a decade of anarchy, perhaps comparable to that which existed during the heyday of the pirates.

THE LOYALISTS AND ABOLITION

Another group of Americans to visit the Bahamas were a number of Loyalists, who fled to Great Britain, Canada, and the West Indies as the war neared its end and their side faced defeat. Among those who came to the Bahamas in 1783 alone were such future leaders as

Abraham Adderley, William Pritchard, and Michael Malcolm; many of these Loyalists were slaveowners who brought their Negroes with them, thus adding greatly to the population of the islands. The Bahamas, like Florida, had fallen into the hands of Spain early in May 1782, but eleven months later, in April 1783, Loyalist Major Andrew Deveaux of South Carolina was to lead an expedition departing from St. Augustine which liberated New Providence. This was in fact the last battle of the American Revolution, and it was won by the Loyalists; even more ironic was the fact that the Anglo-Spanish treaty which had been signed nine days previously had restored the Bahamas to Great Britain. (Conversely, Spain obtained East Florida under the terms of this treaty, thus depriving the Loyalists of a future refuge there.)

As a result of the American Revolution perhaps five to seven thousand Loyalist immigrants from the United States settled in the Bahamas between 1783 and 1787, many of them from the plantations of the Carolinas, Georgia, and East Florida, but others from New York. The latter sought out Abaco Island, which had received the first Continentals. This procession continued in the years which followed; a large number of the newcomers settled in the Out or Family Islands, where they established sea island cotton plantations. Unfortunately for the planters, however, their estates declined in value during the first third of the nineteenth century for a number of reasons: soil exhaustion, insects, droughts, blistering winds.

While the native Bahamians, or Conchs, showed a certain tolerance for the Loyalists from New York, since they were mostly former soldiers rather than slaveholders, they resented the airs of superiority too often displayed by the southern Loyalists. It was almost inevitable that a political clash would ensue between the Loyalists and the Conchs; by 1797 the former had emerged victorious, even forcing the recall of two royal governors, John Maxwell and the aforementioned Lord Dunmore. (The latter earlier had moved to the Bahamas from Virginia.)[5]

With the abolition of slavery in 1833-34 throughout the British Empire, the plantation system also inevitably came to an end in the islands. The white planters there did receive some financial compensation from the government (unlike their American counterparts), and they used these funds to move to Nassau and inaugurate new projects, or to leave the Bahamas for allegedly greener pastures. As a result, the Out or Family Islands became populated largely with the former slaves and the mulatto offspring of the former planters.[6]

THE WAR OF 1812 and "WRECKING"

Important as it was, the American economic impact on the Bahamas during the first third of the nineteenth century was by no means limited to the declining cotton plantations of the Loyalist emigrants. The islands profited commercially from the American Embargo Act of 1807, which restricted U.S. trade with Europe, and from the War of 1812, during which the Americans burned the town on Harbour Island. To cite one key trade route, goods were smuggled into the United States via Amelia Island, then a part of the Spanish province of East Florida. But by 1815 Bahamian cotton was no longer able to compete with cheap southern cotton; from that date onward the trade of the islands was conducted on a rather limited basis, consisting largely of salt, sponges, turtles, and other local produce which made their way to America. Commercial relations between the United States and the Bahamas were regulated by the treaty of 1815 between America and Great Britain, the provisions of which were extended to the islands in 1830. During the decade of the 1820s Bahamian trade with the United States fluctuated widely, while in September 1821 the first official American representative to serve in Nassau, John Storr, assumed his position as the agent for commerce and seamen.

One factor which impeded American trade with the islands was the ever present danger of shipwreck. According to a report of the House Committee on Foreign Affairs dated January 20, 1825, Great Britain was not willing to cede any part of Abaco Island, nor any other island in the Bahamas, for the purpose of erecting lighthouses to aid navigation. The British were willing to build the latter, but only if the United States would pay for their upkeep. In the opinion of this committee, the British plan was not practical. Then during the spring of the following year Democratic Representative Edward Livingston of Louisiana complained on the floor of the House that the Americans had built a string of lighthouses along the coast of Florida after the United States had acquired the latter from Spain in 1819, and that no nation had benefitted more from these navigational aids than Great Britain.[7]

To complicate matters further, sometimes the wrecked American vessels carried slaves, as did the *Comet*. Sailing for New Orleans from Alexandria with 164 blacks on board, this vessel was wrecked on the banks off Abaco Island early in January 1831; the slaves were taken to Nassau, where they were liberated over the protests of the owners.

A similar pattern of events followed the breakup of the *Encomium,*
bound from Charleston to New Orleans with forty-five slaves aboard,
off Abaco Island in February 1834. Among the other ships that
wrecked in the Bahamas during this period were the *De Witt Clinton*
in February 1832, the *Kentucky* in September 1838, the *Russell
Baldwin* in November 1838, and the *Fairfield* in September 1844;
fortunately, the crews and passengers generally escaped with their
lives.

But one man's sorrow is frequently another man's joy, and the
storm clouds which often had accompanied the wrecks had a silver
lining. The salvaging of the contents of these vessels in distress
brought an at times profitable, if irregular, living to the human
vultures who preyed on the carcasses of these dead ships; significantly, this activity had begun as early as 1648 in the islands. Prior
to 1847 the wreckers had no financial claim to either the cargo or
the vessel, but after that date they did receive a share of the recaptured items. A total of 313 wrecks was reported between 1858 and
1864, most of which were either American or British, while during the
nine-year span from 1855 to 1864 £638,864 in recaptured goods was
entered at the Bahamian customs. Most of the wreckers, it should be
noted, were Loyalists or their descendants from the Out or Family
Islands.

THE U.S. CIVIL WAR

The economic impact of the American Civil War on the Bahamas was
to prove considerable, as had that of the War of 1812 a half-century
earlier. A thriving blockade running business arose, centering on
Nassau, while a number of ships (perhaps as many as one hundred) were
built on Abaco. Approximately four hundred vessels cleared Nassau
for the Confederacy during the last two years of the war; W. Adolphe
Roberts has observed that "the profits reaped by Nassau were perhaps
the greatest in the annals of Caribbean ports, size and temporary
prominence considered, since the days of the buccaneers' Port Royal."[8]
Exports mushroomed from £196,000 in 1861 to £1,008,000 in 1862
and to £4,672,000 in 1864, with 72 percent of the latter consisting of
raw cotton destined for Great Britain. Not surprisingly, a number of
the pilots who engaged in the blockade running were grandchildren of
those Loyalists who had migrated from the United States during the
latter part of the nineteenth century. The arriving Confederate agents,
moreover, were able to enjoy the facilities of the newly built Royal

Victoria Hotel in Nassau; constructed with an appropriation of
£6,000 from the Bahamian legislature, it quickly became a year-
round resort.

The continuing export of strategic materials from the Bahamas to
the Confederacy quickly aroused the ire of the Union government.
In this connection, Secretary of State William H. Seward complained
to the minister to England, Charles Francis Adams, on September 10,
1861, about the transportation of arms and powder from Nassau
for the use of the insurgents. The British, like the Americans, had
long before passed a statute opposing armed expeditions from their
territory against countries not at war with them, but the pro-
Confederate activities continued in the islands for the remainder
of the war.

In May 1863 the American consul in the Bahamas, Seth C. Hawley,
lamented that the Governor of the islands was looking with disfavor
upon the visit of such American men-of-war as the *Rhode Island.* The
reply of Governor C. J. Bayley was that Commander S. D. Trenchard
of that vessel had failed to obtain his express permission to anchor;
an earlier gubernatorial proclamation had stated that neither Union nor
Confederate ships-of-war and privateers should be allowed to dock,
except by special permission of the Governor, or in case of bad
weather. (Trenchard had instead applied for permission to a subordinate magistrate on Great Inagua.) Bayley later made an abortive
effort to delay the departure of the *Rhode Island,* thus adding fuel
to the fire.

During the same month, too, the Governor wrote Lord Lyons, the
British minister to the United States, complaining that American customs authorities at New York City were attempting to prevent the
exporting of goods from there to the Bahamas. As a result, the British
prime minister, Lord John Russell, suggested to the American authorities that ". . . a distinction ought to be made between shipments of coal
and other articles . . . the export of which may have been prohibited
as contraband . . . and other articles of innocent use. . . ."[9] The collector of customs at New York, Hiram Barney, took the position in re-
buttal that the character of imports into Nassau had changed drastically in recent years, aside from the fact that they had greatly
multiplied numerically. Seward did placate the British somewhat
by ordering that the instructions by means of which New York port
officials had hampered the departure of vessels be rescinded, but
shortly thereafter a group of British merchants engaged in the New
York City–Nassau trade began to complain of harassment by officials
of the former port.

In Nassau itself American consular authorities attempted to provide the U.S. navy with intelligence, but local crown officials were far from cooperative. To Frank T. Edwards, the latter were "subservient not only to the indigenous merchant class, but sympathetic as well to recently established Anglo-Confederate interests which had become identified with the new-found prosperity of the British colony."[10] What local aid the Americans did receive came largely from abolitionist-minded Negro pilots. After mid-1863 U.S. attempts to monitor the insurgent base at Nassau proved to be increasingly futile; this was to some degree the result of a temporary deterioration in the quality of the American consular representation there, but also was partly attributable to the lack of an amiable relationship between the State and Navy departments.

The question of the handling of wrecked vessels surfaced again in January 1865, when the U.S. man-of-war *San Jacinto* went ashore in a desolate bay of the Bahamas. After the wreckers had performed their act of salvage, it became necessary to compensate them for their services; subsequently another American man-of-war, the *Honduras,* proceeded to Nassau in search of coin to pay the wreckers. The Governor denied this vessel permission to enter the harbor on the grounds that it was faced with neither a grave emergency nor real necessity and distress, despite the fact that it was on an errand relating to a case of actual distress. The American reception of this rebuff was hardly a gracious one, especially since Confederate blockade runners had been docking regularly at Nassau. Refusing to be thwarted in his mission, Captain Harris of the *Honduras* put a small vessel ashore from the mother ship and obtained the money. By this time, of course, the end of the Civil War was only three months distant.

A HALF-CENTURY OF DECLINE

Unfortunately for the Bahamas, once the war ended the foreign trade of the islands reverted to its pre-war level. The main products exported at this time were salt, sponges, pineapples, and cotton; the last three, though, were dealt a severe blow by the hurricane of 1866 which destroyed many of the cotton plants and fruit trees and tore away the sponges. As for the salt industry, it collapsed in 1887 after the United States adopted a high protective tariff. On the other hand, the existence of a resort hotel in theory acted as a stimulus to the tourist trade, but in practice it was not until regular steamship sailings to New York City began after the Civil War that tourism started to

have a significant impact on the economic life of the Bahamas. Even
the once profitable wrecking business declined for a number of reasons: the erection of additional lighthouses, the increasing employment of steamships, and shifting trade routes. It was no wonder,
therefore, that the Bahamas entered an era of economic depression
following the American Civil War.

Between the Civil War and World War 1 references to American-
Bahamian relations in contemporary magazines and periodicals became
rare indeed. One of the most interesting episodes involving the United
States occurred during the years 1872-73, when a printing error in the
American tariff of 1872 enabled fruit dealers in the islands to evade the
intended 20 percent ad valorem duty on their produce, and even to
recover $50,000 in duties already paid. Then in the aftermath of the
Spanish-American War, Republican Senator Henry Cabot Lodge of
Massachusetts proposed that the United States keep Manila and perhaps
all of Luzon, but trade the remainder of the Philippines to Great
Britain in exchange for the Bahamas and Jamaica.

By the end of the nineteenth century American scientists were also
becoming interested in the islands. B. M. Wilson noted at the time of
the Bahamas expedition of the State University of Iowa in the summer
of 1893 that ". . . nowhere in the world, possibly, do the waters of the
sea throb with a more varied and wonderful marine flora and fauna than
around the Bahamas and Florida Keys."[11] This expedition was under
the direction of the professor of biology C. C. Nutting, who brought
with him a hoisting apparatus provided with 300 fathoms of wire rope.
Among the items which the Iowa group collected aboard the *Emily E.
Johnson* were sea fans, gorgonians, rattling crabs, starfish, sea urchins,
and even luminous beetles.

Even more important was the expedition of the Geographical Society
of Baltimore to the Bahamas in the summer of 1903. This was under the
direction of George B. Shattuck; employing a two-masted sailing vessel,
it spent two months in the islands. As a result of this survey a beach
mark was erected at Nassau, which was probably the first of its kind
in the West Indies. Prior to this time it was generally thought that the
Bahamas had been built of wind-blown coral sand, but the Baltimore
group discovered that the lower portions of many of the islands also
contained marine organisms in large numbers. It then concluded that
the Bahamas had been undergoing both subsidence and elevation. Another interesting phenomenon which the Shattuck group investigated
was the degeneracy due to close intermarrying of the inhabitants of
Hope Town, Abaco. The descendants of the original Loyalists there were
now suffering from many disorders, including serious body deformities.

Those months just prior to the launching of this expedition witnessed two or three steamers a week voyaging between Miami and Nassau. By this time there were two hotels in operation in the latter city, both of them owned by the Florida East Coast Hotel Company; many travelling Americans patronized these between November and April. In 1903 the leading Bahamian exports to the United States were pineapples, sponges, and hemp, the leading American exports to the islands flour, cotton, silk and woolen goods, and earthenware and glassware. The United States took $500,000 worth of the total exports (valued at $525,000) of the Bahamas, while America also furnished $600,000 of the total imports (valued at $750,000) of the islands. Probably the most important business of the colony in 1903 was the sponge industry.

Writing over a decade later, in 1916, Chester Lloyd Jones concluded that from the standpoint of international trade the Bahamas were not of much consequence, in comparison with other British Atlantic possessions. The commerce of the islands did not even match that of tiny Bermuda, and was only one-twelfth that of Trinidad. The most important industry at this time aside from sponges was turtle shells, but this had been on the decline in recent years; it, moreover, had been temporarily halted by the outbreak of World War 1. Admittedly, the frequently high American tariff wall had adversely affected the citrus industry in the Bahamas, but an increasing export of canned pineapples and also of vegetables to the United States was developing. Thus, Jones held out hope for a more diversified island economy in the future.

LIQUOR SMUGGLING DURING PROHIBITION

The first World War did not have a highly significant impact on Bahamian-American relations, but the decade or so of liquor smuggling that followed the termination of this conflict did. In 1913 the total value of alcoholic liquors, including beer and wine, imported into the islands was only $76,000; by 1919 it had risen to $228,000, and by the first half of 1920 to $842,000. The American consul Loren A. Lathrop charged in October that the overwhelming bulk of this liquor was then smuggled into the United States, despite the theoretical operation of the Prohibition amendment there; it was, in fact, to the advantage of the Bahamian government to permit this smuggling, since, in the words of Lathrop, its "budget has been lifted by this liquor business from a record of deficit to one of prosperity."[12] Not being a

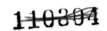

crown colony and having a locally elected legislature, the islands were by no means susceptible to pressure from London.

On May 2, 1923, Lathrop expressed hopes that smuggling from the Bahamas into America would decline in the future, because of competition from Europe, St. Pierre, Halifax, St. Johns, and the Caribbean. Despite his optimism, however, Lathrop was well aware that there was no income tax or land tax in the islands, so that the government was forced to rely on customs duties for the bulk of its funds. To make matters worse, the Bahamian Assembly passed a Tariff Amendment Act in 1923 which included a rebate of 50 percent on alcoholic beverages of imperial origin. Thanks to measures such as this, on June 6, 1924, Lathrop concluded that "if the laws had been made to facilitate the liquor traffic, they could not have been better framed."[13] According to his figures, between 1920 and 1923 over $12 million worth of liquor had been smuggled into the United States illegally from the Bahamas.

The next American consul at Nassau, Harry J. Anslinger, concluded in the fall of 1925 that the liquor smuggling business was on the wane; around the same time a one-time prominent resident of Nassau, Robert Curry, published an article in the *Christian Science Monitor* entitled "Bahamas Rumrunning Boom Fails as Profits Decrease." Anslinger was of the opinion that it would be far easier to reduce smuggling even further, were there a requirement of visaed passports for Bahamians. Although officials in Nassau attempted to take credit for the decline in smuggling, Vice Consul William A. Smale complained on December 19, 1925, that they in fact had denied to the American consulate access to certain courthouse records. Smale also declared that it had been economic conditions and American vigilance rather than Bahamian efforts which had caused the decline of the illegal traffic.

Earlier that month, on December 2, American and British officials had met at Washington to discuss the presence of U.S. Coast Guard vessels at Gun Cay in the Bahamas without the prior permission of the British authorities. Gun Cay was an uninhabited coral island 42 miles off the coast of Florida that was used as a base by smugglers; unfortunately, on at least two occasions an American Coast Guard vessel had either stopped or played its spotlight on a ship carrying an official of the Bahamian government. In addition, the conferees at Washington also discussed the question of the seizure of ships by the U.S. Coast Guard within the 3-mile limit. According to the liquor treaty, enforcement authorities of the United States were allowed to apprehend smuggling vessels outside the 3-mile limit. On March 26, 1926, the British government proposed relative to Gun Cay that the

American cutters call first at Bimini for a one year's license; it took the position that there already had been a crackdown on transfers to the British flag of vessels engaged in smuggling. By September the American and British governments had reached a mutual understanding on this general question, which it was hoped would enable them to work together more effectively.[14]

That attempting to suppress the illicit trade was at times a highly dangerous business was attested to by George Pinder, a Negro member of the Nassau constabulary. When Pinder boarded the rumrunner *Eker* in Nassau harbor on April 10, 1926, to investigate the illegal transhipping of liquor from one vessel to another, he became involved in a fight, was knocked unconscious, kidnapped, put to work at sea, and threatened with death. After the ship had docked at Edgewater, New Jersey, and begun to discharge its cargo, the smugglers released Pinder and gave him the funds to return to Nassau. Unfortunately for the former, authorities later seized the *Eker* with 15,000 gallons of alcohol in her tanks; Pinder then testified against the smugglers at the court proceedings in New York City.

Since there were a large number of rumrunners operating between the islands and the United States, it was only natural that sooner or later an overzealous American pursuer would violate the 1926 agreement between the United States and Great Britain. This did occur in September 1927, at which time Coast Guard Boatswain Laurence Christiansen captured two American-owned and operated vessels five and a half miles from Gun Cay. After the British government had lodged a protest, American officials saw fit to apologize. Christiansen not only was required to turn over the two seized craft with their cargoes of liquor to the British, but also to release six prisoners whom he had captured, without their standing trial. In July 1928 the governments of the two countries agreed on restrictions on the operations of Coast Guard cutters in the Bahamian waters; no longer could the cutters enter Bimini harbor in search of possible smugglers.

It was during the same month, on the ninth, that federal agents seized 200,000 quarts of rye whiskey aboard the *Iriquois* off New York City pier 37, North River. In the aftermath of this capture the American government cast its dragnet for twelve alleged leaders of a liquor ring thought to be responsible for numerous shipments from Miami to New York City by rail, motor truck, and steamship. Back at Nassau custom house figures for the first part of 1928 revealed a 10 percent increase in whiskey imports. Although export totals from Nassau had fallen off to half of what they once had been, this was no victory for the prohibitionists, since most of the other half had been transported to schooners and warehouses at Grand Bahama and Bimini for clandestine shipment to the United States.

Despite these numerous setbacks, on November 2, 1931, Fred D. Fisher, the American consul at Nassau, was able to write Washington that liquor smuggling into the United States had been on the decline since the beginning of 1930, thanks largely to the efforts of the American Coast Guard and Customs Service. As a result, the Bahamian government had been forced to curtail its expenditures; there were even reductions in the salaries of governmental officials and employees. It thus is perhaps not surprising that authorities in the Bahamas were not totally cooperative in furnishing their counterparts in Washington with inside data regarding vessels suspected of smuggling liquor into this country.

Between the repeal of Prohibition in the United States in 1932 and the outbreak of World War 2 in 1939, the Bahamas entered a period of economic depression, now that the islands' main source of revenue was gone. On October 30, 1932, the *New York Times* proclaimed "In consequence of prohibition in the United States, the last thirteen years will probably go down in history as a golden era, eclipsing any other phase in the checkered career of the islands."[15] Fortunately for the Bahamas, Sir Harry Oakes, a Canadian multi-millionaire, emigrated to Nassau around this time; his construction projects employing Bahamian labor gave a desperately needed stimulus to the economy of the islands.

AMERICAN ECONOMIC INVOLVEMENT, 1919-39

Aside from rum smuggling, legitimate trade between the Bahamas and the United States continued to flourish during the inter-war period. In 1929 the government of the islands did clamp a temporary embargo on Florida fruits and vegetables after the Mediterranean fruit fly had made its appearance in that state, but other products from the mainland were not affected. Two years later, on October 31, 1931, the *Nassau Guardian* published an article entitled "Buy British Goods"; its object was the transference of the American trade to the United Kingdom, Canada, and other British possessions. At this time the principal American imports into the islands were apparel, hosiery and cotton goods, meats and poultry, vegetables, metal manufactures, electrical apparatus, and hardware. Only Canadian butter and cheese offered significant challenges to rival American products. The total annual imports of the Bahamas (including liquor) were averaging between $8 million and $10 million, of which American manufacturers were responsible for between 36 to 42 percent. The leading export of the islands, sponges, went mostly to the United States, Great Britain, and the Netherlands.

During the 1920s there was a real estate boom in conjunction with the liquor smuggling. American real estate operators, many of them from Florida, bought land throughout the islands, even purchasing some previously uninhabited ones. As of 1931 the controversial Munson interests (which we shall examine shortly) had investments in the Nassau area totalling approximately $1,500,000, while in 1935 the New Englander A. W. Erickson revived the salt industry on Great Inagua. Then during the following year the *New York Times* headlined a front page story "Americans Investing Huge Sums in Bahamas to Escape Income Tax." Since there was no income tax in the islands, it was to the financial advantage of wealthy Americans to sink their money in property development there; these tropical entrepreneurs often hid their identity behind responsible Bahamian merchants who fronted for their operations. It was reported several months later that the migration of American investors to the Bahamas had been especially vigorous during the last six months.

But for every American investor who made a business trip to Nassau, there were literally dozens of tourists who journeyed there. We noted earlier that the Royal Victoria Hotel there had been constructed on the eve of the Civil War; regular passenger steamship service between New York City and Nassau began with Samuel Cunard around this time and later was maintained by the Ward Line. The Florida East Coast Railway, too, started to operate a winter steamship service between New Providence and Miami, and also purchased both the Old Colonial and the Royal Victoria hotels in Nassau. Prior to World War 1 the government of the Bahamas was granting subsidies of £5,000 to both the Florida East Coast Railway and the Ward Line. When the contract with the latter expired in 1915, that company refrained from signing another one, but continued to operate its vessels down to 1926. As for the Florida East Coast Railway, its contract expired in 1922, about the time that the Old Colonial burned down and its guiding genius, Henry Flagler, died; this firm then decided that it, too, should withdraw from servicing the Bahamian tourist trade.

Thus, a vacuum existed relative to American tourism during the early 1920s, which the United Fruit Company eventually was invited to fill. When United Fruit declined on the grounds that it lacked the proper type of vessels, the Bahamian government turned to the Munson interests. A temporary contract was entered into for 1921 and 1922, providing for service between New York City and Nassau, with a tacit understanding that the Munson interests would also operate between Miami and Nassau and build a first class hotel in the Bahamian capital.

On January 1, 1923, a permanent contract went into effect. Almost immediately friction developed between the Munson interests and the government of the islands. Among other things, it was charged that the supplemental loans to the former were unwarranted, that the construction costs for the hotel had been padded, and that the firm's payments to the Bahamian authorities were too small. As time went on, too, the latter came to feel that the Munson steamships should be larger and more luxurious, especially after they had improved and enlarged the harbor at Nassau. On the other hand, the Munson interests complained that the government of the islands had helped underwrite the Waterloo Hotel Company, which in 1926 opened a competing first class modern hotel, the Fort Montagu. Bahamian officials, too, encouraged the operation of an airplane service during the winter months by Pan American Airways between Miami and Nassau beginning in 1929, which injured the steamship business. Of course, neither the government of the islands nor the Munson interests had any control over the mushrooming cruise ship trade from New York City to Bermuda or the West Indies, most of it in vessels of countries other than the United States. Aside from the tourists arriving by ship or by plane, it was estimated that in 1929 only 186 American citizens permanently lived in the Bahamas.

Still another American group which was active in the islands between the two world wars was the scientists. In 1927 the third oceanographic expedition of the *Pawnee,* directed by Harry Payne Bingham, collected a number of deep sea specimens which were placed on display at the Peabody Museum as the Bingham Oceanographic Collection. Four years later the Bingham Oceanographic Foundation of this museum at Yale University launched a Bahamian expedition under the direction of Gifford C. Ewing of New York City. The schooner employed by the scientists, the *Abenaki,* was equipped with a winch and wire, which enabled them to observe the ocean down to a depth of 1,000 fathoms.

Despite the friction generated by such economically oriented problems as liquor smuggling and the fulfillment of the Munson contract, American relations with the Bahamas generally remained on a harmonious level between the two world wars. In 1919, however, the Bahamian government became so exercised by the circulation there of newspapers, pamphlets, and books from the United States which might have had an inflammatory impact on the racial situation, that it encouraged the legislature of the islands to pass the Seditious

Publications Prohibition Act. This was directed in particular against Jamaica-born Marcus Garvey, then living in New York City, and his *Negro World.*

A more enduring problem was that of American influence in the Bahamas. In 1925 a Miami newspaper published an article entitled "Bahamas Need Prince," in which it asserted that if American business firms continued to inundate the islands, the Prince of Wales would have to visit Nassau as a reminder that the Bahamas were still a part of the British Empire. The local press of the islands reacted vehemently in protest; it noted that there currently was a great crime wave going on in the United States. (Bahamian rumrunners were, of course, contributing their own share to this breakdown in law and order.) But from a more philosophical standpoint, one editor expressed beautifully the dilemma of remaining British in character while becoming to a large degree an American economic colony:

> Here in the Bahamas, we hear a lot about the efficient American methods. Fear is expressed that the Bahamas will become Americanized. True it is that we may buy her goods to an extent, enjoy the friendship of her people who visit our islands; but—patriotism apart—be governed by people who find the greatest difficulty in governing themselves? Never! Were Britain overwhelmed by a subterranean wave, British jurisprudence and freedom of thought would still survive throughout the world, and nowhere stronger than in the Bahamas.[16]

This Nassauvian editorial assessment notwithstanding, the fact remains that by the time of the outbreak of World War 2 the Bahamas had become to a considerable degree an economic colony of the United States, although technically Great Britain still controlled their government. This was perhaps inevitable, since the Bahamas are geographically far closer to the United States than to the mother country; they also are much nearer to the mainland than the American Caribbean outposts in Puerto Rico and the Virgin Islands. Whether the American economic impact on the Bahamas took the form of tourism, investment, or legal and illegal commerce, it was nevertheless more continuous and more significant than were the intermittent U.S. military, diplomatic and scientific contacts. It was an impact, moreover, which as we have seen dated back to the fleeing Loyalists of the American Revolution or even earlier, rather than being the product of the century of "dollar diplomacy."

WORLD WAR 2

Complain as they frequently have done throughout history about the deleterious aspects of the American presence, the Bahamians greeted with something less than an outburst of joy the imminent decline in American tourism following the outbreak of World War 2. Shipping offices were deserted, local merchants overstocked, the large hotels practically empty, and the cost of living up. Another factor aside from World War 2 which had a negative impact on tourism was a regulation of the British government which required passports and visas of all aliens who entered the islands. Among the steps taken by the Bahamian government at this time to revitalize the colony were its attempts to persuade London to relax this regulation, and to develop steamship service between Nassau and New York City.

In September 1939 the American vice consul W. K. Ailshee noted in a dispatch to Secretary of State Cordell Hull that ". . . the preponderance of opinion seems to be that if the United States will repeal the arms embargo and supply the Allies with food and munitions it will have done its share."[17] Two months later John Dye, the American consul, pointed out that the enactment by the U.S. Congress of new neutrality legislation—which included the lifting of the embargo—had won the almost unanimous approval of both the Bahamians and the British. By this time, too, the passport and visa requirement for American tourists had been removed, and frequent passenger and freight service between Miami and Nassau had been contracted for. As a result, two of the three big hotels planned to open as usual for the winter season of 1940, while the Bahamas Development Board and a Bahamian delegation sent to New York City were briskly advertising business as usual. Summing up her impressions of that winter in Nassau, the duchess of Windsor (whose husband had been appointed governor general earlier that year) observed that the American visitors and tourists were pouring in.

By this time, however, American military interest in the Bahamas had begun to develop. Although the islands would place 1,100 men in uniform during World War 2 and contribute £500,000 to the British war treasury, local defense forces were practically non-existent in the Bahamas as late as August 1940. That October a U.S. naval mission paid a visit to inspect possible sites for naval and air bases under the recently signed Anglo-American destroyers-for-bases agreement, and in September 1941 the Duke of Windsor conferred with high-ranking army and navy officials in Washington. But it was not until December of that year, around the time of Pearl Harbor, that construction actually began on a naval air station on Great Exuma at Georgetown. A year earlier F.D.R. had rejected Abraham Bay in Mayaguena as the site because it offered inadequate protection from the weather, while the Army's original desire for a Bahamian base had waned.

Rather than being a transatlantic terminal, Great Exuma was intended for use as a base for seaplanes employed in patrol operations along the southeastern coast of the United States and within the islands themselves. Key operating facilities included a 50-foot timber seaplane ramp, a 180-foot barge pier, and a partly dredged beach. The Great Exuma station, which was constructed without the assistance of the Seabees, was commissioned on May 15, 1942.[18] Early in September the Duke of Windsor, in thanking those Americans responsible for the building of the base, praised them for their wholehearted cooperation and noted that their relations with the Bahamians had been most cordial.

Unlike the United States, the Bahamas experienced no Pearl Harbor, but within the space of a year a hurricane, a riot, and a fire did considerable damage to the islands. The first of these struck on October 4, 1941, wrecking many small ships and fishing boats, and annihilating 90 percent of the fruit crop. On the other hand, the June 1942 riot in Nassau saw a mob of three thousand inflict $40,000 in damage upon the business section of the city; several people lost their lives, while several dozen others suffered various injuries.[19] A single individual, though, was responsible for the fire which gutted a considerable portion of the downtown area of the city several weeks later. Although the theory circulated that this conflagration might have been linked to the earlier riot or even to sabotage, investigating authorities discovered that the culprit was a property owner who wished to collect some fire insurance. He was later sent to jail for arson.

Examining the June riot in greater detail, one needs to point out at least several contributing factors. First, there was the presence in the islands of racial prejudice similar to that long found in the southern United States. As Paul Blanshard noted five years later, "This is the only British colony in the Caribbean which draws a color line comparable to the American color line."[20] Second, there was the iron grip which the Bay Street oligarchy of Nassau was exerting over the islands. It is significant in this connection that the Moyne Commission, which investigated other British colonies in the Caribbean during 1938 and 1939, did not pay a visit to the Bahamas; as a result, many authorities in London may not have been fully aware of the highly conservative atmosphere present in the islands.

The precipitating cause of this June 1942 riot, however, was not any action by the Bay Street oligarchy or any discrimination along racial lines, but rather the differential between what the American airbase contractors paid for common labor (80¢ per day) and what the local inhabitants received for similar work elsewhere. Bahamian workers who had held jobs in the United States prior to this time were well aware that financially there were far greener pastures on the mainland; towards the close of World War 1 hundreds of laborers from the islands had found employment at the Charleston, South Carolina, military facilities, while by 1921 they were working on farms in Florida. It took the actual presence of an American firm paying American salaries, though, to generate widespread discontent in the Bahamas during World War 2. In May 1942 a local federation of labor organized by dissatisfied workers demanded a basic salary of $1.60 a day to combat rising prices, whereupon the local government took the step of setting up an advisory board, an inadequate remedy in the eyes of the labor leaders.

It is not uncommon that a riot or a revolution will break out when the head of state is out of the country; the overthrow of Kwame Nkrumah of Ghana and Yakubu Gowon of Nigeria are but two recent examples. At the time of the June 1942 riot, too, the Duke of Windsor was away from Nassau, conferring with officials in Washington over the Colonial Supply Mission. Flying back to the Bahamas in an airplane placed at his disposal by F.D.R., the duke arrived in the islands' capital after the looting had taken place. Overruling the more cautious members of his executive council, he adopted the tactic of using whatever force might be needed to restore order, and achieved this goal without further bloodshed. The duke then returned to Washington to complete the Colonial Supply Mission negotiations.

One of the most controversial aspects of this riot was the extent to which American troops participated in the stifling of it. Following the close of the war, a member of the Sixth Cavalry Regiment asserted that a 135-man contingent under the direction of Captain David B. Goodwin had flown from Tampa, Florida, to the Bahamas early in June 1942, remaining there for six weeks. According to this account, these troops were sent there secretly by President Roosevelt after the duke had appealed to Washington for assistance. Their precise role was not explained, but their mere presence contributed to order. American officials even at this late date were reluctant to comment on this incident, but it is quite possible that the U.S. government did reinforce its military police unit to protect American interests and property.

But if the duke met force with force, he was no tool of the Bay Street oligarchy oblivious to the need for various reforms, not all of which were at stake in the riot. It will be recalled that his liberalism, as well as his desire to marry a divorcee, was a factor in the successful drive to force him off the British throne a half-dozen years earlier. Pleading for tax reforms, the duke personally informed Bahamian legislators that the time had come to inaugurate direct taxation. Another prominent British official who called for reforms at this time was Sir Allison Russell, the retired chief justice of Tanganyika, whom the Colonial Office appointed to make an outside investigation of conditions in the islands. The Russell report, among other proposed changes, advocated income and inheritance taxes, the secret ballot, labor legislation, and the widespread dissemination of information about birth control.

The result of these reform demands was, if not an entire loaf of changes, at least a few slices of progress. Would-be farmers were offered two grants totalling £54,576 to provide them with tools, seeds, and supervision, while sisal growers were assisted by a governmentally sponsored project. Turning to labor, the Assembly enacted a law which permitted unions to exist but refused agricultural workers the right to join them; it also approved workmen's compensation legislation and restricted the death benefit, but refrained from imposing an income tax. In commenting upon this body's reluctance to institute reforms, the *Nassau Tribune* in May 1943 compared the Bay Street oligarchy with the ruling class in France before the French Revolution, and with Joshua, who commanded the sun to stop in its course. "After all," it observed, "the dinosaur disappeared from the jungle scene because he was unable to adapt himself to a changing world."[21] A few more reforms ensued after the Attlee Labour government came to power in Great Britain at the end of the war, such as the use of the secret ballot in all of the Out or Family Islands, yet the Bay Street oligarchy stood firm in its resolve to maintain its ascendant position in the Bahamas for as long as possible.

While the Duke of Windsor was proposing various reforms to the Bahamian legislature, he also was attempting to line up foreign investment capital. After he had set up the Economic Investigation Committee and written personal letters to a number of American businessmen, he met with General Foods representatives in New York City during August 1943. Prior to February 1942 Axel Wenner-Gren had operated a fish packing plant on Grand Bahama, but the duke seized these facilities after the controversial Swedish capitalist had turned up on the Proclaimed List. Now, eighteen months later, General Foods agreed to lease and operate the plant, and thus give work to hundreds of the islands' unemployed; only 60 miles from Palm Beach, these facilities included a quick-freeze plant and cannery, and a fleet of power-driven fishing boats. Although General Foods planned eventually to diversify their products, the original emphasis was on rock lobster, or crawfish.

Aside from this enterprise, one might cite several other industries which were experiencing growth during this period. Exports of straw work, for example, had reached a total value of $155,647 in 1941, shells and shell work $20,959. The abovementioned sisal industry had been on the decline since the late 1930s, but a representative of an American rope company visited Nassau in 1942 to train inspectors, leading to increased output. An inhibiting factor here was the scarcity of fresh water in the Bahamas. It must be remembered, though, that the now dormant sponge industry had once employed one-eighth of the population of the islands, and its collapse left a king-sized economic vacuum to fill.

While these economic developments were taking place, the war effort also continued. In June 1945, shortly after the termination of World War 2 in Europe and several months before its end in the Pacific, the U.S. naval air station on Great Exuma was disestablished. At a total cost of $273,583, it had been by far the least expensive of the eight military bases which the American government had set up in eight British North Atlantic colonies extending from Newfoundland to British Guiana; from a purely military standpoint, its impact was more limited than that of the other five Atlantic bases which we are examining in this volume. (Only Jamaica was more isolated from the theaters of war.) There also was a British military presence in the Bahamas during this conflict, since the British Air Ministry purchased Oakes Field airport in 1942 and expanded its facilities. But the major impact of World War 2 on the islands, as we have seen, was economic, not military.

THE AMERICAN MILITARY PRESENCE SINCE 1945

In the years which followed World War 2, economic factors continued to dominate American relations with the Bahamas, especially in the areas of tourism and investment, but military and diplomatic considerations occasionally came to the fore. There was, however, a three-year lull in military activity, since in March 1946 the United States post engineers who had been in charge of the maintenance of two air-fields in Nassau built during World War 2 turned over their duties to their RAF counterparts. Similarly, there was a temporary suspension of interest in the islands back on the mainland. Thus, in July 1947 southern Democrat John Rankin of Mississippi complained on the floor of the House of Representatives about the invitation extended by the Speaker of the Assembly of the Bahamas for four members of Congress to visit the islands after Christmas. In the words of Rankin, "This running around all over the globe to find out what somebody else is thinking beyond the boundaries of the United States, and particularly behind the iron curtain, is just about worn thread-bare."[22]

As the cold war heated up, American interest in the Bahamas began to revive. In May 1949 the American government sought permission from its British counterpart to fire missiles across the islands during a series of long-range tests;[23] the two countries eventually signed a twenty-five-year agreement to this effect in July 1950, providing that both the United States and Great Britain were to set up technical and supporting facilities in the Bahamas. The launching site of the unarmed missiles was to be the east coast of Florida near Cape Canaveral, while the flight test range was to extend southeastward across the Atlantic Ocean. This agreement was extended in January 1952 to include the Turks and Caicos Islands, then technically a dependency of Jamaica, and then early in 1956 also to embrace St. Lucia in the Windward Islands group, 850 miles from the Turks and Caicos.

Another joint military operation, of an entirely different nature, involving the Bahamas was the naval research stations; these were to be set up with the objective of obtaining information that could be used in an anti-submarine campaign. (Up to this time there had been a lack of data about water conditions in the Caribbean and the Atlantic.) The original public announcement of this project was made in November 1957. Three years later, in November 1960, the British government agreed to allow the United States to survey the waters in the vicinity of the Bahamas from the standpoint of possibly establishing a naval testing and evaluation center. According to plans, these underwater tests would focus on weapon systems, including submarine detection. But although Congress authorized this project in the same year, and Prime Minister Harold Macmillan of Great Britain was sympathetic to the scheme, the colonial government of the islands was hesitant to grant base rights on Andros Island for AUTEC (the Atlantic Underwater Test and Evaluation Center). Adjacent to this island, the largest in the Bahamas, lies an underwater canyon approximately 100 miles long and 20 miles wide, the so-called Tongue of the Ocean, a natural formation which in theory would be an ideal site for a test range.

Finally, in May 1963 the American and British governments reached an agreement for the construction of a $95 million underwater weapons testing center which would focus on torpedoes, missiles, and sonar tracking. The British were to share in the use of these facilities with the Americans.[24] Far from being a minor operation, this was the biggest joint anti-submarine effort undertaken by the U.S. navy and the Royal navy to date; by mid-1964 the governments of the two countries had formulated an anti-submarine program, although it was estimated that it would take a decade fully to implement these plans.

In related diplomatic developments, in 1959 the American consulate in the Bahamas became a consulate general, and then was elevated to embassy status on July 10, 1973, the day that the islands became independent. During the interim in December 1962, President John F. Kennedy had held a two-day meeting with British Prime Minister Harold Macmillan at Nassau, at which the two men discussed the cancellation of the Skybolt air-to-ground missile program. J.F.K., surprising as it may seem, given the proximity of the islands to the United States, thus became the first American president ever to set foot on Bahamian soil.

INVESTMENTS, GAMBLING, AND TOURISM

During the post–World War 2 era American investors were active in the Bahamas; in fact, more so than ever before. Both tourism and trade have been on the increase during the last three decades. Since such illegal operators as blockade runners and rum smugglers have at different times played a major role in Bahamian-American relations, it is perhaps not inappropriate that after World War 2 the first American to operate on a large scale in the islands was Wallace Groves, who had been indicted, tried, and convicted in the United States for certain illegal stock dealings. Among the other American investors who were to become active there were Huntington Hartford, the Crosby brothers, and Owens-Illinois.

In 1955 Groves persuaded both the British and the Bahamian governments to sell to his Grand Bahama Port Authority 50,000 acres of land at $2.80 an acre on the previously underdeveloped Grand Bahama Island lying off the Florida coast, where for several years he had operated a lumber mill. As a part of the agreement, Groves promised to construct a deepwater port, roads, and schools. To encourage industry and commerce and to stimulate the growth of the new town of Freeport, the agreement prohibited the taxing of its residents' corporate income, salaries, capital gains, and property until 1990, and relinquished the imposition of customs duties on imported business goods until 2054. Similar concessions were extended to the remainder of the Bahamas under the Industrial Encouragement Act; since there were no taxes on foreign enterprises in the islands at the time, what was significant about the agreement with Groves was the contractual long-term promise of no future taxes.

Groves quickly established himself as the leading businessman of Freeport, and closed negotiations for the building of a 30-foot harbor with the U.S. shipowner and billionaire Daniel K. Ludwig. This was opened in 1959, following the early completion of a nearby airstrip capable of accommodating jet planes. By this time Groves and an English partner had invested $6 million in what one contemporary observer described as a desolate stretch of sand and scrub. Looking back today, one might suggest that Groves's creation of the second largest city in the islands out of nothing was the most significant contribution ever made by an American to the Bahamas. From World War 2, moreover, he was the largest employer of islanders in the private sector of the economy, prior to selling his controlling interest in the Port Authority to Benguet in 1968.

By 1959 between twenty and thirty American companies besides that of Groves had established some sort of facility in the Bahamas, many of them having arrived in the last several years. Among these firms were the United States Steel Corporation, the Bethlehem Steel Corporation, the Crucible Steel Company, the Owens-Illinois Glass Company, the Whirlpool Corporation, and the Outboard Marine Corporation. It was not uncommon for companies such as these merely to use Nassau as a headquarters for an overseas sales subsidiary, but Owens-Illinois at this time was beginning to cut pines on Grand Bahama for its paperboard mill in Jacksonville, Florida. In addition, Standard Oil of California and Gulf Oil had invested $3 million in an offshore well, while Morton Salt Company was operating a salt plant on Great Inagua Island after merging with the Erickson firm in the early 1950s. Insurance companies, too, were now becoming more active in the Bahamas; one prime example was the Peninsular Life Insurance Company of Jacksonville. The first American bank to operate in the islands was the First National City Bank of New York, which opened a commercial banking branch in Nassau during February 1961.

More ill-fated were the activities of the A. & P. heir Huntington Hartford, who purchased four-fifths of Hog Island across from Nassau around this time. Banning automobiles, roulette wheels, and honky tonks, Hartford began formulating plans to make Hog a dignified vacation resort which would be attractive to Europeans and Americans. Of course, by investing in the West Indies men like Groves and Hartford were simply following the example of a number of respected American millionaires, such as Laurance Rockefeller, who by this time had holdings in both the Virgin Islands and Puerto Rico. More controversial was the individual from whom Hartford acquired his Hog Island acreage; the abovementioned Swedish industrialist, Axel Wenner-Gren, had allegedly entered into various deals with the Germans during World War 2.

Meanwhile, on the political front the winds of change were beginning to swirl through the islands. In 1962 both the mainly white United Bahamian Party and the wholly black Progressive Liberal Party came out for responsible government in their election manifestoes, and in May 1963 a constitutional convention for the islands convened in London. Here the delegates agreed that the Bahamas were to have full internal self-government; the governor was to retain reserved powers only in the areas of foreign affairs, defense, and internal security, beginning on January 1, 1964. This convention also granted the Out or Family Islands 21 seats in a 38-member Assembly to be elected by universal adult suffrage, while allowing only a 15-member Senate to exercise a suspensory veto over legislation. The general election held on January 10, 1967, produced a tie between the two major parties for Assembly seats, but Progressive Liberal Party leader Lynden Pindling was able to form a government after winning over one of the successful minority candidates.

While Pindling's triumph may have marked a victory for majoritarian home rule, the election was held because the previous ministry was charged with being involved with American criminal interests relative to casino operations on Grand Bahama. From that time onward, moreover, the gambling issue has regularly been at the forefront of both Bahamian politics and Bahamian-American relations. Since gambling was illegal in the islands, it was necessary for the government to grant a special exemption from the colony's penal code to casino operators in Freeport; this was done in April 1963, not by the legislature, but by the governor's nine-member executive council.

In December 1966, just one month before the abovementioned election, Lynden Pindling flew to London personally to request that the colonial secretary set up a royal commission to investigate the various allegations of corrupt behavior. One of these was that there was a tie-in between American gangsters and the Bahamian casino, another that the former had also become involved with certain Bahamian politicians. Colonial Secretary Lee, however, rejected the royal commission concept, instead merely asking for a report from the governor, Sir Ralph Grey, who had recently made a speech in Memphis, Tennessee, painting a rosy picture of the situation in the islands. British officials may well have been alienated by Pindling's going before the United Nations in both 1965 and 1966; on the latter occasion he charged that the people of the Bahamas were being sold out to gangsterism. In any event, according to *The Economist*, there had been no discussion of the islands in the House of Commons for at least two years.

Once Pindling became prime minister early in 1967 after promising to rid the Bahamas of American gangsterism and double dealing, officials there quite naturally expected a cleanup. Yet after two months he had failed to expel three American gambling operators from the islands who had fled the United States to escape indictment for tax evasion. To make matters worse for the Prime Minister, the U.S. Securities and Exchange Commission was preparing to investigate certain activities of the Crescent Corporation; this widely diversified New York company not only owned a blueberry plantation in the Bahamas but also manufactured electronic components and laboratory equipment. As the president of a Bahamian company named Six Ms Pindling had helped to finance Lewis Colasurdo's effort to gain control of Crescent by extending him a $2 million loan in the fall of 1965, and Colasurdo reciprocated by lending him a Crescent-owned airplane to use during his successful election campaign. The Prime Minister's response to these disclosures involving himself was to sever his connections with Six Ms and a number of other companies with which he had become associated as a private lawyer. With respect to the three gamblers, though, Pindling maintained that it was not possible to resort to extradition, since no treaty between the United States and the Bahamas covered their alleged crimes.

Returning to more legal business operations, the most spectacular American investors to appear on the Bahamian scene during this political transition period were the three Crosby brothers, who expanded a small paint manufacturing and retailing business into that thriving concern known as Resorts International. By 1969 the latter was attempting to buy into Pan American Airways. The catalytic factor which precipitated the Crosby brothers' rise to riches was the series of problems which Huntington Hartford experienced in his attempts to develop Hog Island, now renamed Paradise Island. After spending approximately $30 million on this would-be vacation mecca, Hartford was unable to obtain either a license to open a gambling casino or permission to build a bridge from Nassau; he was blocked on both counts by the Bay Street oligarchy, which already had granted a gambling monopoly in that city to Wallace Groves by the special dispensation of the government which it controlled. Hartford then made the mistake of hiring as his attorney Lynden Pindling, who was in the midst of his campaign to drive the oligarchy from power, and whose efforts on Hartford's behalf only further alienated Bay Street.

In 1966 James Crosby of Mary Carter Paint offered to purchase 75 percent of Hartford's interest in Paradise Island for $3.5 million in cash and the assumption of a $9 million mortgage. By this time Paradise Island was costing the latter approximately $1 million a year. Once Crosby had concluded the deal, the Bay Street oligarchy agreed to allow the bridge to be built, and Wallace Groves decided to sell his Nassau casino, the Bahamian Club, to Mary Carter Paint. After erecting a five-hundred-room hotel and a casino on Paradise Island, Crosby then shut down the Bahamian Club. Both the casino and the hotel opened in December 1967; six months later, in May 1968, he sold off the company's paint business to Delafield Industries, and changed the name of his company (Mary Carter Paint) to Resorts International. Crosby then constructed another motel and a 270-room hotel on Paradise Island, although as Hartford had predicted, most of the casino's clients crossed the bridge in taxis or on foot from their hotels and motels in Nassau. (Some of the latter were far less expensive to tourists.)

Less successful were the sugar operations on the island of Great Abaco which Owens-Illinois and its wholly-owned subsidiary, Bahamas Agricultural Industries, conducted between 1966 and late 1970. Owens-Illinois had decided to go into the sugar business when it became apparent that it would be profitable to cut its timber holdings there for only a limited number of years. Despite governmental encouragement of this monopoly, which it was hoped would help to diversify the economy of the islands, this enterprise failed when its operators were unable to obtain expanded markets for the sugar which they were producing.[25] Owens-Illinois nevertheless built 1,500 miles of primary and secondary roads there, including the Great Abaco Highway, through its subsidiary Bahamas Agricultural Industries.

This episode to the contrary, many U.S. business firms have thrived in the Bahamas during the last decade or so. According to one estimate, almost $800 million was invested in Freeport alone between 1963 and 1970; U.S. Steel, for example, built a $40 million cement factory there.

Elsewhere, early in 1968 the Precision Valve Corporation of Yonkers, New York, the leading manufacturer of valves for aerosol spray containers, purchased Walker Cay, the northernmost Bahama island. Aside from expanding the living facilities there, Precision Valve planned to experiment in sea farming and to test new plastic products. With respect to joint enterprises involving American firms and the Bahamian government, by the end of 1971 the latter had completed negotiations with Seabulk International of Fort Lauderdale; this new firm was to be known as the Bahamas Government Industrial Estates, 51 percent of which was to be owned by the government of the islands. Its first major project was to build a deepwater petroleum terminal designed to accommodate the world's largest tankers.

With this mushrooming of American investment in the Bahamas and the growth of Freeport, it is not surprising that there also has been a surge of tourists to the islands as well. In 1963 only 26,000 Americans visited the Bahamas; three years later the total passed the 200,000 mark. By 1968 it was reported that route integration, heavy promotion, and improved service were producing sharp increases in passenger traffic on Eastern Airlines between the United States and the Bahamas. (At this time the round trip economy fare between Miami and Nassau was only $27.) Other airlines flying between America and the islands included Pan American, British Overseas Airways, and Northeast Airlines; during the summer of 1970 Bahama Airways scheduled daily service between New York City and Nassau, only to suspend operations by October, thanks largely to a breakdown in negotiations with the islands' government. Despite this stepped-up air service, 86 percent of the estimated 1.3 million visitors to the Bahamas in 1971 came from the United States, exactly the same proportion as in 1961. The average visitor stayed five days, with Florida, New York, New Jersey, Pennsylvania, Illinois, Michigan, and Ohio furnishing the most visitors.

American exports to the Bahamas also increased sharply after 1955, totalling $15 million in 1955, $49 million in 1960, $107 million in 1965, and $179 million in 1969. Similarly, imports from the islands grew from $2 million in 1955 to $8 million in 1960, and from $24 million in 1965 to $48 million in 1969; the leading Bahamian exports at the end of this period were pulpwood and crawfish, oil (from the new refinery), salt, rum, fruits, and vegetables. According to a U.S. government publication issued in 1971, American consumer goods "normally have a competitive edge despite their higher prices because Bahamian consumers are familiar with them through Miami television advertising and shopping trips to Miami."[26] But it was not just the individual Bahamian citizen who was interested in American products.

In 1966 the Export-Import Bank of Washington authorized $9 million and $4 million loans to the government of the islands for the purchase of machinery and equipment to improve Nassau harbor and of assorted telecommunications equipment to modernize facilities in the Bahamas.

Thanks to increased American commerce, tourism, and investment, the existence of a tax refuge, the presence of gambling interests, and the movement of the Bahamas towards self-government, the U.S. Congress began to pay more attention to the islands after 1960. Thus, Democratic Senator Albert Gore of Tennessee complained on March 7, 1961, that tax dodging was flourishing in the Bahamas, citing them along with Panama, Switzerland, Liechtenstein, Bermuda, the Netherlands Antilles, Liberia, and Venezuela as the most popular tax havens. Democratic Representative Wright Patman of Texas offered some remarks along a similar line on January 31, 1964, entitled "Hot Money Hideaway Booming," in which he made reference to the role of the underworld. But it was not just illegal operations which were subjects of criticism on the floor of Congress. In October 1965 Democratic Representative Joseph Resnick of New York attacked a request by Owens-Illinois for a sugar quota for its holdings on Great Abaco, with Republican Representative Charles Gubser of California taking the opposing position that the company's action demonstrated a compassion for its employees. Resnick's sentiments to the contrary, a sugar quota of 10,000 short tons from the Bahamas per year was included in legislation.

In January 1967, at the time that Lynden Pindling took over as prime minister, Republican Representative Paul Fino of Michigan introduced a mass of material into the *Congressional Record* in an attempt to establish the existence of a complex series of financial relationships between the United States and the Bahamas. Here reference was made to former New York Democratic Representative Adam Clayton Powell's Huff Enterprises; by that date the black Harlem leader had become a frequent visitor to the islands. That fall Republican Senator John Williams of Delaware, long a critic of waste and corruption in government, complained about the August issue of *Esquire,* in which an advertisement appeared proclaiming that the savings which American citizens deposited in the Bahamas could earn a 6 percent tax free income. The Treasury Department, though, pointed out that this advertisement was in error, and that this interest would not be tax-exempt. In more recent years congressional interest in the Bahamas has continued to flourish, since until the mid-1970s the islands have remained a tax haven.

RECENT DEVELOPMENTS, FUTURE PROSPECTS

On July 10, 1973, the Bahamas became independent from Great Britain. Lynden O. Pindling, who had become prime minister in 1967, had led the drive for separation; Prince Charles, representing Queen Elizabeth, was in attendance at the ceremonies, as were Secretary of the Interior Rogers C. B. Morton, actor Sidney Poitier, and Foreign Minister Raul Roa of Cuba. Although Pindling took the position that for the present the islands would continue to emphasize tourism and banking, he also stated that he wished to diversify the Bahamian economy, possibly through an increased emphasis on fishing. From the American standpoint, independence for the islands did not mark an immediate and abrupt shift in the generally harmonious relations which the United States enjoyed with them, although these had been disturbed briefly during the final days of British rule in January 1972, when U.S. customs officials in Miami searched Bahamas Finance Minister Carlton Francis. Francis, who was on a private trip to Florida, had failed to bring along any documents indicating his position. In apparent retaliation officials at the Nassau International Airport shortly thereafter delayed the departure of approximately two-hundred American tourists for three hours.

Nearly a half-millennium ago Christopher Columbus observed of the Bahamas that "this country excels all others as far as the day surpasses the night in splendor."[27] Despite the natural beauty of the islands and the more recently acquired man-made wonders, an atmosphere of illegality continues to hover over the Bahamas, as it did in the days of the blockade runners and the rum smugglers. To cite only one example, in September 1973 Elliot Roosevelt was accused of conspiring to assassinate the Prime Minister; this charge was made during hearings of the Senate Permanent Subcommittee on Investigations headed by Democrat Henry Jackson of Washington. According to Louis P. Mastriana, a 51-year-old convicted stock swindler and a one-time Roosevelt employee, the former Miami Beach mayor and Mike McLaney, a Haitian casino operator, who had been convicted once on income tax violations and once for securities fraud, had offered Mastriana $100,000 to assassinate him in 1968 after Pindling had allegedly failed to honor a promise to McLaney that the latter would receive a gambling permit in the Bahamas. This promise allegedly was made during the 1966–67 election campaign in the islands, at which time McLaney supposedly contributed nearly $1 million to the future Prime Minister's campaign chest. Mastriana told the senators that the murder was not attempted because of the difficulty in escaping from New Providence Island safely.

Replying angrily from his ranch outside Lisbon, Portugal, where he had been writing, promoting tourism, and breeding horses, the former president's son labelled Mastriana's story fantastic, and accused the subcommittee of using his name to obtain a cheap, sensational headline. As for Chairman Jackson, his position was that attempts to interview Roosevelt in Florida about this matter the previous August had been unsuccessful, but he did allow the former President's son to deny the murder plot charges before his subcommittee on October 3, with McLaney following suit the next day. (McLaney did confirm the gambling permit-campaign funds deal, however, setting the amount donated at $65,000.) In Nassau, Prime Minister Pindling disclaimed any knowledge of the alleged assassination plot, and also stated that he had never received any campaign contributions from either McLaney or Roosevelt.[28]

The amount at stake in this episode dwindles into insignificance, though, when one contemplates the total personal fortunes of two Americans who temporarily took up residence in the Bahamas during the early 1970s, the late Howard Hughes and Robert Vesco. The billionaire Hughes, most of whose business dealings remain a closed secret, purchased the Xanadu Princess Hotel on Grand Bahama after leaving Las Vegas in late 1970, and then lived there until he fled the island by yacht in March 1972 to escape possible deportation. Earlier, during the late 1950s, Hughes had expressed an interest in acquiring control of the Nassau airport and the telephone communications from the islands.

With respect to Vesco, this controversial international financier allegedly contributed $200,000 to President Richard Nixon's 1972 reelection campaign via Attorney General John Mitchell and Secretary of Commerce Maurice Stans; in return he supposedly received promises that the Securities and Exchange Commission would drop its investigation of him. In large part because Vesco was not produced at the Mitchell-Stans conspiracy trial in New York City, both men were found innocent by the jury. Moving to the Bahamas, he may have invested $40 to $50 million in Nassau-based holding companies and banks (where he offered liberal credit terms for small loans), including $2 million in renewable ninety-day Bahamian Treasury bills. The U.S. Justice Department did attempt to extradite Vesco from the islands, but a magistrate's court in Nassau ruled that mail fraud was not a crime in the Bahamas; there also was the question of the applicability of the 1931 extradition treaty between America and Great Britain, now that the islands were independent.

One reason why Bahamian authorities were hesitant to hand over Vesco was the fact that his total investment in the islands was so enormous in relation to the annual governmental budget. Since the latter for 1974 was only $122.5 million, and the Bahamian economy was in a state of deep recession, the abrupt removal of Vesco's influence from the economic life of the islands might have proved disastrous. Despite Prime Minister Pindling's loudly proclaimed policy of Bahama for Bahamians, a considerable portion of Vesco's money allegedly ended up in the hands of associates and friends of Pindling, while the Prime Minister himself supposedly enjoyed the use of a Vesco jet aircraft. Pindling himself admitted that Vesco had made a substantial contribution to his political party, but denied that the Vesco interests had been favored. Summing up the situation on March 30, 1974, *Business Week* sarcastically observed that "with Vesco's investments, observers wonder whether a new era of Bay Street Boys has begun—only this time the 'boys' are black."[29] After that Vesco moved his base of operations to Costa Rica, only to be forced out in 1978.

While the clouds of controversy swirled about the world of high finance on New Providence and Grand Bahama, it being difficult if not impossible at times to separate rumor from fact, on Great Abaco there had developed strong reservations about the new independent Bahamas, especially among those inhabitants who were descendants of the early American settlers. First colonized in 1785 by Loyalists from New England, Scotch-Irish from New York, and planters from Eleuthera, the second largest island in the Bahamas more recently (since 1959) has been the site of various Owens-Illinois operations, ranging from cutting pine to processing sugar cane. The future relationship of New Providence and Grand Bahama to Great Abaco and other Out or Family Islands may prove increasingly troublesome, especially if the latter come to feel that they are being relegated to a subordinate position by authorities in Nassau and Freeport.

As for the U.S. connection today with the islands as a whole, in 1972 Robert D. Crossweller noted that "the Bahamas contain more strategic U.S. military installations than any other area in the Caribbean, and they control hundreds of miles of northern approaches to that sea. . . ."[30] Thus, the islands remain of interest to the American government for military as well as economic reasons; it is not surprising, therefore, that the United States has attempted to cooperate with the Bahamas in various ways during the age of independence. One good example is the BARTAD (Bahamas Agricultural Research Training and Development Project) begun in 1973, to which the American government to date has made available $10 million as its share of a joint undertaking to develop a system of agriculture based on commercial family farms. One specific aspect which one might cite is the North Andros cattle project, which has involved experimenting with sorghum sudan.

Yet there are indications that as the Bahamas move further and further into the post-colonial era, friction with America may increase, if only because the government of the islands has taken the position that it will apply the archipelagic principle in determining its territorial sea, while the United States through its consul at Nassau has expressed the need to minimize the economic damage to the Florida fishing industry which would result from its application. By the summer of 1975 the attempt by islands officials to restrict lobster fishing in Bahamian and international waters had incurred the wrath of both Florida lobstermen and expatriate Cuban-Americans. As of August 1 the spiny lobster was to be considered a creature of the Bahamian continental shelf; in adopting this measure, the islands merely copied a 1973 U.S. law protecting Maine lobsters. It has been estimated that the value of lobster tails at stake here is in the neighborhood of $15 million annually.

On January 4, 1976, the *Washington Post* published an article by Gaylord Shaw and Robert L. Jackson entitled "Bahamas Haven for U.S. Riches." The gist of this essay was that the 300 banks in the islands—280 of which were private institutions with restricted charters—were offering a refuge for American tax evaders by providing secret accounts. There was, of course, little, if anything, new in these charges. On the other hand, in the Bahamas the *Nassau Guardian* was headlining a story only two days later "Permanent Residence Will Now Cost $5,000"; the accompanying text revealed that one-year residency permits were to cost $1,000.[31] These new Ministry of Home Affairs rules will most likely drive a large number of foreigners (including many Americans) from the islands and thereby deprive the public treasury of some sorely needed funds. Thus, if the U.S. influence there is to remain strong, it will have to overcome the obstacles raised by Prime Minister Pindling's Bahamianization program, of which this apparently is only one phase.

3

JAMAICA
Land of Wood and Water

When Christopher Columbus first viewed Jamaica in 1494, the mountainous character of the island led him to describe it as a crumpled piece of paper. In contrast, the original inhabitants of the islands, the Arawaks, looked upon Jamaica as the land of wood and water: Xamayca. During the years following 1500, though, the island won the nickname of the white man's grave, thanks to the at times severe tropical climate as well as the dissolute life which many of the Europeans led there.

In 1509, fifteen years after Columbus had discovered it, Juan de Esquivel conquered and settled Jamaica, inaugurating 146 years of uninterrupted Spanish rule. Beginning in 1517, Negro slaves were imported to take the place of the native Arawaks, whom the Spanish were already in the process of exterminating. In 1523 the conquerors built St. Iago de la Vega (later renamed Spanish Town), which remained the capital until Kingston usurped its role in 1872.

During the century and a third which followed, Jamaica continued to develop under Spanish rule. In 1655, however, Admiral William Penn and Robert Venables conquered the island for Great Britain, and under the Treaty of Madrid of 1670 the Spanish recognized the claim of Great Britain to Jamaica. Already in 1656 the British had founded Port Royal, while during 1662 the first Assembly meeting had taken place. Unfortunately, in 1692 an earthquake destroyed most of Port Royal, leading to the foundation of Kingston. Another important development occurred back at London in 1672, when the Royal African Company was given a monopoly over the slave trade; from that time onwards the island was to be one of the world's greatest slave marts.

This was, of course, long before the modern Jamaican economy emerged with the development of the banana and the bauxite-alumina industries.[1]

EARLY TRADE WITH AMERICA

At the time of the British takeover of the island in 1655, New England played a major role in provisioning the invading force, while Robert Sedgwick, a merchant from Charleston, served as a major general over part of the expedition. American contacts with Jamaica between this date and the American Revolution were primarily commercial in nature, but trade statistics for this period unfortunately are scattered, so that it is difficult to offer any meaningful generalizations. Richard Pares, though, has concluded that at the beginning of the eighteenth century the cheaper Barbados rum had begun to lose out in popularity to its Jamaican rival on the mainland.

By 1730 a considerable number of Jamaican vessels had begun to visit such ports as Boston, Philadelphia, New York City, and Newport annually. Conversely, Kingston by this time had become an important market for American produce, although some Boston merchants preferred to obtain homeward cargoes of molasses in the French port of Cap François or of logwood in Honduras. By the eve of the American Revolution slave trader Aaron Lopez's men had gone beyond mere trading contracts on the north side of the island, and were now spending more and more time in Jamaica itself by assuming the role of factors.

On December 1, 1774, the Continental Congress banned British Caribbean produce from the ports of the Thirteen Colonies. Alarmed by this drastic step, the radical mercantile element in Kingston pushed a memorial through the Jamaican Assembly that month in the absence of the conservative, rural members. Endorsing colonial rights in general on behalf of the Americans, this document went so far as to deny Parliament's claim of the right to legislate for the colonies. As one might have expected, the memorial caused a furor when its contents became known in London, but the Connecticut House of Representatives and the Continental Congress itself expressed their appreciation to the Jamaicans.[2]

Unlike Bermuda and the Bahamas, Jamaica was to play a rather negligible role in the American Revolution, aside from becoming a haven for departing Loyalists. As early as October 1775 one London paper reported that several American families had arrived there; the evacuation of Savannah brought 400 white families and 5,000 slaves to Jamaica, while the surrender of Charleston triggered an exodus of 1,278 whites and 2,613 blacks to the island. This movement of U.S. Loyalists helped to swell its population from 18,500 whites, 3,700 free colored people, and 190,914 slaves in 1775 to 30,000 whites, 10,000 free colored people, and 250,000 slaves in 1787. Loyalists continued to arrive in small numbers in Jamaica from both the North and the South until the following year. Aside from the inevitable planters, there were gentlemen, widows, surgeons, tradesmen, and Quakers as well; an examination of the refugee certificates issued 174 arrivees in 1783 reveals that most of these newcomers came from the South and settled in Kingston, and that 61 of the 145 who made the latter their final destination brought slaves with them.[3]

COMMERCIAL EXPANSION AND THE WAR OF 1812

Turning next to commercial contacts between the United States and Jamaica in the three decades between the American Revolution and the War of 1812, a British Order in Council dated July 2, 1783, restricted to English vessels the importation into the West Indies of American lumber, grain, and livestock, while also prohibiting the entry of salt beef, pork, and fish from the United States. Although it was by no means the only island legislature of Great Britain to do so, the Assembly of Jamaica took the position that free trade with the United States was an absolute necessity: "We claim it as the birthright of every member of the empire; we demand it as one of the gifts of nature, to enable us to avert impending ruin." By August 1784 Jamaica was on the verge of famine as the result of a series of hurricanes which had struck the island since 1780, and the Lieutenant Governor issued a proclamation allowing the importation for four months (later extended) of provisions in foreign bottoms.[4] Between July 1783 and February 1785 253 vessels of British register brought from the United States large amounts of bread and flour, rice, and corn and peas, as well as great quantities of lumber, staves, headings, and shingles. In contrast, only thirty bottoms arrived during this period from Nova Scotia and Canada.

A decade following the Treaty of Paris, in 1793, the outbreak of war between England and France resulted in a Royal Proclamation dated February 11 which unleashed both British naval vessels and colonial privateers upon American commerce in the West Indies.

Unlike Bermuda, however, Jamaica showed little interest in enforcing this proclamation, even opening her ports to salted provisions which previously had not been permitted entry; one Captain Townsend reported from Barbados in 1794 that "by late accounts from Jamaica we learn that no American vessels had been condemned there and the people, not interested in privateering, were exceedingly exasperated that the Americans were even detained."[5] Since the island had legally meticulous Admiralty courts, the latter usually did not find any special grounds to condemn vessels.

By 1803, though, the British government had begun to adopt a slightly more liberal attitude towards imports from the United States, and between June of that year and July 1807 150 barrels of flour and 120 barrels of bread entered Jamaica in British bottoms. During this period a mass meeting was held there at which it was advocated that several Caribbean ports should be kept open to American trade under the discretionary clause. Many Kingston merchants took the opposite position, but both Lieutenant Governor Nugent and his successor, Eyre Coote, admitted vessels from the United States.

As was the case with the American Revolution, from the military standpoint Jamaica did not play a leading role during most of the War of 1812. Although in 1809 the Governor of Jamaica rejected a request from the Spanish commandant in Mexico for arms and ammunition to defend the latter against an expected American attack, four years later privateers from the United States did almost blockade the coast of Jamaica. Then towards the end of this conflict British strategists formulated a plan to drive the Americans out of Louisiana and Florida, after which they changed the advance base for the attack from Bermuda to Jamaica. Instead of purchasing their supplies in Europe, thoughtless military officials bought them instead in the West Indies, thus further broadcasting their intentions to the United States; this contributed to the British defeat at New Orleans in January 1815.[6]

FROM ABOLITION TO INSURRECTION

During the generation between the abolition of slavery and the Morant Bay Uprising of 1865, economic contacts between the United States and Jamaica did continue, although they fluctuated in intensity. According to Robert Greenhalgh Albion, "For a while the Aymars and other New York merchants maintained a fair amount of trade with Jamaica and ran packets to Kingston, but this dwindled to a minor part of New York's Caribbean commerce."[7] In 1860, of the 211,000 tons of sugar imported at New York, only 5,000 came from Jamaica, in contrast to 171,000 from Cuba and 22,000 from Puerto Rico; the abolition of the tariff protecting colonial produce in the British market in 1846 had lowered sugar prices and wiped out profits. On the other hand, a decade earlier Jamaica had been exporting 28 percent of its coffee and nearly half of its pimentos to the United States, but by the time of the Civil War it was selling as little coffee as sugar in the American market. Out of the 72 million pounds of coffee imported at New York in 1860, Jamaica furnished a mere 2,600,000, while Brazil led with 46 million.

Looking at attempts to recruit labor for the island elsewhere, in 1842 the Select Committee on West India Colonies, meeting in London, discovered during the course of its investigations that as of that date approximately two-hundred immigrants had arrived in Jamaica from the United States, most of them former residents of Philadelphia or Baltimore. In general, American laborers showed little interest in coming to the island, since the wages there were not as high as they were on the mainland; some who did make the trip later returned to the United States. On the other hand, no attempt had been made to purchase southern Negroes for employment as free laborers in Jamaica, since blacks from Africa were available.

During 1860 the *New York Times* speculated as to whether the recent opening of steamship communication between New York City and Jamaica might cause a large number of American blacks to emigrate there, much to the delight of the planters. But since the latter were known to be in dire financial straits, and thus not always able to fulfill their promises, the writer concluded that their offer of free passage and a daily wage of 25¢ to 60¢ probably would prove an insufficient inducement. Of course, the establishment of regular steamship service between the mainland and the island had far more significance for both nations than the purely racial aspect discussed by the editorialist.

In the spring of 1861 overt war broke out in the United States between the North and the South. On August 17, 1861, the Kingston correspondent of the *New York Times* pointed out that the island's trade had been crippled as a result, Jamaica being almost totally dependent on the mainland for the breadstuffs and provisions which it consumed. During the year ending September 30, 1862, there was a decrease of 20 percent in the aggregate U.S. tonnage arriving at Kingston, but a number of other American vessels with American officers flew British flags as a safety precaution. At the beginning of the con-

flict Governor Charles Darling had issued a government notice that
Jamaica would maintain a neutral position, but this did not always
prove easy to maintain.

Nevertheless, serious incidents were at a minimum during the
American Civil War, despite a number of minor irritations. Perhaps
the most important exception to this generalization was the controversy surrounding the 118 prisoners from the U.S.S. *Hatteras*
whom the *Alabama* brought into Port Royal under French colors
in January 1863. Confederate Captain Rafael Semnes, who stayed six
days in Kingston while his vessel was being repaired, received a greeting from the islanders approaching hero worship, and one firm even
gave him a public reception. The northern prisoners were freed upon
disembarking; afterwards they were dispatched to the United States
on the *Boradin,* which vessel was not totally safe because it pos-
sessed only a limited number of lifeboats. Jamaican authorities denied
that they had exhibited favoritism towards the Confederacy, yet they
turned away from port the U.S.S. *Vanderbilt* when it approached the
island in search of coal and other supplies.

Jamaica, too, was to experience a more limited insurrection of its
own in 1865, when decades of discontent there led to the outbreak
of the Morant Bay Uprising. The leaders of this revolt were Paul
Bogle and George William Gordon. They afterwards were executed
with four hundred other insurgents before being declared national
heroes a century later in 1965; the precipitating cause of this Morant
Bay Uprising was an outbreak in October which led to the death of
the chief magistrate of the parish and eighteen other whites. Many
Britishers throughout the West Indies applauded the ruthless suppres-
sion of this revolt. Nevertheless, the Governor who had presided
over Jamaica during the years preceding, Edward John Eyre, was recalled and replaced because of his apparent use of unnecessary force
and brutality in combatting the revolutionaries.

In the United States word of the Jamaican riots spread slowly;
the reports which appeared in the American press at first minimized
Eyre's over-reaction and dwelt instead upon alleged black misdeeds.
Not only did the Charleston, South Carolina *Courier* complain that
the "fiendishness and downright barbarity" of the Jamaicans was
"paralleled by nothing in living memory," but the Portland, Maine
Eastern Argus referred to the revolt as the "act of fiends, enacting
most brutal atrocities."[8] Back on the island the Kingston *Colonial
Standard* blamed the teachings of British missionaries and American
newspaperman Horace Greeley for the insurrection, while reports
circulated there that blacks from the United States had gone to the

Caribbean and spread revolutionary ideas. It was not until November that the *Chicago Tribune* noted that Jamaica was run by a few English landlords, supported by the military, at the expense of the blacks, and that the riots demonstrated that the ballot should be extended to Negroes in the United States. By mid-December Congress had begun to debate the implications for America of the Jamaican disturbances, with Democratic Representative John W. Chanler of New York opposing and Republican Senator Charles Sumner of Massachusetts favoring black equality.

Prior to leaving Eyre had persuaded the island legislature to dissolve itself and the British parliament made Jamaica a crown colony in 1866. The new governor, Sir John Peter Grant, instituted a number of important innovations with respect to the police, the courts, health care, public works, education, and agriculture. In 1872 the capital was transferred to Kingston, the same year that the mongoose was introduced as a check against the now abundant rats and mice. A dozen years later, in 1884, a new constitution went into effect which provided for limited participation at the local level in the governmental process; reformers added nine elected members to the legislature in that year, a number which they increased to fourteen in 1895. During this post-insurrection period the Anglican Church also was disestablished.

THE GOLDEN AGE OF BOSTON FRUIT

American relations with Jamaica between the U.S. Civil War and World War 1 were dominated by the activities of Captain Lorenzo Baker, Andrew Preston, and later Minor Keith, who were the three principal figures in the expansion of the island's banana industry. This story is a long and complex one. Its origins date back to 1871, when a 30-year-old Cape Cod sea captain, Lorenzo D. Baker, docked his over-age fishing schooner at Port Morant on his return trip from Venezuela. Looking for a cargo to take back to the United States, he made the fateful choice of a load of bananas, and what had originally promised to be a one-shot gamble soon evolved into a regular marketing run. Back in Boston Baker made the acquaintance of the 23-year-old Andrew Preston, an employee of the Boston commission firm Seaverns and Company; although the latter concern had never sold bananas previously, it was soon advertising for sale "Fine Tasteful Yellow Bananas Fruit on Direct Import from the Antilles." Preston later entered into a partnership with Baker which was to last 27 years.

Despite the facts that Boston was far removed from Jamaica and that he initially employed sailing schooners rather than steamships, Baker's enterprise quickly began to grow in scope. In 1877 he moved with his family to the island, where he set up the L. D. Baker Company; besides bananas he also planned to buy and sell coconuts, oranges, ginger, pineapples, and sisal on commission. It was also during this year that Baker invaded the New Orleans market. In the summer of 1882 the governor of Jamaica, Sir Anthony Musgrave, observed to a *New York Times* reporter that "the fruit trade . . . with the United States is still in its infancy, but is growing at a really marvellous rate."[9] He went on to point out that the banana exporting business on the north side of the island had been built up entirely through the efforts of such men as Captain Baker, but also noted that the exporting of oranges was keeping pace.

The next significant episode in the banana saga took place in 1885, when Baker, Preston, and eight other individuals contributed $2,000 apiece to the formation of the Boston Fruit Company, a partnership. Business boomed during both 1885 and 1886; thus far there had been no hurricanes to destroy the Jamaican crops or ships lost at sea. But in 1888 cargoes began arriving too late and too ripe, and New York City merchants started to invade Boston by rail. Faced now with a real competitive challenge, Andrew Preston bought two new steamships, the *Ethelred* and the *Ethelwold,* while Lorenzo Baker purchased four banana plantations in Jamaica with an annual production of at least 150,000 bunches. With the firm now worth a half-million dollars, the Boston Fruit Company was incorporated in Massachusetts with Baker as president and tropical manager and Preston as Boston manager. The latter attributed the success of Boston Fruit to both good management and good luck.

During 1888 2 million bunches of bananas were exported to America, a staggering increase over the less than a million bunches of the previous year; pineapple exports also were up, although the sale of oranges in the United States was on the decline because of competition from Florida. By 1891 two-thirds of the island's exports made their way to America, while the latter sent Jamaica around one-third of its imports. Since 1880 the amount of sugar exported to the United States had increased in value from $320,000 to $745,000, coffee from $230,000 to $825,000, and fruits from $200,000 to $1,730,000, while dye-woods sales there had doubled.

But in October 1890 the McKinley Tariff became law. This measure not only raised the overall average of duties to 49.5 percent, but also granted to the president the authority to impose duties on goods from those countries which discriminated against American products. The bounty of a 2 cents per pound on the production of domestic sugar injured the Hawaiian economy, as well as posing a threat to the sugar producing islands of the West Indies, including Jamaica. In March 1891 the *Kingston Gleaner* reported that commercial relations between the United States and the island were likely to be strained, and encouraged the sending of an island delegation to Washington. Two months later, however, the Kingston representative of *The Times* of London reported that American manufactured goods (locomotives being a prime example) had begun to replace their British counterparts.

On December 2, 1891, H. H. Hocking and C. F. Farquharson arrived in Washington on the steamship *Alvo* to discuss the reciprocity provisions of the McKinley Tariff which were to go into effect on January 1, 1892. The two Jamaican commissioners admitted that fruit was not affected, but wished to guard against a future emergency. As a result, the island did sign a treaty with the United States removing a 12½ percent ad valorem duty on American imports; on the average, these concessions cost Jamaica £35,000 a year.

Treaty or no treaty, many islanders continued to worry about the future of Jamaican commerce with the United States. As of July 1893 British trade with the island remained on the wane, while there had been an increase in commerce with the United States. Leading American imports at this time included foodstuffs, tobacco, building materials, machinery for sugar mills, and other machinery and tools; on the other hand, Jamaica was exporting to America fruits, sugar, coffee, and pimentos. The following year the Wilson-Gorman Tariff of 1894 reimposed the duties on raw sugar which the McKinley Tariff had suspended.

On March 31, 1895, the American consul at Kingston, Q. O. Eckford, declared that the United States was the natural market for the island, but complained at the same time that the United States was furnishing Jamaica with only 10 percent of its cotton imports. Had he delayed his report for several months, he would have been able to observe that orange plants from Louisiana and Florida were faring even worse than cotton. In August the Governor of Jamaica banned their further entry into the island on the grounds that a parasitic disease in epidemic form was present in the American groves; he exempted only those plants which the curator of the Jamaica Institution had proclaimed to be disease-free. Thanks to recent frosts in Florida, a number of American orange growers had been exploring the possibility of transferring their base of operations to the island, but found the native orange to be distinctly inferior in type.[10]

In discussing the island's economy on January 6, 1898, the *New York Times* observed that "in common with the other West Indies islands, the industry of Jamaica—sugar—has been ruined by the free admission into the market of the mother country of bounty-fed European sugar."[11] Thus many Jamaicans had begun to seek reciprocal trade with the United States, whose commerce they regarded as desirable. The first inaugural address of President William McKinley dealt in part with the tariff, further kindling interest among the Kingston newspapers in reciprocity, but opponents of the scheme precipitated a bitter struggle in the legislative council.[12] Back in Washington the enactment of the Dingley Tariff of 1897 hardly proved a blessing for Jamaica, since according to the *New York Times* it threatened the island's fruit trade with extinction. It was at this time that the British colonial secretary, Joseph Chamberlain, attempted to interest a leading British fruit trading house in driving the American firms from the Jamaican trade. Two months later it was reported that the Elder-Dempster combine had failed to achieve positive results, probably because of Chamberlain's advocacy of local enterprise, but a new Fruit Trading Association directed by A. M. Nathan and backed by a number of British and Scotch capitalists had come to the fore.

On July 1, 1899, though, a series of reciprocity treaties (including one with Jamaica) were concluded in Washington between Commissioner John Kasson, representing the United States, and Mr. Tower, the British chargé. That November the collector general at Kingston was able to report that for the most recent financial year the total value of American imports into the island had surpassed that of their British counterparts, 45.1 to 44.7, the first time that the mother country had been thus outdistanced in Jamaican history. When the terms of the reciprocity treaty with the island were released in December, it was learned that Jamaica had agreed to admit duty-free a long list of American products, while the United States was to reduce by 20 percent the import duties on the following island products: citrus fruits, pineapples, fresh vegetables (including potatoes and onions), and rum.[13] The following February the Jamaican Assembly approved this treaty. As a result, a British commission from Bristol which arrived that fall with the object of developing trade between western England and the island was told by the acting Governor and leading businessmen that it would have to inaugurate new business enterprises, rather than compete directly with the established U.S. trade in various items.

It was also at the turn of the century that the Boston Fruit Company, which was now active in exporting bananas from Cuba and Santo Domingo as well as Jamaica, joined forces with the Minor

Keith interests, which raised bananas in Costa Rica and Colombia. The result was the United Fruit Company, formed via an amalgamation of the two groups in 1899; United Fruit paid Boston Fruit $5,200,000 for its assets, and the Keith firms $4 million for theirs. Between 1890 and 1899 the direct imports of Boston Fruit had doubled, and dividends had averaged 20 percent annually for eight years. But in 1898 and 1899 hurricanes did hit Jamaica, as well as the Dominican Republic during the latter year, wiping out most of the banana crop. The climate of Cuba, on the other hand, was in the opinion of Keith too cold for successful banana raising; as a result, sugar eventually superseded bananas there under the direction of United Fruit, which also abandoned its Santo Domingo properties. Of the Caribbean islands, only Jamaica continued to produce the fruit on a large-scale basis.

OTHER CONTACTS WITH THE UNITED STATES, 1865–1900

During the last third of the nineteenth century American contacts with Jamaica were developing in areas other than the raising and exporting of sugar, bananas, and citrus fruit. During 1872 the Jamaican government reached an agreement with the Pacific Mail Steam Ship Company providing for one of the latter's vessels to stop twice monthly at Kingston. Nevertheless, the steamers carried only one-fifteenth of the banana exports between 1878 and 1882, and island authorities discontinued the subsidy in 1884. Pacific Mail, however, continued to stop at Jamaica after that date.[14]

Unlike Bermuda, where there was no railroad system in operation until 1931, Jamaica had a railroad dating back to 1843. In October 1889 the latter was sold two-thirds incomplete to a syndicate of American citizens, only 63 miles of it being in operation,[15] after the Jamaican government had ordered a special election so that the people could vote on the matter. A number of anti-Yankee posters then went up, with a typical one reading: "Do you want America to own us? People of Jamaica, arouse! Go to the polls and vote against permitting Americans to get control of our Island. Buying the Railroad is the first step in that direction."[16] These warnings were to no avail; the voters gave the American capitalists a big vote of confidence. Under the railroad agreement the new owners were to build 30 miles of track yearly until the entire line was finished, while in return the Jamaican government (following the American example) was to grant them valuable tracts of land along and near the line. Despite these auspicious beginnings, by 1899 the New York West India Improvement Company had surrendered its control over the railroad to other parties. Profitable as the line had proved at times, completing it in mountainous areas was no easy feat.

Far less official interest was shown at first by the United States towards the international exhibition which opened on January 27, 1891, at Kingston, four decades after the American participants had paraded their technological genius before the world at the Crystal Palace Exhibition in London. When asked why the American government had displayed so little enthusiasm towards it, Secretary of State James G. Blaine (a leading figure in the Pan-American movement) took the position that the United States had not been officially invited. Technically this was true, since the British government did not make a practice of inviting countries to any exposition throughout the Empire which it did not itself organize. Nevertheless, in a series of maneuvers independent of the American government the Boston Trust Company subscribed $1,000 to the exhibition and displayed a number of fruit-carrying whale boats and banana carts; the Boston Fruit Company also offered its space to forty-seven New England firms, while seventeen New York companies sent representatives. In praising the Canadian displays, the *New York Times* complained that "as a rule the American exhibits are meager in quantity, badly arranged and displayed, crowded and uncared for."[17] In June *The Times* of London likewise shed tears, not only because the exhibition's overall balance sheet showed a loss of $100,000 but also because Great Britain itself did not take much interest in the event.

Annexation talk also was in the air at this time. On January 6, 1898, the *New York Times* reported that: "There has long been an undercurrent of public opinion in this island setting strongly in favor of its annexation to the United States."[18] In August of that year Senator Henry Cabot Lodge of Massachusetts proposed that America trade the Philippines apart from Manila or the island of Luzon to Great Britain in exchange for Jamaica and the Bahamas. The following January Phil. Robinson observed in *Harper's Weekly* that the British should sell the island to the United States, since "Jamaica does not reflect any glory upon England, nor does she contribute to the imperial revenue, nor does she absorb officials in any appreciable numbers."[19] The previous October, however, *The Times* of London declared that pro-annexation sentiment in the island had been overestimated by the New York City press, it being confined largely to a few disgruntled sugar and coffee planters, fruit growers, and professional men who were experiencing economic hardships.

THE SWETTENHAM INCIDENT

Unlike such non-British nations as Cuba, the Dominican Republic, and Haiti, Jamaica suffered no temporary takeover or military intervention by the United States during the Progressive Era. Nevertheless, on January 16, 1907, a natural calamity struck the island; in the words of the American consul, Nicholas B. Snyder, "Fearful earthquake followed by fire; Kingston destroyed; hundreds of lives lost; food sadly wanted."[20] Learning of this disaster, the chief engineer of the Panama Canal works dispatched a steamer laden with supplies and tents to the island. When Rear Admiral C. H. Davis arrived on the *Missouri,* accompanied by the *Indiana* on the following day, he conferred with Colonial Secretary Bourne and Deputy Inspector-General Wedderburn. The latter reported a serious mutiny at the local penitentiary, and with the blessing of Bourne asked Davis for aid.

The admiral then landed an armed force which put down the mutiny, repaired the lighthouse on Plumb Point, and fed several hundred American and British travellers; he also sent 200 men to clear the streets, tear down unsafe walls, and recover the dead. (A later report by Snyder on January 22 placed the total number of deaths at 1,800, with 30,000 homeless.) On the same day the British chargé, Esmé Howard, wrote Washington expressing "the thanks of the governor and people of Jamaica for the sympathy of the American people, and for the very prompt and valuable service rendered by Rear-Admiral Davis and the officers and men of the American naval squadron who visited Kingston for that purpose."[21] As for the British navy, none of its vessels reached the island for a week.

But what had been initiated as a noble humanitarian gesture became an ugly international incident, thanks to the over-reaction of Governor Sir Alexander Swettenham, who looked upon the American activities on shore as an illegal encroachment upon his authority and wrote Admiral Davis to this effect. The 61-year-old Swettenham was not only a Cambridge graduate, but also had served for forty years in the colonial service in the Straits Settlements and British Guiana, as well as Jamaica, and had published a well received work on the Malayan archipelago. According to *Current Literature,* he frequently made enemies by the score, but even the latter recognized his fairness and ability; to his friends he was a splendid horseman, a fine sportsman, and a lavish host.

No episode in the history of Jamaican-American relations has ever caused such a flurry of journalistic reactions in either the United States or Great Britain. The cartoonist Opper in the *New York American* had

Uncle Sam rejecting "Salome" John Bull's offer of Swettenham's head on a platter, while Bartholomew in the *Minneapolis Journal* portrayed the Governor as a human volcano erupting insolence and sarcasm. The *Independent* noted on February 7 that even in Kingston resolutions censuring the Governor had been unanimously adopted at a mass meeting of citizens, with the vice president of the Merchant's Exchange presiding; an earlier account had claimed that Swettenham withheld the pay of government clerks who were absent from their official duties caring for their dead or injured relatives. With respect to England, *Harper's Weekly* reported that no one had a good word to say about Swettenham there, "the cross-grained Governor of Jamaica [being] the recipient of almost universal disapprobation and rebuke at the hands of his countrymen."[22]

Yet *Blackwood's* magazine, in corroborating this assessment the following month, described Swettenham as "a grave man, sorely tried by calamity and impertinence,"[23] and there were other British publications which either praised him or downgraded the significance of the incident. Typical of these was the *Spectator,* which had early in the controversy opined: "The worst that can be said of Sir A. Swettenham is, not so much that he showed himself pedantic when pedantry was undesirable, as that he seems to have lost his temper, and conveyed his wishes to the Admiral in a letter of which the flippancy is hard to defend."[24] Perhaps the kindest endorsement of all came from a Toronto newspaper, which suggested that "if Swettenham be recalled, he should try to make a *detour* through Canada on his way home, as there are people in this country who would like to have a good look at the last of his kind."[25]

The Governor, in fact, did apologize to Admiral Davis under orders, and then offered his resignation on grounds of age. On February 12 the king himself (Edward VII) expressed his satisfaction with Swettenham's courage and devotion, but the British government merely inquired of the latter as to whether he would like to reconsider his resignation, rather than openly ask him to do so. On the other hand, President Theodore Roosevelt officially extended to Admiral Davis the highest commendation, after calling British Foreign Secretary Lord Edward Grey on the transatlantic telephone to protest Swettenham's behavior. (Grey had already directed the Governor to withdraw his protest.)[26]

Overlooked by many observers was the fact that Roosevelt, who had long been pursuing an activist policy in the Caribbean Basin, had previously become disenchanted with the Governor. Thus, in his recent canal message to Congress, the President had complained that "one of the governors of the islands in question has shown an unfriendly disposition to our work, and has thrown obstacles in the way of our getting the labor needed."[27] But Swettenham himself was by no means a disinterested observer of global developments, either, considering his wide diplomatic experience. Most understanding was *Harper's Weekly,* which observed: "We can easily forgive Governor Swettenham when we comprehend him. The truth is that in his latent enmity to men and things American he is not precisely individual."[28]

THE PROGRESSIVE ERA AND THE FIRST WORLD WAR

But even before the Swettenham incident had occurred in Jamaica itself, a situation had been developing in Panama which led to an explosion there two years earlier. Island laborers had been making their way to the isthmus for several years, where they worked under the auspices of the Canal Commission; at first things went smoothly, but a rather nasty incident occurred on April 26, 1905, when 50 Panamanian policemen attacked 200 Jamaican waterworks laborers. The former had been called by the American foreman after the workers had objected to the food given to them and had refused to return to their jobs. On May 8 the U.S. minister there, John Barrett, wrote the Panamanian minister of government and foreign affairs that ". . . the responsibility for the first incident at the Chiriqui Barracks rests with the American foreman and the laborers and not with the Panama police." He added, though, that "I must say in all frankness that I saw the police there act in a way which would have caused me to censure any police, whether they were in Panama, the United States, or Europe."[29] The Panamanian minister for foreign affairs, Don Santiago de la Guardia, subsequently informed the American chargé, W. F. Sands, on June 10 that the commanding police officer at the time of the altercation would be severely punished, and that an apology and expression of regret would be sent to the British consul. In fairness to the police, however, it must be admitted that they did not unleash their attack until one of their comrades had been wounded, at which time they proceeded to beat and even to bayonet some of the workers.

The years to follow witnessed a return to more normal conditions in U.S. diplomatic relations with Jamaica, as the outbreak of war in Europe neared. In February 1912 Great Britain extended to America the privilege of engaging in torpedo practice within the territorial waters of Jamaica, on the condition that advance notice be given.

Jamaica, however, failed to play an important role in American military operations after the United States entered World War 1 on April 6, 1917. Towards the end of that conflict, in August 1918, the American government did agree to have its consuls at Kingston and Port Antonio protect the Chinese populations residing there.

Returning to the economic sphere, the provocative American author Brooks Adams had observed in a book published in 1900, *America's Economic Supremacy,* that "Germans and Americans, who were more diligent, succeeded in making the island of Jamaica profitable after its owners had given it up as hopeless." Adams went on to attack the London tradesmen for their slackness, and suggested that confidence had begun to crumble with the failure of British agriculture there. Another object of ridicule in this work was the railroad system, "built at vast expense over the mountains where no traffic goes"[30] and charging prohibitive rates. In contrast, the banana exporting activities of the Boston Fruit Company had in the opinion of Adams been a brilliant success.

At the time of the great earthquake Jamaica was primarily agricultural, with the production of sugar being the leading industrial enterprise, although this was now playing only a minor role in the American market. Among the more important imports from the United States at this time were boots and shoes, foodstuffs, office and household furniture, household hardware and kitchen ware, cooking stoves and sewing machines, and barbed wire and wire fencing. On the other hand, Great Britain rather than America was now furnishing the island with most of its textiles, sheetings, cheap prints, and cottonades.[31] As of February 1908 both the Atlantic Fruit Company and the United Fruit Company were operating a line of steamers between the United States and Jamaica, which carried passengers as well as fruits; the Hamburg-American Steamship Company and the Royal Mail Steam Packet Company were also active. But Jamaican commercial relations with the United States at this time were not always tranquil and harmonious. Among the most frequent complaints levelled against American goods by islanders were with respect to bad packing and consequent pilfering, the terms of payment, and the high price of drugs and medicines.

Jamaica experienced a real economic scare in June 1913 when word was received through the headquarters of the United Fruit Company that the American government was preparing to impose an import duty on its bananas. That March the island Assembly had rejected a proposed export tax on these, and by order of the Governor the ban was lifted from the export of fustic (a dye material) to the mainland. A report then arrived in July that the proposed American tax was to be five cents on each bunch. Islanders were of the opinion that British representatives in Washington had not been supporting their position vigorously enough; they found the tax inexplicable, since bananas for commercial purposes could not be grown in the United States. That September Jamaica breathed a sigh of relief when the congressional Tariff Conference Committee kept bananas on the free list, as President Woodrow Wilson had requested.

At the time of the outbreak of World War 1, in the summer of 1914, Jamaica led the world in the production of bananas. Despite the activities of the United Fruit Company, which had planted 8,000 acres, many independent farmers were also laboring on tiny plots. (Aside from the bananas United Fruit was also cultivating 9,000 acres of coconut groves and 4,000 acres of sugar cane.) Unfortunately, in September 1916 a hurricane destroyed the entire banana crop of the island, ruining hundreds of growers, and ending exports of the fruit for more than two months. One of the surviving firms was United Fruit, which if anything found that its position had been strengthened by the natural disaster. Writing during the same year, Chester Lloyd Jones commented that "if it were not for the banana industry the plight of Jamaica would be sad indeed,"[32] since its fruit exports to the United States had been responsible for the island's steamship connections. Jamaica, though, was not then and never has been a typical one-product West Indies colony; one might cite the example of island coffee, which at this time was marketed in France, since it was unpopular in the United States.

COOPERATION AND CONTROVERSY, 1919-39

During the post-war years the best-known Jamaican in America was the tragic Pan-African leader Marcus Garvey. Born on the island in 1887, Garvey visited the United States around the time of the outbreak of World War 1; upon his return to Jamaica in 1914 he began to publish a newspaper and also set up the Universal Negro Improvement Association. The objective of this organization was to "take Africa, organize it, develop it, arm it, and make it the defender of Negroes the world over."[33] Garvey then returned to New York City in 1916, where he held the first international convention of the UNIA in 1920, while the following year proclaiming himself president of the newly formed Empire of Africa. Unfortunately for Garvey, the collapse of his Black Star Steamship Line led to his imprisonment after he had been convicted of using the mails to defraud in connection with the sale of stock. Forced to leave America for Jamaica after his release from jail in 1927, Garvey died in London shortly after the outbreak of World War 2, a largely neglected prophet.

While Garvey was experiencing his difficulties in the United States, Jamaicans also were critical of America on occasion. On February 15, 1921, the U.S. consul reported to Washington that there had been a "tendency on the part of the *Daily Gleaner* of Kingston to publish news articles and editorials, the principal effect of which is likely to be that of stirring up feelings antagonistic to the United States and American policies."[34] At this time the *Gleaner* was the only important daily newspaper on the island. Among those issues which were agitating relations between the United States and Jamaica, according to the consul, were the cancellation of the British war debt, the possible annexation of Jamaica by America, and commercial rivalry between Great Britain and the United States. Despite its occasional anti-American outbursts, this newspaper frequently copied news articles and pictures from the U.S. press without giving it credit, and even derived some of its most profitable advertising from American sources.

Especially critical of the United States was a Mr. Allan Taylor, who by reversing the letters in his last name penned a column under the pseudonym "Rolyat" for the *Gleaner*. On April 27, 1931, "Rolyat" observed, "She [the United States] has her eye on Jamaica, too—and would like to see the Stars and Stripes flying over the Government Buildings." He then charged that America wanted to cripple local industry, flood the market with U.S. goods, bar British goods via a high tariff, and destroy the rum and sugar industries.[35] The following year, on January 19, 1932, an editorial critical of American reparations policy appeared, which downgraded U.S. contributions to the war effort in Europe with its sneering reference to "an entirely untrained army, commanded by a fool called General Pershing, who prevented his soldiers from playing any really effective part in the struggle."[36] Three days later the *Gleaner* watered down its indictment somewhat with the observation that "many another living leader of men is so described."[37]

During the 1930s several controversies of varying importance disturbed Jamaican-American relations. Thus, on July 28, 1931, Paul C. Squire, the American consul, complained to Washington that Pan American Airways, which since 1930 had been carrying incoming mail, was experiencing discrimination at the expense of Caribbean Airways, which had been handling the outgoing mail. (The latter was a local British company.) To make matters even worse, the Jamaican government had blocked

Pan American from leasing a landing site, with the result that the latter's planes had to land at a float in Kingston Harbor. "I have nothing against the Pan American," observed the Governor in the consul's account, "but this Company must not think it can run this Island";[38] the Governor also took the position that air mail service might not prove beneficial to Jamaica, and that businessmen could always use the cable. It was around this time, too, that air service between New York City and Bermuda began, fortunately under far more auspicious circumstances.

An even more complex dispute, which came to a climax in 1936, involved the Rockefeller Foundation, which had been providing the island with health services since 1918 and which the Governor had praised in 1929. With quinine available at any post office, the foundation had been largely successful in stamping out malaria; on the other hand, the Jamaican medical superintendent had failed to take any steps to wipe out yellow fever, while the campaign against yaws was still in mid-course. But the real focal point of contention was the foundation's anti-tuberculosis drive. Dr. E. L. Opie had made a scientific investigation of this disease between 1927 and 1932 with its backing, and this had resulted in a subsequent report which won the approval of the Jamaican government. On May 27, 1935, the governor, Sir Edward Denham, suggested that a tuberculosis sanitarium would be a fitting memorial in honor of the silver jubilee of King George V. Long Mountain near Kingston was Denham's choice for a site; but when the proposal went before the Assembly it was attacked by a rural black legislator named J. A. G. Smith, with the result that the Governor had to withdraw it. The American consul then suggested in his report to Washington that Smith was acting as the spokesman for several leading members of the medical profession in Kingston who did not want to spend all the money on a single sanitarium.[39]

A totally different type of controversy erupted the following year, in 1937, when Jamaican censors prohibited the showing of the American motion pictures *Winterset* and *We Who Are About to Die*. Under censorship laws passed in 1913, 1925, and 1926, the censors did not have to explain why they banned certain films. It was the opinion of the importer of these two motion pictures that censors had placed them on the prohibited list because they contained scenes which might encourage criminal behavior on the part of those who viewed them.

The fear of violence on the part of Jamaican authorities, moreover, was by no means groundless. During the summer of 1938 there occurred a series of riots and strikes in Kingston which led to a number of police shootings; over the past several decades political, social, and economic discontent had been building up on the island. It was in the aftermath of the flareup that William Alexander Bustamante and Norman Washington Manley emerged as leaders, dominating island politics for the next twenty-five years. As for American involvement in these disturbances, the Reverend Ethelred Brown, secretary of the Jamaican Progressive League of New York, represented that organization at the subsequent British Royal Commission hearings. This was perhaps the first time that Jamaicans in New York City had taken an active role in island politics.

TRADE, INVESTMENT, AND TOURISM, 1919-39

In October 1919 the United Fruit Company announced that it was closing its wholesale and retail stores on the north side of the island, thus removing itself from the merchandising business. The Kingston *Daily Gleaner* observed in this connection, "We are delighted that this decision has at last been arrived at; delighted that one of the causes of a great deal of discontent in this island has been at last removed."[40] Nevertheless, when the attorney general of Jamaica journeyed to the United States in a search for tourists in 1922, he planned a stop at United Fruit Company offices, where he was going to ask for a liberal contribution to a fund for publicizing the island. That October, too, the Pan American Society wrote to the Jamaica Tourist Association on behalf of an unnamed individual who desired to purchase a large amount of land. This was no isolated episode; many other American investors also were involved in similar negotiations at this time.

From the standpoint of trade, in 1921 Jamaica was importing approximately two-thirds more than she was exporting. The United States was still the major source of foodstuffs and most raw materials imported into the island, while America also was the destination of 66.7 percent of Jamaica's coconuts and 82.9 percent of its bananas.[41] Trade statistics for the following year, however, revealed that Great Britain bought 60 percent of the island's cocoa, 85 percent of its logwood extract, and 78 percent of its rum, while Canada purchased 75 percent of its sugar and 80 percent of its coffee. Over the years, of course, there occurred fluctuations in the role played by America, England, and Canada with respect to the island's commerce.

The following year, 1923, Mr. J. L. Wilson-Goode, the British trade commissioner in the British West Indies and Central America, observed that "American influences on the trade of Jamaica shows no sign of abatement," and that "the domination of American products over a period of several years has left an enduring mark upon the trade of Jamaica." Wilson-Goode concluded that islanders had a decided preference for British goods from the standpoint of quality, but that this had been more than offset by American advertising techniques. At this time, moreover, the major hotels for both American and British tourists were the property of the United Fruit Company (which sometimes ran them at a financial loss), while the rival Atlantic Fruit Company had recently purchased a number of banana and coconut plantations in the parish of St. Mary.[42]

By 1927 most foreign investments in Jamaica were either American or Canadian rather than British, although the London market had processed colonial loans at times. The Jamaica Railway Company, representing an investment of $12 million, was now in the hands of American investors; in addition, United Fruit owned 80 miles of railroad and 124 miles of tramways. The total American investment in the island at this time was approximately $25 million, with $6 million of this being concentrated in the Jamaican Consolidated Copper Company.

Despite the fact that Jamaica was exporting over 22 million stems of bananas in 1929, constituting 54.5 percent of its total exports, in 1928 the Republic of Honduras had usurped its leadership as the leading banana exporting nation. Six months prior to the outbreak of the Great Depression in the United States, on April 1, 1929, over six thousand investors led by Negro planters with small plots of land formed the Jamaica Banana Producers' Association. For the remainder of that year this new organization sold over 5 million bunches of bananas, and in 1930 over 7 million. According to Peter Abrahams, the years between 1929 and 1938 were the peak ones for the Jamaican banana exporting trade.

In an episode reminiscent of the ban on the importation of orange plants a generation earlier, in August 1929 the Jamaican government prohibited the entry of *all* American fruits and vegetables, unless it could be proved that they were free of the Mediterranean fruit fly.[43] In contrast, during the following year the Legislative Council ordered forty special railway cars from the United States, charging that British firms could not guarantee prompt delivery; this episode led to an exchange in the English parliament in February. Then in the spring of 1931 the Legislative Council reduced its annual appropriation for the Tourist Bureau from £1,500 to £1,000; one unnamed Jamaican official observed in this connection that "we don't want to raise the cost of living, and

American tourists spoil servants and others with whom they come into contact."[44]

Six years later, in 1937, the United Fruit Company and the Jamaica Banana Producers' Association signed a highly important agreement which had far-reaching consequences. Under this the association was to become an ordinary trading organization rather than a cooperative, while in return one U.S. cent on every bunch of bananas exported from the island was "to be used in such a way as to be of real help in the cultural development of the island and of the peasants."[45] Norman Manley, who had been the association's lawyer, later took charge of the setting up of an organization to administer this fund, Jamaica Welfare, Limited.

In assessing the overall American impact on the island between the two world wars, economic and otherwise, one might again turn to Consul Paul C. Squire's lengthy letter dated July 28, 1931. Among other things, Squire pointed to "the popularity of American goods, more especially cinema films . . . and motor cars." At that time trucks and bicycles sometimes displayed the Stars and Stripes, while there were autobuses named New York Special and Broadway; the pushcarts of beverage peddlers frequently carried such mottos as "E Pluribus Unum" and "In God We Trust!"[46] If, therefore, the Jamaican government at times did take actions of an anti-American character, it may well have been out of a well founded fear that U.S. influences were gradually penetrating an island whose sheer geographical size and natural resources theoretically should have militated against it becoming an American appendage. Yet as we have seen, the banana saga was but a single—if perhaps the most important—aspect of this growing domination as World War 2 approached.

WORLD WAR 2

While Jamaica was experiencing a series of riots and strikes in 1938, which disturbances were largely responsible for the start of the political careers of some of the island's most distinguished political leaders, Germany was moving towards the inauguration of hostilities a year later which were to precipitate a global holocaust. It is noteworthy that the British did not attempt to institute the draft in Jamaica during World War 2; Paul Blanshard has suggested in this connection that "hundreds of colored volunteers in World War 1 had come back to the island with tales of race discrimination in British armed forces."[47]

Generally speaking, Jamaica was relatively unaffected by World War 2, just as it had been relatively unaffected by World War 1.

Nevertheless, there was an American military presence, since on April 4, 1941, officials commissioned the Vernam Naval Air Station. This station, which was located on Little Goat Island, 30 miles from Kingston on the south side of Jamaica, was designed to provide base facilities for two squadrons of seaplanes patrolling the Windward Passage approach to the Caribbean. The original base site to the east of Galleon Harbor had been abandoned because of malaria, frequent flooding, and a nearby leper colony. From the standpoint of general layout and buildings, Vernam resembled the station at Great Exuma in the Bahamas; engineers dredged a total of 2,800,000 yards in preparing the Little Goat Island base for use. After the original contract had been terminated because of waste and inefficiency, work was completed during the summer of 1942, with the total cost of the base reaching the sum of $17,869,553. Even by the end of the war, though, no lease had been signed for a number of reasons, including the confused status of landholdings in several areas.

Aside from Trinidad, Jamaica for a number of reasons was the only British island colony in the Caribbean which had a sizable local defense force during World War 2. (A Canadian infantry battalion had been present since early in the war.) There being fewer Americans than Canadians, in January 1942 the brigadier in command of the Canadian and British troops was given control over the Combined Local Defense Forces "until such time as the strength and composition of the United States garrison . . . warranted the assumption of command by an appropriate United States Army Officer."[48] Both Admiral Hoover and Colonel Ewert, the local U.S. commander, were displeased at this arrangement, especially after October of that year, when reinforcements raised the number of American troops to a level slightly higher than that of the British and Canadian forces combined. But both the War and Navy departments decided to preserve the status quo, the latter taking the position that a change in command might aggravate the possibility of a labor disturbance. There was a slight increase in the U.S. garrison in Jamaica early in 1943, but by June a definite reduction in American forces was well under way.

In the *History of Jamaica Base Command 17 November 1941 to 12 May 1945,* the anonymous author observes that "relations between the base and local authorities have always been cordial and there has existed a spirit of co-operation that has worked for the good of all concerned."[49] However, a tempest in a teapot did develop in October 1943 when the post exchange thoughtlessly placed an advertisement in the local newspapers for white workers only at Fort Simonds. The commanding officer, who was absent at the time of the incident, wrote a letter to the daily which more or less calmed tempers, but not before the Kingston City Council had sent a protest to President Franklin D. Roosevelt. Then in 1945 a colored journalist travelling from Jamaica to Miami was banned from the segregated Pan American restaurant in the latter city, causing a leading citizen of Kingston to complain that the United States was "devoid of any decency, devoid of any culture, and devoid of any of that human feeling that makes for a respectful citizenry."[50]

Among the more prominent visitors to the island from America during World War 2 was Mrs. Franklin D. Roosevelt, who arrived at Fort Simonds by airplane in March 1944. After addressing American forces at the base, she was the guest of the Governor at King's House, where a reception was held in her honor. Six months later, though, in September 1944, authorities placed the Naval Air Station on Little Goat Island in caretaker status, as the war focused more and more on Europe itself.

Tied in with the construction and operation of the Jamaican base was the labor question. Unlike Bermuda, where 86 percent of the workers were on loan from America, Jamaica supplied 93 percent of the laborers; out of the 44,399 workers at the base in October 1941, only 7,400 were Americans. Labor unions, which were active in the island by that time, became quite irritated at the American refusal to deal with the Trades Union Council. It was the position of the War Department that it would accept a consultative committee on which there were labor representatives, but would not recognize a single union as the sole bargaining agency for island workers. So potentially explosive was the situation that the first units of the American garrison were sent to Jamaica because of labor troubles and impending riots, not because of the threat of external attack.

THE LAST DAYS OF COLONIAL RULE

In the years between the end of World War 2 and the granting of independence, Jamaica struck out in new directions in a number of areas, although the social, political, and economic ferment had begun to boil in the years prior to World War 2. Island government was evolving during these years, since the ministerial system went into operation during 1953, while Jamaica obtained complete internal self-government in 1959, two years after the executive council had become a cabinet. (Universal adult suffrage had arrived as early as 1944.) The first Jamaican prime minister was Norman Manley, who took office after the July 1959 election, and whose son also became prime minister at a later date.

Perhaps the most controversial issue to emerge during this era of political change was the role of Jamaica vis-à-vis the West Indies Federation (WIF). The island joined this ten-nation organization in 1958, only to withdraw after a national referendum held on September 19, 1961, had rejected continued membership. Apparently, a critical factor in the eventual Jamaican secession was the designation of a U.S. naval base at Chaguaramas, Trinidad, for the ultimate capital site of the WIF rather than Kingston. According to Wendell Bell, many members of the island's ruling class were alienated by this decision. As a result, the government itself registered a loud protest,[51] while in 1960 Sir Alexander Bustamante's Jamaica Labour Party called for the island to secede from the federation.

It was during this same year that the Reverend Claudius Henry, the "Repairer of the Breach," ran afoul of the Jamaican government. The previous October Henry had begun enlisting twenty thousand bearded natives as new members of an already established back-to-Africa movement, the Ras Tafarians, but this soon evolved into a drive to make Jamaica itself into a Ras Tafari-controlled republic. In April 1961 a raiding police unit uncovered a cache of firearms and missiles stored in the basement of one of his churches; although the island government jailed Henry himself as a result of this discovery, his son Reynold and ten previously deported American Negroes from Brooklyn continued to operate out of the Red Hills region northwest of Kingston. When an unarmed British patrol was captured by the Ras Tafarians, two Tommies were shot and killed in cold blood by the latter. Enraged by this act of violence, Prime Minister Norman Manley unleashed a retaliatory force of one thousand men against the terrorists, backed by aircraft, mortar and rocket crews, and police dogs.[52] Those unfortunate enough to be captured were later hanged for murder. In addressing the National Press Club of Washington in May 1961, Manley attempted to link the Ras Tafarians with Fidel Castro; at this time the Prime Minister observed of Jamaica that "nowhere in the world has more progress been made in developing a nonracial society."[53]

Let us turn next to military and diplomatic relations between the island and the mainland in the years between 1945 and 1962. Little Goat Island was disestablished as a naval air facility on June 1, 1947, with the American government retaining physical possession of the property itself. During this seventeen-year period the United States expended a total of $8 million in grants and credits to Jamaica.

On January 9, 1953, a mission sent to Jamaica at the request of the Governor by the International Bank for Reconstruction and Development published its recommendations for the economic development

of the island. This mission, consisting of seven experts under the direction of John C. de Wilde, had been in Jamaica during March and April
of 1952. Among other things, it proposed a ten-year development
program which would nearly double island goods and services during
the next decade; "Contrary to widely prevalent belief," its report
observed, "we are convinced that the potentialities of agriculture in
Jamaica are far from exhausted."[54] In the opinion of the mission,
the chief problems facing the island at that time were chronic unemployment and widespread poverty.

Two years later, in June 1955, the Foreign Operations Administration
allocated $35,000 in U.S. funds to Jamaica during the coming twelve
months under an agreement providing technical assistance for the long-
range development of the island. During both 1956 and 1958 Jamaica
explored governmental loans in Washington as a result of poor experiences
in the London market; this marked the first time in the history of the
British Empire that a colony had attempted to float a loan in America.
Then in February 1959 Jamaica filed a registration statement with the
Securities and Exchange Commission in connection with the proposed
public sale of $12,500,000 in bonds in the United States. Kuhn, Loeb
and Company was to market these bonds beginning February 26, the
proceeds from which were to help finance agricultural development in
such areas as livestock, cocoa, bananas, coffee, and citrus fruit.

Concurrent with this move to seek funds in the United States was an
attempt to attract American industry to the island. Thus, Prime Minister
Norman Manley's spring 1956 budget proposals included a tax exemption program for U.S. private investment, featuring an optional seven-
year tax holiday for new manufacturers. (At this time most of the
$50 million total American outlay was in bauxite.) Also of major im-
portance were a proposed reciprocal agreement ending double taxation, various tariff concessions to new exporting companies, and a
program of total construction. It was not until 1958, however, that
the U.S. Senate extended the double tax convention between America
and England to the island.

American economic assistance to the contrary, a poll of Jamaican
leaders taken during this year as to whether the Soviet Union or the
United States was more effective in winning over to its point of view
the people living in underdeveloped nations revealed that 56 percent
chose the former and only 24 percent the latter.[55] As Wendell Bell
points out, the majority may have felt that large-scale economic reforms in underdeveloped countries were incompatible with political
democracy. On the other hand, the same leaders came to the conclusion that from the standpoint of moral rightness the United States had

a decided edge on the Soviet Union; fully five-sixths of the sample backed Uncle Sam in this connection.

During 1962, the year of independence, another poll of Jamaican leaders showed that 71 percent favored a national alignment with Western nations, while only 25 percent advocated cooperation with neutralist states and 4 percent with Communist regimes. By 1974, though, the pro-Western percentage in still another poll had slipped to 36, the neutralist to 7, and the Communist to 1; two new categories—Jamaica's self-interest and Third World countries—received 27 and 29, respectively. One should keep these shifts of opinion in mind, since they help explain changes in official governmental policy following 1962.

THE BAUXITE CHALLENGE

As Jamaica moved closer and closer towards independence, its commercial dependency on the United States increased rather than decreased. Although American exports to Jamaica doubled between 1955 ($23 million) and 1960 ($48 million), imports from the island experienced an even greater growth, from $22 million in 1955 to $54 million in 1960. By 1961 the United States had replaced Great Britain as the chief purchaser of Jamaica's exports, a significant development on the eve of the latter's independence from the mother country.

Bananas were still being shipped from Jamaica to America following World War 2, but their ascendancy was challenged by bauxite after the great hurricane of August 1951. As early as 1947 Kaiser Aluminum and Chemical Corporation had sent its first search party to Jamaica in quest of the raw material which yields aluminum, but it was not until 1950 that an agreement was reached between the island government and two U.S. bauxite companies, Reynolds Jamaica Mines and Kaiser. Under the auspices of the latter a remote southern fishing village, Little Pedro, was renamed Port Kaiser and a railroad cut through the Santa Cruz Mountains to the world's largest bauxite mine; in 1953 alone 665,671 short wet tons of the raw material were shipped to the United States. Accumulating a total of 67,000 acres of land by 1960, Kaiser soon diversified its operations into such non-mining areas as land reclamation, resettlement projects, cattle raising, tree planting, and farming.

By 1957 the Jamaican government had become highly dissatisfied with the overly generous terms extended to Kaiser, Reynolds, and Alumina Jamaica, a Canadian company. Under a new agreement negotiated by Prime Minister Norman Manley with the American firms, there was to be a combined payment of an income tax and royalty amounting to 14 shillings on bauxite mined and exported from the island, rather than the initial royalty of 1 shilling per ton and the previous income tax of 1 shilling, 8 pence per ton.[56] One must question, though, whether this new agreement was, as Thomas Balogh argued at the time, "a turning point in the relationship of governments of underdeveloped or formerly colonial territories and large-scale businesses,"[57] since it did not begin to approach expropriation.

It will be recalled that the Korean War had broken out in 1950, the same year that the initial contract was signed between the Jamaican government and the American bauxite companies. Since the United States had depleted most of its bauxite reserve during World War 2, it thus had to turn to such foreign producers as Dutch Guiana (Surinam), British Guiana (Guyana), or the Dominican Republic to supply its needs during the Korean War; unfortunately, the first two countries were further distant from America than Jamaica, while the latter was less democratic. By 1958 the stockpiling of Jamaican bauxite in the United States for strategic purposes had reached the desired level, but American officials continued to purchase the island's output as a form of economic aid. A quite different consideration was the post-war desire of the United States government to challenge the leadership of Alcoa over the North American aluminum industry.

Another beneficiary of American cold war diplomacy was Jamaican sugar. In 1960 the United States government placed an embargo on Cuban sugar, with Fidel Castro now in control of the island. As a result, Jamaica was able to market sugar in America at prices in excess of those obtained from the negotiated price quota under the Commonwealth Sugar Agreement. While the island sold only 39,362 tons of sugar in America in 1960, this figure grew to 102,372 in 1961 and 82,925 in 1962.

Turning next of all to labor, with more and more Jamaicans employed in the bauxite industry it is not surprising that union organizers would become increasingly active on the island. Here one should note that the United Steel Workers of America, an affiliate of the AFL-CIO, financially assisted the National Workers Union in its recruiting drive; far from opposing this unionizing effort, the companies favored a shop steward system to settle disputes in an orderly manner. In addition, many members of the Jamaican labor force had been union members while working in the United States. Unemployment, however, continued to plague the island, since in 1955 alone 15,000 workers sought jobs in Great Britain.

TRANQUILLITY AND TURMOIL, 1962-73

During 1962 Jamaica obtained its independence from Great Britain, thus becoming the first new nation in the Western Hemisphere since Panama. As a result, on August 6, 1962, the United States consulate general of Kingston was raised to the status of an embassy. Among those present at the independence ceremonies was Vice President Lyndon B. Johnson, representing President John Kennedy; also on hand were Mrs. Lyndon B. Johnson, future Ambassador William Doherty, and Democratic Representative Adam Clayton Powell of New York. Back on the mainland New York's Republican Governor Nelson Rockefeller proclaimed August 5-16 as Jamaica Independence Week in New York, while on the following day L.B.J. visited two Peace Corps camps on the island.

On August 7, too, Sir Alexander Bustamante, who had become prime minister following an election held in April, announced that the United States was free to establish a military base on Jamaica without offering any aid in return. Bustamante, who described his new nation as pro-American, Christian, and anti-Communist, visited both London and Washington in the months ahead. He earlier had paid a call on the U.S. Senate in June, and had conferred at this time with President Kennedy, Acting Secretary of State George Ball, Secretary of Labor Arthur Goldberg, and Secretary of Agriculture Orville Freeman.

On November 28, 1961, Ambassador Ivan B. White, the U.S. special representative in the West Indies, had observed in the course of a ten-day visit to the island that Jamaica had been doing a very progressive job. This sentiment was shared by most Americans following independence; the island's biggest booster in the U.S. Congress was perhaps the abovementioned Adam Clayton Powell, who in the years which followed annually made a little address celebrating the events of August 6, 1962. Less ecstatic was Chester Bowles, who as a special advisor to President Kennedy wrote a memorandum listing Jamaica as a country "whose problems were sufficiently acute to require U.S. aid, but whose difficulties resulted mainly from 'misuse and maldistribution' of their wealth."[58]

The decade and more since 1962 has witnessed the signing of a number of treaties between the Jamaican and American governments. These include the investment guaranties and Peace Corps agreements of 1962, and the defense and economic and technical cooperation agreements of 1963. The defense agreement, which was signed in lieu of the establishment of a military base, was criticized by Opposition Leader Norman

Manley on the grounds that it might compromise Jamaican sovereignty; under it the Jamaican government received four Cessna Skywagon aircraft and twelve medium machine guns. Also from that year one might cite the bilateral agreement of 1963 on the export of textiles, in which the United States agreed to ease the order limiting the volume of imports of island products to the 1962 level.[59] Then another note dealing with this trade in cotton goods was signed in 1967, setting an overall ceiling of 2 million square yards annually and specific ceilings on eleven apparel categories.

Official American contacts with the island were by no means limited to the above agreements. In 1962, for example, the Agency for International Development loaned $2.2 million to Jamaica to modernize and expand five water systems serving more than eighty thousand rural islanders. During the following year AID agreed to insure all U.S. investments furthering economic growth, the Export-Import Bank extended a $5 million credit for the Development Finance Corporation, and the American government approved a $1,700,000 loan for low cost housing.[60] In contrast, Peace Corps activities were less successful. Regional Director Jack H. Vaughn observed in February 1963 that the Jamaican project had been his main headache in Latin America, while two professors at the University of the West Indies labelled it a fiasco. Among the factors contributing to this situation were the Peace Corps's failure to obtain $10,000 worth of shop equipment and tools, the lack of customary field training on the part of its volunteers, and the overly plush atmosphere of tourist-oriented Kingston.

Early in 1964, on March 22, the United States surrendered its last defense area on the island, 100 acres of Portland Ridge. This had been set aside for the creation of the long-range navigational communication station program Loran; nevertheless, it had never been used for that purpose, and was now being sought by the Jamaican government for agricultural projects. Thus, of the six islands surveyed in this monograph, it was Jamaica which had its base closed first.

While the American military was withdrawing from the island, the first U.S. ambassador to Jamaica, William Doherty, also was preparing to make his departure. The former head of the National Association of Letter Carriers, Doherty had been the first representative of organized labor ever to be elevated to ambassadorial rank. Assessing his tenure in office, the *Kingston Star* on April 25 of this year evaluated as outstanding the assistance which he gave to Jamaica's economy. *Newsday*, the monthly magazine of the West Indies, had entitled an article on Doherty in its December 1962 issue "Mailman Making Good." His achievement was even more impressive in view of the fact that he was a

Catholic ambassador to a country where members of the Catholic Church were distinctly in the minority.

AID again made a loan to Jamaica in 1965, this time for $3.8 million to assist the expansion of the island's dairy industry over the next five years. During the same year the Jamaican government opened a permanent Trade Centre in New York City to exhibit the island's industrial products. In 1968 Jamaica joined CARIFTA, the Caribbean Free Trade Association.

By this time Prime Minister Bustamante's health had begun to decline. In the first general election held since independence, on January 21, 1967, Bustamante's Jamaica Labour Party retained power with Donald Sangster, who had acted as prime minister under his ailing chief, assuming office in his own right. Sangster, however, died two months later, and Hugh Lawson Shearer assumed the prime ministership. Despite these changes in leadership, the Jamaican government continued to pay homage to black nationalism. Thus, in November 1968 it presented the Marcus Garvey Prize for Human Rights posthumously to the Reverend Dr. Martin Luther King, Jr. Garvey had earlier been made the fledgling country's first National Hero after his body had been returned to his birthplace in 1964, twenty-four years after his death.

American economic involvement in Jamaica continued during the Nixon years, and if anything surpassed that of the Kennedy-Johnson ones. In November 1969 the recently created Jamaica Development Bank opened a branch in New York City. Desirous of attracting capital from Jamaicans residing in the United States as well as from American investors attracted to the island, the New York City office was set up to provide information, determine legal requirements, and improve the machinery for selling national development bonds in the manner of Israel.

The continued interest of the Nixon administration in the island was reflected in the work of a specially appointed commission headed by career diplomat Maurice Bernbaum, which made an on-the-scene investigation at the end of 1970 to determine how America could help Jamaica remain politically stable and a safe place for foreign investment. This commission had been sent to the island at the request of Prime Minister Shearer, who had conferred with the President in Washington during July. Bernbaum and his associates were assisted in their investigation by experts in labor training, farm economics, nutrition, and public administration.

As of May 1972 the AID had loaned the island government $30.5 million since 1961, the Export-Import Bank $60 million. The AID loans had gone for community water supply development, low cost housing, dairy farms, feasibility studies, rural feeder roads, and a secondary mortgage bank, while the Export-Import loans had been made for a number of industrial and infra-structure projects. At this time approximately two hundred Peace Corps volunteers were active in Jamaica, primarily in education, but as we have noted, their record was a mixed one.

Despite these American contributions to the new Jamaica, not every ambassador who followed William Doherty won the universal respect and admiration accorded him. A case in point was the late Long Island millionaire and heavy Republican campaign contributor Vincent de Roulet, whom the new Jamaican prime minister, Michael Manley, declared persona non grata in the summer of 1973. De Roulet, who according to *Time* kept a 90-foot yacht in Kingston harbor and seventeen racehorses at the local Caymanas track, climaxed his four years as ambassador by testifying before the Senate Foreign Relations Subcommittee on Multinational Corporations. According to de Roulet, he had made a deal with Prime Minister Manley before the 1972 election in Jamaica; Manley allegedly had promised that he would not nationalize the American bauxite companies if he emerged victorious, while the ambassador in return committed himself not to attempt to sway the outcome of the campaign. After the Prime Minister denied these claims and de Roulet was forced to leave the island, the Jamaica *Daily News* observed: "What the public needs to know is why the ambassador was allowed to remain as long as he did."

Even retrospectively American journalists have not dealt sympathetically with de Roulet, who died of a heart attack in 1975 at the age of 49 and thus is no longer able to defend himself. According to *Harper's,* the ambassador supposedly observed that "until I arrived, Kingston used to be the repository of the dregs of the Foreign Service"; his response to living in a city with a high crime rate was to carry a gun in his lap while driving the streets of the capital. As ambassador, de Roulet's major undertakings were his strenuous effort to limit black immigration from the island into the United States (he also tried to block visas for musicians Miriam Makeba and Mick Jagger) and his vigorous attempt to force the chief executives of American aluminum companies to improve their firms' public standing in Jamaica. Even the highly critical George Crile has described the latter effort as a remarkable success. More important, in the spring of 1971 a team of career foreign service officers observed of the unconventional ambassador's tenure on the island that "under the vigorous, skillful, and intelligent leadership of a non-career Chief of Mission, Embassy Kingston gets highest marks for its achievements with respect to U.S. objectives."[61] Summing up his stay in Jamaica, de Roulet declared that he would have been looked upon by posterity as the outstanding U.S. ambassador to the island, if only he had resigned his position sooner.

RECENT COMMERCIAL TRENDS

While island laborers were harvesting American crops, Jamaica itself continued to export agricultural produce to the United States. In 1962 the United Fruit Company entered into an agreement with authorities in Kingston to resume the cultivation of bananas; under this the firm was to make an initial investment of £700,000, in an attempt to increase the island's production by 2 million stems a year. The Jamaican sugar industry also was given a boost in November when the U.S. Department of Agriculture asked for 11,000 long tons of sugar after some of the permanent foreign quota holders had failed to supply America with 200,000 short tons. Three years later, in 1965, a five-year Sugar Act went into effect in the United States. Exports of rum from the island to America also had increased from 95,000 proof gallons in 1963 to 705,000 in 1965, with a corresponding decline in shipments to Great Britain.

Writing in 1967, however, Sir Harold Mitchell observed: "The great campaign to re-establish the [banana] industry with the aid of Government grants, after the 1951 hurricane, had met with only partial success. The heavy cost of combating disease and competition from other countries had weakened the industry."[62] On the other hand, there had been a slight increase in sugar exports during 1966 and 1967 as a result of the abovementioned American legislation; nevertheless, the island did not profit as much as it might have from American sugar needs because of low production. A somewhat different situation existed with respect to ginger, since by 1970 the United States was absorbing over one-half of the island's total output.

Following independence, the bauxite industry continued to flourish, and in 1964 the Aluminum Company of America began operations in Jamaica. The absence of cheap electricity in the island made difficult the conversion of alumina into aluminum, but in 1967 Reynolds Metal Company, the Anaconda Company, and Kaiser Aluminum and Chemical Corporation announced plans for a $175 million alumina plant near Port Kaiser. The total annual capacity of this facility was to be between 875,000 and 1,300,000 tons. This step by the three firms was endorsed by the Jamaican government, which obtained a larger tax revenue as a result.

During 1974 the Manley administration moved towards nationalization of the holdings of the bauxite and alumina companies, after the increase in global oil prices had posed a threat to the solvency of the island's economy. In January Michael Manley announced that his government would renegotiate the present contracts with these foreign firms; in April the Leader of the Opposition endorsed a higher rate of royalty payments, while in June the Jamaican House of Representatives passed a sharply increased bauxite levy act, which multiplied the island's annual take from these companies eight-fold ($25 million v. $200 million). That March the International Bauxite Association had been formed in Conakry, Guinea, with headquarters in Kingston. By November the government of the island was purchasing for $20 million in Jamaican currency 51 percent of the Kaiser Bauxite Company, with Kaiser continuing to manage the operation, and was moving towards the acquisition of a similar interest in Reynolds Jamaica Mines.

On May 25, 1974, *Business Week* noted that bauxite-producing countries perhaps have the best chance after the oil-producing nations of keeping prices at a high level. At this time Jamaica was supplying the United States with 40 to 60 percent of its bauxite needs, and the American companies had an $800 million investment in the island. While accepting the additional bauxite levy under protest, the U.S. firms did request that the International Center for Settlement of Investment Disputes rule on the legality of the Jamaican government's action; the Prime Minister announced that he would defy an adverse ruling from that body. The American companies also employed as their agent in the talks the experienced labor negotiator Arthur Goldberg, a long-time acquaintance of Manley. Viewing the situation from the Third World standpoint, James Nelson Goodsell noted in the *Progressive* that Manley's slowness in taking action reflected both his patience and his fairness in dealing with the aluminum companies. The U.S. firms, of course, saw matters somewhat differently.

But American interest in developing the island's economy by no means has been restricted to bauxite since independence. In March 1964, for example, an $18 million Esso Oil refinery was completed. As of January 1963 approximately $60 million of the total $270 million foreign investment in Jamaica had come from the United States; a Boston firm had constructed a $6 million jute manufacturing plant, while an American company had opened a $2 million resort hotel in

Kingston. In April 1965 it was announced by the Jamaican government that the Goodyear Company had been given a franchise for the manufacture of tires and tubes in the island.

Among the American banks operating in the island as of 1970 were First National City Bank of New York, Citizens and Southern of Atlanta, First National Bank of Chicago, and Continental Illinois (an investment bank only). In 1974 the third of these led a group of seventeen international banks syndicating a $50 million twelve-year loan for Jamaica. Active U.S. business firms at this time included the bauxite companies, Esso, Texaco, Goodyear, IBM, ITT, General Cigar, Johnson and Johnson, and a number of garment manufacturers; in 1972 General Electric sold the Jamaica Public Service Corporation two small steam generating power plants. By May 1972 no less than 150 American companies were functioning in the island, with a total investment of $850 million, most of it in bauxite and alumina.

Thus, it is not surprising that in 1970 the United States took $245 million of Jamaica's total exports of $370 million, again much of it in bauxite and alumina. (Great Britain took $108 million, while $51 million went to Canada.) America also furnished the island with 43.4 percent of its imports. Both figures marked pronounced increases over 1962, the first year of independence; at that time imports from the United States had totalled $61.7 million and had included such items as dairy products, cereals and preparations, petroleum products, chemical elements and compounds, and lumber and cork. The following year (1963) America had taken $66 million of Jamaican exports, which were headed by sugar and bananas as well as bauxite and alumina.

The need for the ever quicker transfer of merchandise led in 1965 to the inauguration of twice-a-week jet freight service between Kingston and Miami, as well as a once-a-week service between the Jamaican capital and New York City. Between 1965 and 1969 both American exports to and imports from Jamaica doubled, with Great Britain being the loser in both instances. Despite the importing of Jamaican agricultural products into the United States, American exports of agricultural products to the island also increased two-fold between 1963 and 1968, from $14.6 million to $29.1 million, with the United States by the latter date being Jamaica's principal supplier.

Unlike Bermuda, Jamaica did not become a true tourist attraction until after World War 2. Besides Kingston on the southeastern coast, Montego Bay, Ochos Rios, and Port Antonio on the northern coast have become popular; since the mid-1960s the tourist trade has not been so much confined to the winter months as it once was. A factor stimulating additional tourism has been increased air service. Air Jamaica began operation in 1966, while under the Air Transport Agreement of 1969 between the United States and Jamaica, American airlines were given the right to service Montego Bay and Kingston. Delta Air Lines and Pan American World Airways were already active at this time; Air Jamaica, which then flew to New York and Miami, also was permitted additional stops at Philadelphia, Detroit, and Chicago.

By 1972 Jamaica was attracting 400,000 tourists a year, approximately 80 percent of them from the United States. The number of Americans who visited the island rose from 201,790 in 1968 to 316,191 in 1972; those states furnishing the most visitors were New York, Florida, New Jersey, Illinois, California, and Pennsylvania. Some who came originally as tourists even bought homes on the island, but the relationship between tourist and native has not always been ecstatic in character. In the opinion of one American diplomat (who will remain unnamed), "There is the usual presence of 'ugly Americans,' whose manners away from home are sometimes offensive to the Jamaicans, who work for low wages. . . . Returning tourists complain frequently of surliness, bad service, thievery and other crime as part of their vacation experience."

Inevitable problems aside, Jamaica since independence nevertheless has gone a long way towards fulfilling its national motto "Out of Many, One People." Unlike the Bahamas and Bermuda, it has had both a revolutionary tradition (the Morant Bay Uprising and the riots of 1938) and a strong labor movement; nor is one of the major political parties the ally of a dominant, white conservative ruling aristocracy, as was long the case in the other two islands.[63] Jamaica's geographical size and natural resources also are extensive enough to allow it to stand on its own two feet more firmly than many other island republics. Then, there is the human element, as summarized by former Ambassador Walter Tobriner: "Jamaicans are an extraordinarily gifted and proud people. The educated among them can hold their own with any similar group in the world."[64] Having made these points, we must regretfully note in conclusion that the pronounced leftward drift of Prime Minister Michael Manley—and his friendship for Cuba's Fidel Castro—has dampened U.S. enthusiasm for this island republic in recent years.

That this disillusionment is mutual is revealed by a series of episodes which took place in 1976, a year during which both the United States and Jamaica held national elections. In March, for example, there were various demonstrations on the island against the Central Intelligence Agency. Then in July the *New York Times* reported that American businessmen were becoming increasingly cautious with respect to new Jamaican investments; Prime Minister Michael Manley had charged that certain business elements were trying to "destabilize" Jamaica by undercutting its economy. By this time U.S. investments there had reached the $1 billion mark, but bauxite production was on the decline in the wake of sharply increased governmental levies. A new controversy also arose in July, when the People's National Party admitted that it had received $20,000 from Alcoa for its 1972 campaign but denied that the payments had been made through the late Ambassador Vincent de Roulet.

In August health and climate hazards, rising costs, living conditions, crime, and a number of other factors led the U.S. Embassy at Kingston to declare Jamaica a diplomatic hardship post. This move allegedly had nothing to do with the recent wave of rioting and shootings, and the declaration of a state of emergency by the Jamaican government. In November Prime Minister Manley went on television to defend his nation's relations with Castro's Cuba, stating that he wished for the United States and Jamaica to be friends; Manley added that he had been working towards the relaxation of tensions between the American and Cuban governments. Nevertheless, despite his protestations the decline in both U.S. and Canadian tourism continued during 1976, a phenomenon which the Jamaican government blamed on the press of these countries, which tended to over-emphasize the island's problems rather than its good points. Despite the widespread unemployment, inflation, and unrest in Jamaica, however, Prime Minister Manley emerged triumphant at the polls in December—a development which more or less guaranteed a continuation of heightened Jamaican-American tensions.

4

BERMUDA
Prospero's Magic Island

"Where the remote Bermudas ride," once wrote Andrew Marvell,
"In th' ocean's bosom unespied."[1] While Christopher Columbus discovered America in 1492, it was not until 1609 that the British vessel
Sea Venture under Sir George Somers shipwrecked there on the way
to Virginia; this episode led William Shakespeare to mention the "still
vex'd Bermoothes" two years later in *The Tempest*. As late as the time
of the American Revolution Bermuda was still being referred to in some
quarters as the Somers Islands, but during the sixteenth century many
individuals labelled it the Isles of the Devil.

Although the first date of European contact with the islands is still
an object of speculation, the Spanish apparently had knowledge of
Bermuda as early as 1511; the islands take their name from Juan
Bermudez, a Spanish sea captain, who sighted them at least twice by
1515. In 1527 there was an abortive attempt at settlement by the
Spanish, after which Bermuda remained unoccupied by Europeans[2]
until the shipwreck of the Somers party there. In 1612 Bermuda was
included in the Virginia Company's third charter and sixty settlers
were sent there, but in 1615 the islands were transferred in return
for a payment of £2,000 to another group, the governor and Company
of the City of London for the Plantacion of the Somer Islands. Under
order no. 212 of its 1622 laws, the Bermuda Company obtained from
the Virginia Company a piece of land in Chesterfield County, Virginia,
which even today local inhabitants describe as the Bermuda Hundred.

With the exception of that of Virginia, the representative Assembly
which Bermuda set up in 1620 was the first ever to convene in the
empire outside of Great Britain. At the time of the execution of

Charles I of England in 1649, the Bermudians refused to accept Oliver Cromwell as their ruler, instead proclaiming Charles II as their king; it took the conquest of Barbados by the forces of Cromwell to persuade them to change their minds. Then numerous complaints about company operations from 1670 on led British authorities to annul the company's charter in court proceedings held at London in 1684. Although the company had demanded that the colonists raise tobacco, the latter disliked farming and the tobacco proved to be of low quality. Bermuda then became a colony of the crown; yet, since the Assembly was reestablished after a ten years' hiatus, it was not technically a crown colony.

EARLY CONTACTS WITH THE THIRTEEN COLONIES

Apart from its earlier contacts with Virginia, Bermuda from 1645 on attracted the attention of New England merchants, who attempted to open up the islands by establishing trade relations and by sending a £400 letter of credit to an agent there. Thanks to competition from Virginia, however, the tobacco industry of Bermuda went into eclipse; by 1700 it was largely defunct, with the result that the residents of the islands were impoverished. After that date the Bermudians turned to exporting salt to the mainland colonies. Vessels from Bermuda gained an increasing hold on the mainland's commerce with the West Indies for the next six decades. Nevertheless, statistics covering the years 1714–72 reveal that trade between Bermuda and such mainland ports as Boston, New York City, Philadelphia, and Charleston was not so great as that between these cities and the Bahamas at the end of the period, although Bermudian commerce with the South Carolina city in particular was relatively thriving.

Cultural ties also existed between the islands and the mainland, especially the southern colonies. Most of the clergy occupying pulpits in Bermuda came from North America, while the sons of the well-to-do often went to the mainland in search of an education, or in quest of a profession. This two-way migration for often extended periods was in marked contrast to the present-day, almost invariably one-way traffic of American tourists to the islands for brief periods.

But it was the economic ties which assumed an increasing importance at the time of the French and Indian, or Seven Years' War. Having subordinated agriculture to commerce during the eighteenth century, the inhabitants of Bermuda were forced to import as much as three-quarters of their supplies. With the outbreak of hostilities threatening their very subsistence, Governor William Popple twice sent a petition to the Provincial Congress of Pennsylvania in 1756 requesting permission for Bermuda to import foodstuffs. Once the threat of starvation was overcome, however, Bermudian merchants did a thriving business during the course of this conflict, while privateers were also active; in fact, the termination of the war had an adverse impact on the islands' economy, since many ships were reduced to idleness.

The migration to the mainland colonies of individual Bermudians to the contrary, a plan to transport a large number of islanders to East Florida in 1764 proved abortive. Here the key figure was John Savage of Charleston, who entertained high hopes of settling them at his own expense on 10,000 acres of arable land; the site which he tentatively selected was at Mosquito Inlet, approximately 60 miles south of St. Augustine. Although every man and woman and child who relocated there was to be given a bounty of £5 sterling, by 1766 only forty families had migrated to Mosquito Inlet, instead of the two or three thousand that Savage once had envisaged.

THE AMERICAN REVOLUTION

Within a decade the American Revolution had erupted on the mainland. Bermuda quite naturally was affected, as it had been two decades earlier by the French and Indian War. The noted journalist Philip Freneau, who was to assume the editorship of the anti-Federalist *National Gazette* of Philadelphia in 1791, has left us an "Account of the Island of Bermuda" dated May 10, 1778. Freneau reported that at this time there were fifteen or sixteen thousand inhabitants in Bermuda, some families containing as many as fourteen or fifteen children, and that the chief products which they obtained from the newly independent United States were corn, flour, and pork. He added that the only thing of value being cultivated was cedar trees, lumber from which was used in building ships which they sold in the West Indies and in America, at a very high price.

Unlike the mainland colonies, Bermudian officials remained faithful to the mother country during the American Revolution, but there nevertheless was a strong undercurrent of insurgency. As early as the time of the Stamp Act of 1765, the inhabitants of the islands had expressed concern that the stamps would have an adverse impact on their commerce with the Atlantic seaboard; Governor George Bruere, however, refused to disregard the tax on ships' papers, since under the system of government by instruction the colonial governors were required to implement the orders sent them from London or face removal from office. Two years later the enactment of the Townsend Acts by Parliament triggered an orgy of smuggling on the part of many Bermudian merchants.

Although both the Stamp Act and the Townsend duties posed a problem for the islands at the time, their impact was minor compared with the outlawing by the Continental Congress in October 1774 of commerce between the mainland colonies and Great Britain and Ireland, the British West Indies, and the Bahamas and Bermuda. As a result of this action the inhabitants of the latter faced starvation, and they immediately petitioned the Continental Congress to allow them to have certain necessities. Some British officials, it would appear, were willing to look the other way when Bermudians obtained food from the mainland. In this connection, the House of Assembly informed the governor that ". . . we might be compelled by hard necessity to quit these islands for some country that might furnish us with the necessities of life."[3]

After placing a one year's embargo on goods leaving Bermuda,[4] the House of Assembly appointed a delegation headed by Colonel Henry Tucker, which then left the islands for Philadelphia. While persuading the Americans to furnish them with a supply of food, the Bermudian delegation made it known that it was willing unofficially to make available to the United States pertinent information about a large cache of gunpowder then sitting unguarded at a powder house on St. George's. Fortunately for the islanders, this was one military prerequisite then in short supply in the mainland colonies; according to Henry Wilkinson, as much as 90 percent of the gunpowder employed by the Continental troops during the first two years of the war came from overseas. The future ally France supplied the bulk of this, either directly or indirectly through St. Eustatius.

On the night of August 14, 1775, a group of Americans in connivance with a number of leading Bermudians—who wished to keep their role secret—led a clandestine raid on the St. George's powder house. But this time the latter had become quite critical of the islands' governor. One hundred barrels of gunpowder were trundled down the hill by the raiders to a fleet of small boats, while a dozen or so battered barrels were left behind as an insult to Governor Bruere; the powder magazine, moreover, rested on land owned by the Bruere family, which gave the burglary a highly personal touch. On August 26 the *Lady Catherine* docked at Philadelphia with 1,800 pounds of gunpowder, of which only two-thirds was usable. Nevertheless, according to one account, the Bermudian supply helped George Washington to recapture Boston on the following March 17.

Governor Bruere, who was far from amused by the incident, on August 16 called a meeting of the House of Assembly to investigate the matter. That body in a display of mock indignation appointed an investigating committee which included Henry Tucker, its leading member and a ringleader of the group of Bermudians which had aided the Americans; much to the disappointment of the Governor, the offer of a reward of £100 failed to dislodge any information from the participants or any witnesses. The British, though, did send the *Scorpion* to Bermuda in October to assist Bruere, and other police ships arrived in the months that lay ahead, with three vessels patrolling the waters after January 1777.

Previously, on August 1, the Continental Congress had adopted a resolution specifically listing various British islands and colonies with which commerce was prohibited, including Bermuda. But the seizure of the gunpowder sharply altered the climate of opinion towards the islands on the mainland; on September 6 George Washington penned a personal address to the inhabitants of Bermuda, and on October 2 a committee of the Continental Congress came out in favor of exports to the islands. Then on November 22 the Continental Congress approved an exchange in which Bermuda would make available to the United States salt, arms, and ammunition, and the United States in return would supply the islands with bread or flour, beef or pork, peas or beans, and rice. Bermuda as well as the Bahamas was exempted when the Continental Congress reaffirmed its embargo on July 24, 1776, while vessels from the former were also protected from capture by American privateers under a November 1777 decree of that body.

Even before the first of these measures was enacted, Silas Deane, the secret U.S. agent to France, had paid a visit to the islands on his way to Paris. Observing that the governor was obnoxious, Deane concluded that famine loomed; he therefore recommended that the United States should seize and fortify the islands.[5] (His continuing interest led the British ambassador to France later to report that in some quarters Mr. Deane referred to himself as a native of Bermuda.) His plan was not adopted by the United States, but during the summer of 1777 two armed American vessels from South Carolina, supposedly commanded by Bermudian captains, hovered off the west end of the islands over the bitter objection of the Governor. After their eventual departure frequent contacts between Bermudian collaborators and American vessels continued. According to a letter from Lieutenant Colonel Edward Smith dated October 22 of that year, "All American ships . . . must stand for the West end, and by their hoisting a jack at the main topmost head, a Mr.

Tucker would send off a boat, and procuring them, as required, assistance, would give them orders or satisfactory information."[6]

A turning point in the war for both the United States and Bermuda occurred on July 17, 1778, when the former entered into its only permanent alliance with a foreign nation prior to the end of World War 2: that with the France of Louis XVI. Articles 5 and 6 of this treaty were of critical importance, since under the first of these the United States obtained the right to seize for itself Canada (part of which France had once controlled) and Bermuda, while under the second France renounced any future claim to either. At one time the Marquis de Lafayette had expressed an interest in assisting the United States in seizing the islands, but these tentative plans never went into effect.

One major result of this alliance was that the British were forced to defend their possessions in the West Indies. During the months which followed they no longer patrolled the waters of Bermuda to the extent that they once had, although to maintain a full squadron there would have required only a minimal part of their navy. But while British vessels were now generally absent, a contingent of English troops arrived on November 2, 1778, followed by another party of one hundred men on December 1, 1779. Their efforts in suppressing the commerce between the mainland and the islands proved less fruitful than those of the earlier naval forces, but they nevertheless were a constant nuisance if not a perpetual threat to the Americans.

Ironically, just at that moment during the war when maritime contacts between the United States and Bermuda became more easy, the activities of Bermuda-based privateers owned by Loyalists caused the American government to take a less hospitable stance towards the islands. As early as the fall of 1778 the Continental Congress adopted a new set of export regulations which deliberately omitted a list of exempted colonies, although it did authorize the shipment of 1,000 bushels of corn to the islands in May 1779. No less than ninety-one prizes went through the Admiralty court at Bermuda by 1780, and in March 1781 the Continental Congress repealed all exceptions favoring the islands, the order to be effective May 1. Virginia won permission to import 50,000 bushels of salt; following this, relations between the United States and Bermuda were suspended for the remainder of the conflict.

Another factor which chilled American enthusiasm for the islands was the treatment of Americans there who had been captured by the privateers. Their daily diet at times consisted of a single meal of raw rice. In this connection the House of Assembly complained to the

Governor on November 19, 1779: "Unhappy are we to find . . . that men thrown among us by the calamities of war alone should be suffer'd to remain in a situation shocking to every principle of humanity." But the prisoners were to have their revenge, since a fever which had originated in the jail spread throughout Bermuda, causing a number of deaths and interfering with the operations of the government itself.[7] In the decades to come the treatment of captive Americans by the Barbary pirates led to widespread protests throughout the United States, but the example of the islands indicates that inhumanity was by no means confined to non-Christians.

As was the case at its beginning, the closing years of the revolutionary war witnessed a continuation of the tug-of-war between pro-American and anti-American forces in Bermuda. George Bruere wrote Lord George Germain on October 17, 1781, "I have the pleasure to inform your Lordship of a change among part of the Inhabitants, they have joined Mr. Goodrich and fitted out a fine ship against the Enemy. . . ."[8] Yet only four months earlier, on June 19, Bruere had accused "a misguided & deluded people" of doing "all they could do to serve the Americans."[9] St. George Tucker, who wrote George Washington on October 23, characterized the British sympathizers as being "held in so great Detestation as to give rise to a general Association not to deal with them on any Account whatsoever."[10] Tucker also presented George Washington with a complete plan for the seizure of the islands, the American leader being definitely interested in the project at this time.

On January 4, 1782, Colonel William Brown, an eminent journalist from Salem, Massachusetts, who had left the United States because of his Loyalist sympathies, became the governor of Bermuda. Brown discouraged the harassing of American commerce on the grounds that "the spirit of privateering will draw the resentment of the enemy."[11] But during that summer armed vessels from America were present in the waters surrounding the islands, while the Governor was preoccupied with actions designed to facilitate the latter's defense; in the retrospective judgment of Wilfred Kerr, Bermuda and the United States were finally approaching a state of war. Meanwhile in August Robert Livingston sounded out the French relative to the possibility of Admiral Vaudreuil joining forces with the Americans to launch a joint attack on the islands.

But war between the United States and Bermuda was not to become a reality, since peace between America and Great Britain was at hand. Following the signing of the Treaty of Paris in 1783 Bermuda experienced an economic relapse, and by 1784 its position had become at least temporarily precarious. A return to normalcy, however, was well under way; the good price received for Turks Island salt, in the words of the Governor, "diffuses an air of cheerfulness and contentment over the countenances of those who were left at home."[12]

THE NAPOLEONIC WAR AND THE WAR OF 1812

In 1793 the war that was to poison relations between England and France for more than two decades broke out. Under the Royal Proclamation of that year, American trade with the French West Indies was subject to harassment from both British naval vessels and colonial privateers, and the latter soon began to implement it on the high seas. According to a report published in the *Salem Gazette* in December 1793, the Bermudians often went so far as to strip the U.S. ships which they had halted, even if there were no grounds for taking them into port. A representative example of excessive Bermudian vigilance was the seizure of Captain Baker's schooner *Swallow* in 1795, after it had been regularly cleared by the British authorities from a port in Hispaniola. It is thus not surprising that the Bermudian captains arriving in American ports were not greeted with open arms; a mob in Boston seized one vessel suspected of being a privateer, set it afire, and cut it loose, after which it burned up on Charlestown Point. Apparently, officials in London also became quite perturbed about the islanders' actions, as a reversal of some of their Vice Admiralty decrees and the execution of writs of attachment upon the property of several leading privateersmen led to a noticeable slowdown in privateering around August 1796.

During 1789, four years before the outbreak of hostilities between Great Britain and France, more than 175 ships had been registered at Bermuda. The coming of war quite naturally led to an increasing number of British naval vessels on the scene in addition to the privateers. In 1795 Vice Admiral Sir George Murray enthusiastically advocated the setting up of a naval base there, and in 1797 Bermuda obtained a military garrison from the mother country. But it was not until the eve of the War of 1812, in 1810, that the construction of the British dockyards actually began, after the English government had obtained the land for this purpose the previous year.

At the time of the outbreak of this conflict, feelings in Bermuda were again mixed, as they had been at the time of the revolutionary war. This time, however, there probably was less pro-American sentiment in evidence than there had been at the time of the earlier war, if we are to accept contemporary sources at their face value. It was in

1812, too, that the capital of the islands was transferred from St. George's to Hamilton; the American commodore was present at the town hall of the latter, where he was a guest of honor at a ball held to celebrate the occasion.

Contrary to the situation which prevailed throughout the American Revolution, an order in council dated October 13, 1812, permitted Bermudians to export to America in licensed foreign vessels sugar grown in the British West Indies, as well as coffee imported into Bermuda. In return, these ships might bring back from the United States certain products. Unfortunately for the Bermudians, their own direct trade with the B.W.I. and Newfoundland was frequently disrupted by American privateers; during the course of the war no fewer than thirty-nine vessels from Hamilton alone were seized. Enterprising American captains, moreover, sometimes visited Bermuda, as when the schooner *George Washington* from New Haven offered to supply the Governor with forty head of cattle. Nor was this an isolated case by any means, since the *Niles Weekly Register* of Baltimore reported on April 24, 1813, that provisions from the United States arrived frequently.

But Bermuda privateers were also active, and by the end of the conflict the islanders had taken as prizes forty-three foreign-built vessels. According to Lieutenant Colonel Thomas Melville Dill, "The war had brought American shipping to a complete standstill, St. George's harbour was full of prizes, and the *Romulus,* prison hulk in Murray's Anchorage, was full to overflowing."[13] (By this time the treatment of American prisoners seems to have improved over what it had been a generation before.) To add insult to injury, the British expeditionary force which burned Washington was launched from the islands; conversely, the American Congress considered a plan to capture Bermuda, but that body narrowly rejected this in favor of an alternate proposal to attack merchant vessels which were returning to England from the West Indies.

Among the American prisoners taken by the Bermudians was the previously unknown Henry King. King was transferred afterwards to the guard ship *Ruby.* In a daring feat resembling Captain Bligh's crossing of the Pacific in *Mutiny on the Bounty,* King bought a pocket compass from a shipmate, stole a small boat from the *Ruby,* and set sail for America with two loaves of bread and a few quarts of water. Miraculously escaping disaster, he landed in the vicinity of Cape Henry nine days later.

A far more famous prisoner was Captain Stephen Decatur, who already had won immortality for his exploits against the Barbary pirates. His vessel, the *U.S.S. President,* was captured by the British ship *Endymion* off Long Island a day after he had left New York on January 14, 1815. Technically, the War of 1812 was now officially over, and its last battle (New Orleans) had been fought. Bermudian authorities took Decatur to Murray's Anchorage, whereupon the *Royal Gazette* published a libellous article that impugned his character; this charged that he had concealed sixty-eight men in the hold of the *President*, who were to make a sneak attack on the British after they had taken over the vessel. Not only did the colonial secretary, Robert Kennedy, write a scathing letter to the editor, Edmund Ward, challenging this article, but several weeks later Midshipman Randolph of the *President* attacked Ward in King's Square.[14] The unfortunate editor later suffered the further indignity of losing his position as king's printer.

COMMERCE, ABOLITION, AND POLITICAL REFORM

Between 1815 and 1822 Bermuda became the focal point of a rather vigorous commerce; this trade was largely attributable to the exclusion of U.S. ships from the British West Indies, and the subsequent use of Bermuda as an entrepôt for produce from both America and the B.W.I. Commercial relations with the United States, though, were not always harmonious, as is evidenced by the seizure of an American vessel in 1815 following the unauthorized landing of a cargo of hams. The Bermudian fleet now numbered more than two-hundred vessels, approximately half of which were privateering prizes. Shipbuilding and sailmaking flourished in the islands. But after 1822 U.S. vessels were permitted to trade with the British West Indies, a step which had an adverse effect on Bermudian commerce, as did the introduction of steam during the 1830s. Tonnage figures which are available for the year 1835 with respect to foreign arrivals into New York, Boston, and Philadelphia reveal that those from Bermuda were fewer than those from the Bahamas and Jamaica.

The mid-1830s were traumatic years for the islands, as they were for the British colonies in the West Indies, thanks to the emancipation of slaves throughout the empire. When Bermuda abolished slavery in 1834, it was the only English colony aside from Antigua to do so outright; during the same year there was an increase in the property qualifications for voting, a step taken to lessen the chances of the newly enfranchised blacks gaining political power.

As for Bermudian relations with the United States, there was an international cause célèbre when the brig *Enterprise* bound for Charleston with seventy-eight slaves aboard was driven by foul weather into port at Hamilton early in 1835. According to an account sent to Lord Palmerston, "On her arrival there, she was seized by the colonial authorities, on the pretext of her having slaves on board; . . . the slaves . . . on disembarking were . . . proclaimed free, for having been landed in a colony where slavery had ceased to exist."[15] As late as the latter part of 1836 the British government had apparently not done anything of consequence in response to the American complaints.

In 1839 there arrived in the islands William Reid, frequently referred to as "the good governor." At this time there were only two plows in Bermuda, an indication of the backward state of agriculture then. Reid introduced both the plow and the harrow into the islands, and by 1843 Bermuda had begun to export a considerable amount of agricultural produce, especially to America.[16] But during that year the facilities which were available under the warehousing system began to disappear. Another factor which had an adverse impact on the carrying trade of the islands was the repeal of the Navigation Acts by the British parliament in 1849; led by Sir Robert Peel, England was now entering a free trade era. By the eve of the U.S. Civil War potatoes had become the staple crop of Bermuda, and in 1858 alone 22,648 barrels were exported to the mainland. The coming of the "Irrepressible Conflict," however, dealt a serious blow to this particular trade.

THE U.S. CIVIL WAR

Unlike the American Revolution, the Civil War did not lead Bermuda into an active role. Her sympathies, however, lay with the South; in the words of David White, "These two leisurely, 'old world' areas were opposed to the progressive, industrial North."[17] But vessels from both the North and the South visited the islands during this conflict. Thus, on October 26, 1861, the Confederate steamer *Nashville* docked at St. George's to take on coal, while during the following month a Union warship, the *Keystone State*, began to cruise the waters of Bermuda in an attempt to hamper Confederate commerce. In the winter of 1862–63 Major Norman Walker arrived on the scene to act as the Confederate agent there; the Union government had already dispatched Charles M. Allen to the islands as the American consul. This enterprising rebel was to weather physical attacks and even attempts on his life during the war in carrying out his duties in a most effective manner.[18] Mrs. Walker left us a valuable diary.

During April 1862 the U.S. navy seized New Orleans from the Confederates, depriving the South of its largest port and dealing a crippling blow to its commerce. With the federal blockade of the Confederacy in operation, small vessels departing from such ports as Wilmington, North Carolina, frequently docked at St. George's, which had a larger harbor than Hamilton.[19] Up to approximately August of that year the Bahamas were more important from the standpoint of blockade running than Bermuda, but after that date increased vigilance on the part of the U.S. made the use of Nassau as a port highly dangerous.

By the beginning of 1862 officials in Washington had begun to complain to their counterparts in London about Confederate vessels docking in Bermudian waters. In writing to the U.S. minister to Great Britain, Charles Francis Adams, on March 22, the British foreign minister denied that the Governor of Bermuda had gone on board the *Nashville* when that Confederate ship arrived in the islands. But the North itself was hardly in a position to cast stones at others' behavior; one needs only to cite here the activities of Admiral Charles Wilkes of the U.S. navy, who ten months earlier had taken the Confederate agents James Mason and John Slidell off the *Trent*, a British steamer. Arriving at St. George's on the U.S.S. *Wachusett*, accompanied by the U.S.S. *Tioga* and the U.S.S. *Sonoma*, Wilkes almost immediately complained that the officers on shore at Fort Cunningham had failed to give him the customary salute. The American captain then requested permission to re-store and to re-coal two of the vessels, although he had left Hampton Roads only four days earlier; in the meanwhile the *Sonoma* patrolled the waters around Bermuda, obviously in search of Confederate vessels. When Wilkes reported that the *Sonoma* needed repairs before it could leave, and that the *Wachusett* had a blown boiler tube, Bermudian tempers reached a boiling point. Fortunately for all parties concerned, the American captain departed before an incident occurred.

Wilkes, however, had every reason to be concerned about Bermuda from the standpoint of blockade running. According to a report which appeared in the Bermuda *Royal Gazette* for January 5, 1864, the key development during the past year had been the expanded trade resulting from this activity. A less desirable by-product was the nightly presence of a group of rowdy sailors in Shin Bone Alley, the scene of innumerable fights and riots.

Profitable as the year 1863 was for the blockade runners, 1864 was even more so; by this time the Confederacy had been thrown on the defensive, and had grown desperate for supplies. This climax in Bermudian commerce took place in spite of a yellow fever epidemic, which killed approximately 5 percent of the inhabitants during the summer. If one established an index figure of 100 for 1860 relative to imports into the islands, then for 1864 the corresponding total would be 330.6. During that year 369 ships docked at St. George's, compared with 158 at Hamilton; the value of imports from the United Kingdom and the United States was approximately the same, while total exports had a value 285 percent that of 1863.

Unquestionably, the most horrifying episode that occurred in the islands during the Civil War took place at the very end of this conflict. At this time a fanatical southerner, Dr. Luke Blackburn, conceived a vicious plot to infect the poor people of New York City by shipping there a quantity of infected clothing once worn by yellow fever victims. Just prior to Blackburn's placing this diabolical scheme into operation, the ever vigilant American consul, Charles M. Allen, learned of the plot; this time the Bermudian and British authorities were quite cooperative, and even Confederate officials there expressed their shock. By April 1865 Blackburn had departed, but his accomplice, one Swan, was arrested. The clothing was buried with a solution of oil of vitriol at the quarantine station on Nonsuch Island.

Even before the U.S. Civil War officially came to an end on April 9, 1865, when General Robert E. Lee surrendered to General Ulysses S. Grant at Appomattox courthouse, Virginia, blockade running between Bermuda and the mainland had declined, thanks to the fall of Fort Fisher near Wilmington. By 1866 an economic depression had set in, and by 1868 the index figure for imports into Bermuda had fallen to 133.5. Despite the peak commercial activity experienced by the islands in 1864, the Bahamas still probably benefited more from the abnormal conditions then prevailing than did Bermuda. In fact, the Governor of the latter expressed the opinion in 1867 that "the fictitious prosperity of the Civil War was a great calamity, one of the least evil results of which was an increase of permanent burdens devolved upon the colony on account of its apparent and temporary riches."[20]

WHISKEY, ONIONS, AND POTATOES

During the final generation of the nineteenth century, economic issues dominated the relations between the United States and Bermuda to the almost total exclusion of other concerns. In 1869 the first regular steam freight service between New York City and Hamilton went into operation, and this development opened an entire new market for Bermudian produce. By this time, however, the production of potatoes in the islands had begun to fall off, thanks to American competition; taking their place were Bermuda onions, which had been shipped abroad as early as 1843.

A decade later, in 1881, the *Bermuda Almanac* for that year reported that "the establishment of direct regular steam communication with New York has done much to aid our agricultural exports, as expedition is all important in handling perishable freight and in reaching a highly sensitive market."[21] Nevertheless, six years later the same publication had begun to complain about the lack of financial success of the agricultural exports program; such Bermudian products as onions and potatoes had to compete in the New York market not only with American produce but also with that imported from other countries.

Other aspects of U.S. trade with Bermuda were more devious. By 1883 ships were shuttling back and forth between New York City and Bermuda which were carrying barrels of whiskey. Since whiskey in bond was not taxed in the United States until several years after its manufacture—or its arrival in America—the whiskey was shipped to the nearest foreign port (Bermuda) and back again when the time of reckoning approached, thus enabling it perpetually to escape taxation. The Quebec Steamship Company played a leading role in this somewhat tainted if legal enterprise, with the *Orinoco* one of its most active vessels.[22]

As we have seen above, Bermudian exports of agricultural produce to the United States had begun to wane by the time of the passage by Congress of the McKinley Tariff in October 1890. This measure contained the first tariff duties ever imposed by the American government on farm imports; this was the tariff, too, which dealt a heavy blow to the Hawaiian sugar planters by authorizing a bounty of 2 cents a pound on homegrown sugar cane. Not surprisingly, Bermuda quickly began to suffer from its impact, since the McKinley Act taxed all the islands' leading agricultural exports, with the exception of arrowroot. The Bermudians complained with great bitterness that while the islands levied an ad valorem tax of only 5 percent on American imports, which made up four-fifths of the total, the corresponding U.S. taxes were in effect prohibitive, although fresh vegetables grown in Bermuda did not compete seasonally with those grown in America. When two delegates from the islands arrived in Washington during July 1893, they speculated that the tariff on potatoes had been placed in the McKinley bill to keep out ones from Canada, but that its effect had been to exclude ones from Bermuda as well.[23]

While the marketing of Bermudian agricultural produce in the United States was experiencing hard going, between 1883 and 1893 America had lost to Canada the market for supplying shooks for crating the onions, beets, and tomatoes raised in the islands. The reason for this turnabout was that although the Bermudian farmer was able to buy Canadian shooks for 9 to 9.5 cents a pound, the American ones cost 9.5 to 10.5 cents. Shook demand in the islands, however, was only a seasonal one, lasting from the beginning of January to the end of June, when the crops were all harvested.

The somewhat less protectionist Wilson-Gorman Tariff of 1894 had a more favorable impact upon the Bermudian economy, although it did affect Cuban sugar growers adversely, thus contributing to the general deterioration of conditions there as the Spanish-American War neared. Then in 1897 the U.S. Congress enacted the Dingley Act, which placed duties on Bermudian produce roughly comparable to those of the McKinley Act. Again, as seven years before, the islands sent a delegation to Washington, this time to attend a reciprocity conference. Although Joseph Chamberlain, the British secretary of state for the colonies, was not enthusiastic about these negotiations, on June 27 the Bermuda Commission completed a reciprocity agreement with officials of the American government, which was then submitted to the Bermuda Parliament. Under this there was to be a 20 percent reduction in the U.S. duties on island potatoes, onions, bulbs, flowers, tomatoes, and other vegetables.

Prior to 1903 Bermuda more or less enjoyed a monopoly on early onion production for the American market, but around the turn of the century a man named Nye decided to grow the same type of onions from Teneriffe seed in Laredo, Texas. Within approximately a decade, in 1909, 550,000 crates of Texas Bermuda onions were being shipped all over the United States. To quote David White, "This whole situation is comparable to Virginia's destruction of Bermuda's tobacco industry in colonial times."[24] The Payne-Aldrich Tariff of 1909 maintained the high levels of the Dingley Tariff of 1897, but the Underwood-Simmons Tariff of 1913 lowered the duties on onions and potatoes. As a result, during World War 1 Bermuda was able to market its farm products—and 92 percent of the islands' exports in 1914 were vegetables—in New York City with considerable success. On September 28, 1917 *The Times* of London reported that the Bermuda Commission had asked the United States to help it export the greatest crop in the history of the islands.

SCIENTISTS, PRISONERS, TOURISTS, AND YACHTSMEN

By the end of the century American scientists were beginning to take an interest in the islands. It is a little-known fact that the first person to transport live Bermudian fish to the United States was the famous showman Phineas T. Barnum. After Barnum had sent expeditions to both Honduras and Bermuda which ended in failure, he was persuaded by W. E. Damon, one of his associates, to send the *Pacific* on a voyage to the latter, with Damon in charge. Arriving in the islands in the summer of 1862 during the midst of the American Civil War, Damon quite naturally aroused suspicion, and it required the intervention of the American consul before authorities there would withdraw a peremptory order halting his work. A total of six hundred live Bermudian fish were eventually shipped by Damon to New York City, where much to the delight of its patrons they swam in the tanks of the Ann Street Museum.

P. T. Barnum, of course, was more of a businessman than a scientist, unlike the members of the Alumni Biological Expedition of New York University, which visited the islands in the summer of 1897. Bermuda was chosen as the focal point of this group's activities for several reasons; among these were the ease of transportation via the Quebec Steamship Company, and the relative absence of the malarious diseases which intermittently struck such West Indies islands as Jamaica. The director of this expedition, Dr. Charles L. Bristol, established his headquarters at the Harrington House six miles from Hamilton. Confining its work mainly to the lee shores, the Bristol group collected a large number of specimens, as well as a large number of live fish, which were later displayed in the Aquarium in New York City.

In 1903 a biological station opened at the Flatts under the joint sponsorship of New York University and Harvard University, with Professor Edward L. Mark as its first director. After it had proved impossible to obtain public financing for the construction of a public aquarium and a biological station, the Bermuda Natural History Society obtained a lease from the War Department on Agar's Island, where it converted an old powder magazine into an aquarium. Since the agreement with both N.Y.U. and Harvard had been abrogated in the meanwhile, the Bermuda Natural History Society invited Professor Mark to move his operation there. From then until 1917 biologists were active at the Agar's Island aquarium. Upon the entry of the United States into World War 1, however, the island was used as a supply station for the American navy; at that time the biological station moved temporarily to Dyer's Island.

A somewhat more unusual presence in the islands at the turn of the twentieth century was that of six thousand prisoners captured by the British in South Africa during the course of the Boer War (1899–1902). The funding, maintenance, and guarding of these Boers temporarily contributed to the prosperity of the islands.[25] Back in the United States, though, Republican Senator George Frisbie Hoar of Massachusetts introduced a resolution into the U.S. Senate on January 15, 1902, requesting that the Department of State determine ". . . whether the British Government exact duties on goods intended for prisoners of war in Bermuda in violation of Article 16 of the convention at the Hague."[26] It had recently been brought to the attention of Hoar, a senator whose section usually displayed far more interest in the Canadian fisheries than in the Bermudian tariff, that several charitable organizations in America were transmitting supplies to the Boer prisoners of war. The U.S. Senate unanimously agreed to Hoar's resolution, but on the following day Hoar requested that it be reconsidered, since the U.S. Senate had not acted on the second Hague convention (which included Article 16); the Governor of Bermuda, moreover, had unofficially stated that it was his intention to ask the Parliament of the islands to eliminate the disputed duties via appropriate legislation.

The number of American tourists visiting the islands remained minimal until 1890. Even between 1890 and 1905 the annual total of American tourists was generally less than a thousand, but after the introduction of steamship travel this figure sharply increased from 5,418 in 1908 and 12,509 in 1909 to 15,482 in 1910 and 27,045 in 1911. In July 1909 Consul W. Maxwell Greene reported from Hamilton that during the height of the current tourist season more Americans were lodged there at one time than had visited the islands over a four months' span during the previous year. Then in September 1910 it was reported from London that the Quebec Steamship Company and the Royal Mail Steam Packet Company had reached an agreement to conduct a joint service between New York City and Bermuda, to be augmented during the winter months.[27]

Of all the American tourists who visited the islands in the years immediately preceding World War 1, none were more prominent than Mark Twain and Woodrow Wilson. The famed humorist was then in the twilight years of his life; after having made a trip to Bermuda thirty years earlier, Samuel L. Clemens paid several more visits to the islands between 1907 and 1910. Surrounded by such companions as Henry Rogers, Clemens often voiced his rather pessimistic opinions of mankind, or read aloud from the poetry of Rudyard Kipling. It was here that he prepared an article, "The Turning-Point in My Life," for *Harper's Bazaar*.

During 1910 the callers at Clemens's Bay House included Woodrow Wilson, who on occasion engaged him in games of miniature golf. Wilson himself, then on the eve of his political career, was also experiencing health problems, having temporarily lost the sight in his left eye in 1906. While recuperating in the islands, the then president of Princeton University wrote several lectures and preached a sermon in a local church. Wilson, who looked upon the possible use of automobiles in Bermuda with disfavor, even drafted a petition to the legislature in which he observed: "It would . . . be a fatal error to attract to Bermuda the extravagant and sporting set who have made so many other places entirely intolerable to persons of taste and cultivation."[28] Following his election as president and before his inauguration, he wrote there a preface to a selection of excerpts from his campaign speeches entitled *The New Freedom*.

In addition to the scientists, prisoners, and tourists, another group which began to take an interest in the islands from 1906 on were the maritime enthusiasts: the schooner and motor boat racers. The first ocean race between Bermuda and New York City involving the former took place in 1906; Sir Thomas Lipton offered as the prize a $500 cup, and T. F. Day's schooner *Tamerlane* came in ahead of two other entries. Mr. Day also emerged the victor the following year, when James Gordon Bennett presented a £200 cup to his *Ailsa Craig*. As we shall see later on in this narrative, such ocean regattas were to become regular biennial occurrences in future years.

WORLD WAR 1, THE TARIFF, AND ANNEXATION TALK

Late in 1916 and early in 1917 the Governor of Bermuda dealt a minor blow to harmonious relations with the United States by successively banning the importation into the islands of fifteen American newspapers and ten U.S. magazines.[29] The diplomatic correspondence unfortunately offers no explanation for this action. But after the United States joined the war on the side of Great Britain in April 1917, such episodes were soon forgotten; several months later Bermuda became Base 24 of the American navy, a way station for submarine chasers, which were often repaired at the local dockyards.[30] The presence of the U.S. military base there, moreover, stimulated the Bermudian economy. Walter H. Brownell has written in this connection: "The American blue-jacket was a welcome visitor in Bermuda. He spent his money with characteristic freedom, his discipline was excellent, and he upheld the finest traditions of the United States Navy, making many friends for himself and his country."[31]

These friendly relations were maintained in the years following World War 1, thanks to such actions as the presence of the American battleship *Kansas* at the tercentenary celebration of the Bermuda House of Assembly in 1920. The Prince of Wales, who stopped off at the islands on his way home from Australia during the first part of October, commented favorably with respect to the presence of Admiral Hughes and his vessel. During 1920 and 1921, however, Republican Senators William Kenyon of Iowa and Albert J. Beveridge of Indiana proposed respectively that the United States should either purchase Bermuda or obtain it in partial payment for the war debts owed to America by Great Britain. These suggestions were not received with favor in the islands.

Then on July 4, 1920, an episode occurred which had a more deleterious effect on Bermudian-American relations. On that date several drunken English sailors attempted to rip off, or lower, the U.S. flag above the entrance of the American House in Hamilton; as one might expect, the British embassy in Washington took the position that the seriousness of this prank had been exaggerated. It is true that this tempest in a teapot eventually quieted down, but it did not prove so easy to halt the controversy over liquor smuggling from Bermuda into the United States. After rumrunners had begun hiding whiskey bottles in barrels of potatoes, the islands' parliament passed a special law in June 1921 imposing fines on those individuals found guilty of this illegal activity.

At the end of that decade the Great Depression engulfed the United States, and a desperate Congress raised protection to the highest level in American history by passing the Hawley-Smoot Act. Bermuda suffered as a result, since this measure for all practical purposes drove its agricultural products out of the American market and into the arms of the Canadians. The islands themselves, though, had practiced a bit of discrimination in January 1927, when the Bermuda legislature passed a measure which prohibited the importation into the islands of raw carrots from both Canada and the United States; later that year there was an unsuccessful attempt in the House of Assembly to place a 50 percent tax on American imports. Nevertheless, as late as 1926 92.1 percent of Bermudian exports were marketed in America.[32]

Perhaps the most mysterious episode in Bermudian-American relations between the two world wars was the so-called Log Conference, which took place between Prime Minister Ramsay MacDonald of Great

Britain and President Herbert Hoover at the President's Rapidan Camp in October 1929, with Secretary of State Henry Stimson also in attendance. Here, according to Republican Representative Louis McFadden of Pennsylvania, MacDonald in a secret conversation offered Bermuda to the United States in partial payment of the British war debt, only to have Hoover decline it after careful deliberation. On the other hand, Cedric Joseph has written more recently (November 1973) that it was Hoover who sought not only Bermuda but also British Honduras and Trinidad. The reaction of governmental officials and businessmen in Bermuda to rumors eminating from this conference was one of solid opposition to annexation by the United States; there was speculation that what actually had occurred at Rapidan was that MacDonald had assured Hoover that the islands would not be fortified. Oblivious to this negative reaction, isolationist Democratic Senator Robert Reynolds of North Carolina later was to propose in 1938 that the United States acquire Bermuda, Newfoundland, and an access strip across western Canada to Alaska in return for a debt settlement with Great Britain. Yet the Rapidan conference remained the only discussion at the official level of the war debts/British islands exchange proposal.

Turning to the New Deal years prior to World War 2, a contemporary State Department memorandum reveals that there were a number of disputes featuring U.S. employees in Bermudian hotels. Other incidents involved an American tourist losing an eye after being attacked by several black youths, and a U.S. citizen protesting a court decision against him with respect to a butcher's bill of several hundred dollars. More serious, perhaps, was the confrontation between the Governor of Bermuda and Major Henry von Rhau, an American, who spoke on "What is Right with Great Britain" at Hamilton; when the former interrupted the latter's remarks about the English general strike, von Rhau refused to continue his address. But Bermudian-American relations generally remained harmonious as World War 2 approached. In March 1936 the Bermuda House of Assembly made a modest goodwill gesture by unanimously approving the "American Red Cross Society Resolve," a measure which provided £1,020 for flood relief in the United States.[33]

As for trade, during the four-year period ending in 1934 imports from the United States into the islands had totalled $2,745,970, as compared with $2,531,915 from Great Britain and $1,434,640 from Canada. In 1932, however, 75 percent of Bermudian exports went to Canada, only 25 percent to America. Thanks to the fostering of trade throughout the British Empire via the Ottawa Agreements, the

United States had now begun to lose some of the economic supremacy which it once had enjoyed relative to the islands. Despite strong opposition in the House of Assembly, the Bermudian parliament in December 1932 approved the preferential duties in favor of empire products; American exporters and U.S. congressmen immediately proposed such retaliatory measures as requiring passports for travel to the islands, or even taxing steamship tickets.

Of equal significance was the fact that in July 1936 the Legislative Council of Bermuda killed an investment companies bill, a measure which was designed to enable foreign-owned enterprises to operate in the islands. Since this bill would have aided U.S. tax dodgers by creating a pro-investment climate similar to that in the Bahamas since 1945, opponents looked upon its defeat as an anti-American gesture.[34] But back in the United States the Canadian-American Trade Agreement had gone into effect on January 1, 1936; under this, low-priced U.S. produce was allowed to enter the Canadian market, thus annulling the benefits enjoyed by Bermuda under the imperial preference system. Between 1935 and 1936 Bermudian sales in Canada decreased by half, and in the years that followed the islands largely abandoned agriculture except for the production of lily buds and bulbs. By 1939, moreover, a greater percentage of Bermudian exports were sold in America (48.1) than in Canada (43.8).

OTHER INTERWAR CONTACTS

Following the close of World War 1, the temporarily halted pastime of yachting revived and flourished in the islands. In June 1923 the first Newport-Bermuda race took place, with John Alden captaining the schooner *Malabar IV* to victory over twenty-one other starters; beginning in the following year, this 635-mile race has been held biennially during June, aside from the World War 2 years. In addition, in 1926 Bermudian one-design yachts began racing their Long Island counterparts in Bermudian waters, while the islanders also started to challenge the Americans in contests held off the U.S. coast. But as colorful as these developments were, an even more important event in the field of transportation dating from this period was the successful completion in April 1930 of the first air flight from New York City to Bermuda by Captain Lewis A. Yancey and a crew of two. The Board of Trade of the islands presented each of the flyers with a $1,000 check at a farewell dinner held at the Princess Hotel; in return Captain Yancey turned over his plane's compass to the Bermuda Historical Society.

Communication between the islands and the mainland also became more frequent at this time, thanks to the wireless telephone. As early as July 22, 1882, Republican Senator Henry Anthony of Rhode Island had introduced a resolution advocating "that the Committee on Military Affairs be instructed to inquire into the expediency of having a telegraphic cable laid between Bermuda and some convenient point in the United States."[35] But it was not until December 21, 1931, that wireless telephone service began operations between Washington, D.C., and the islands; on this occasion the Governor of Bermuda exchanged greetings with the under secretary of state. "Tell Wall Street to get to their offices earlier," observed a member of Parliament, "for there are thousands of orders from Bermuda awaiting them."[36]

As we have previously noted, the first air flight between New York City and Bermuda took place in 1930. Six years later the United States entered into reciprocal agreements with Great Britain, and the Irish Free State for transatlantic air service; but during the negotiations flights into and out of Hamilton became a bone of contention. According to the final agreement, there was to be a separate local service between the United States and Bermuda, but this was to run concurrently with the transatlantic service and was not to become a part of any other through routes. In the summer of 1937 Democratic Representative Louis Ludlow of Indiana and Democratic Senator William Gibbs McAdoo of California were guests on the inaugural flight of the *Bermuda Clipper* between New York City and Hamilton; Ludlow had been the chairman of the Appropriations Subcommittee which had sponsored the legislation establishing transatlantic air mail and passenger service. Ludlow and Gibbs later attended a banquet given by the Governor at the Belmont Manor Hotel.

Although the Bermudian government did not begin making an annual grant to the Furness-Bermuda shipping line until 1932,[37] 53,713 American tourists came to the islands during 1930, a sharp increase over the respective 1922 and 1926 totals of 24,589 and 31,594.[38] Since the days of Mark Twain and Woodrow Wilson a number of prominent Americans had visited Bermuda, including William Howard Taft, Charles Evans Hughes, John W. Davis, Gifford Pinchot, Samuel Seabury, Helen Hayes, Katherine Cornell, and Gene Tunney; Eugene O'Neill, in fact, wrote a large part of *Strange Interlude* in the islands, making use of the library facilities there. In 1929 twenty-seven American citizens were permanent residents of the islands.

Unfortunately, there were those Americans who were not welcome in Bermuda. One of these was perennial Socialist Party presidential candidate Eugene V. Debs, who was warned in 1936 that he would be deported if he attempted to make a speech or engage in propaganda. On the other hand, in 1937 District Attorney-Elect Thomas Dewey of New York City amicably exchanged views with the commissioner of police there, and this episode was far more representative of the reception received by Americans in the islands. During the March 1933 bank holiday in the United States, moreover, the Bermuda Chamber of Commerce agreed to give as much assistance as possible to American visitors.

While yachtsmen and aviators were active in or above the waters off the islands, and tourists were visiting Bermuda itself, Dr. William Beebe was exploring beneath the surface of the ocean in a large steel cylinder known as a bathysphere. Marine study in the islands had been given a significant boost by the Rockefeller Foundation, which in November 1929 made a £50,000 grant to the Bermuda Biological Station for Research; this institute's trustees then purchased the Shore Hills Hotel property and converted it into a laboratory which they formally opened on January 6, 1932. During this year, too, Dr. Charles H. Townsend of the New York aquarium brought to the islands several hundred American fish for release in local waters. But Beebe, the director of the Department of Tropical Research of the New York Zoological Society, had already begun his operations off Nonsuch Island in 1929, where he explored the ocean's depths over the course of three summers.

One could easily dwell upon the more spectacular aspects of Beebe's submarine exploits, and then devote just as much space to the scientific findings that were the end result of his investigations. Endorsed by the Governor and parliament of Bermuda, Beebe chose the islands for research partly because deep water approaches closer to shore off Bermuda than anywhere else. Although he did study deep sea life quite exhaustively off Bermuda, Beebe investigated the shore fishes as well, which differed markedly from their abyssal counterparts; through July 31, 1929, he had already taken two hundred species of true deep sea and pelagic fish, representing thirteen orders and fifty-two families, in the waters off Nonsuch Island. Two of his most important findings were that the density of marine life changed perceptibly from stratum to stratum and that the abyssal fishes and other organisms were just as lively as their surface counterparts. His third expedition (1931) also encountered strong evidence of submerged sea beaches at a depth of 1,450 to 1,550 fathoms.[39]

Given the increasing presence of a wide variety of Americans in the islands, it is not surprising that more than one writer would examine their impact in print. Thus, in March 1930, the same year that the

Hawley-Smoot Tariff was enacted, John R. Tunis published an article in *Harper's* magazine entitled "Bermuda and the American Idea." Here Tunis boldly proclaimed that "in Bermuda the American idea has taken specific form; it has applied standardized American customs to social life."[40] He noted, however, that as a rule the inhabitants of the islands were being educated in Great Britain or Canada, not in America. Writing in *Harper's* magazine eight years later Frederick Lewis Allen similarly noted that Bermuda was becoming less and less self-sufficient. He observed in this connection that "it imports American vacationers and tourists—and with them their spending money on the grand scale. Meanwhile its exports have shrunk."[41] As remedies Allen suggested intensive agriculture and a manufacturing program based on native materials. For Bermuda to have ended this U.S. domination over its tourism and trade, though, would have required drastic reforms and significant changes of which Bermuda perhaps was not capable at that time.

Three years before the outbreak of World War 2 in Europe, American Consul Harold L. Williamson observed privately in an annual political report that "geography, smallness of population, and the legal status of the Islands combine to create an atmosphere of provincialism on the one hand and of lack of the usual highly elaborated political organisms on the other."[42] Despite the relatively limited population, moreover, the density thereof had become so great that it was already a cause of great concern on the eve of World War 2. As today, the colored element in Bermuda was larger than its white counterpart, while among the latter Portuguese and Azoreans were present as well as Canadians and Americans. Many of the Portuguese and Azoreans worked on farms or as domestics; the Canadians, like the Americans, generally came to the islands as tourists or as merchants.

Presiding over this social pyramid of wealthy British and Americans, white collar Bermudians, Portuguese, and Negroes was a conservative native aristocracy zealous of maintaining its power: the so-called Forty Thieves. In reality hardheaded businessmen possessing great acumen, this group included such prominent families as the Treminghams, Trotts, Coxes, Dills, Pearmans, Goslings, Smiths, Tuckers, Norths, and Spurlings. It was under their leadership that in 1939 only about 8 percent of the population was eligible to vote; those males holding property in more than one parish could vote in more than one parish. "This was the Bermuda," observed Jim Bishop during World War 2, "of beautiful estates and yachts, of stingers at noon and gin-and-tonic in the evening, a Bermuda which wants Mother England to clothe her, Daddy America to feed her, and God to send enough rain for drinking purposes."[43]

WORLD WAR 2

Even before the Germans invaded Poland in September 1939, the American government had begun to negotiate with officials in London with respect to certain military facilities in the Atlantic. In June the British granted the United States extraordinary rights to lease airfield sites in Bermuda, St. Lucia, and Trinidad, while in August the American government obtained the authority to lease property in Bermuda for auxiliary seaplane bases. (A contract for Morgan's Island was signed in September.) The commencement of hostilities in Europe quite naturally had an impact on non-military travel to and from the islands, and the *Monarch* and the *Queen of Bermuda* were soon thereafter withdrawn from the Bermuda-New York tourist trade, rather than confront possible German submarine attacks.

During World War 1 the islands had sent 122 white soldiers overseas, of whom one-third lost their lives; it also created the Bermuda militia artillery of over 240 blacks, the only such group in the British army. A quarter-century later the islands failed to pass a conscription law, although anyone was free to volunteer for overseas duty if he so desired. During World War 2 the whites served in the volunteer rifle corps, the Negroes in the islands militia.

By the beginning of 1940 the British practice of stopping the Pan American Clippers at Bermuda and removing foreign mail for the purpose of wartime censorship had become the focal point of discussions among high governmental officials in Washington. Only four years before, in an attempt to cooperate in the enforcement of American laws, the Bermudian government had forbidden the transmission of Bermuda and West Indies sweepstakes tickets by mail. At the later date, however, the interception of the clippers caused adverse reactions in the halls of Congress; Democratic Senators Bennett Champ Clark of Missouri and Robert Reynolds of North Carolina and Democratic Representative Jennings Randolph of West Virginia were among those who were the most critical. Clark, who charged that half the mail on a recent flight had been confiscated, introduced a bill into the Senate to prohibit aircraft transporting mail from landing at the islands. Leading the journalistic assault was the isolationist *Chicago Tribune,* which after asserting that it was an American island, observed that "Bermuda is the spot where the British blockade, with its censorship of the mails, rubs the rawest."[44]

In February Pan American Airways cancelled the Hamilton stop on the eastbound trip to Europe. Yet within a year American censors were cooperating with their British counterparts there, as the war on the continent spread nearer and nearer to the British Isles. In fact, U.S.

authorities even established their own censorship office, which was staffed mainly by the wives of men stationed in Bermuda; this unit examined the mail of the construction workers as well as that of the military personnel.[45]

Strictly speaking, the destroyers-for-bases deal of September 3, 1940, between the United States and Great Britain did not include Bermuda and Newfoundland. Instead, the base sites in the two latter islands were leased to the American government for ninety-nine years, freely and without consideration. Far from greeting this development with an outburst of enthusiasm, the House of Assembly of the islands adopted a memorial expressing the following misgivings: "The people of Bermuda are deeply disturbed lest some new conception of American hemispheric defense may affect the status of this ancient Colony as an integral part of the British Commonwealth."[46] Among the major objections of leading Bermudians to the proposed U.S. base was that it might lead to severe economic, social, and political dislocations throughout the islands.

Philip Goodhart, who has written a full-length book on the destroyers-for-bases deal, has observed that the problem of locating the American military bases was most acute in Trinidad and Bermuda. In October Admiral John W. Greenslade arrived at the latter as the head of an American naval mission entrusted with surveying possible sites; earlier F.D.R. had warned him not to mutilate the islands. Greenslade, however, originally chose a location which would have cut the main island in two, before deciding to build an army base and airfield in the northeast north of Castle Harbour, and a naval air station and operating base in the southwest south of Great Sound. The Greenslade mission made its official report advocating a Bermuda base on January 6, 1941.

By early 1941 work was underway at the two locations; on March 27 the Bermudian House of Assembly officially authorized the U.S. military presence "very grudgingly and at heavy cost," in the words of Samuel Eliot Morison.[47] The naval operating base on the now joined Morgan's and Tucker's Islands was commissioned on April 7, with a part of the new base becoming the naval air station on July 1. This installation was to play a vital role in the anti-submarine campaign against Germany. On April 16 the U.S. army base on St. David's Island was activated and named Fort Bell; the airfield area was designated as Kindley Field on June 25.[48] The official opening of Kindley Field did not take place until November 29, but it soon became a key link in transatlantic air traffic. By the time the U.S. military facilities in Bermuda had been declared 100 percent complete, on August 11, 1943, the U.S. government had spent $42 million on their construction, $9 million for dredging alone.

Despite the action of the House of Assembly of the islands on March 27, 1941 the ruling oligarchy continued to look with some misgivings upon the American presence there. On August 4 the *New Republic* published a letter charging that "already America is at war in the Atlantic—not with the Axis powers, but with the Bermuda parliament, backed up by the British governor and his council."[49] While asserting that the great majority of islanders, both white and black, were pro-American, John Hall alleged that the single contribution which Bermuda had made to the war was to lend money without interest to England. This sacrifice, according to Hall, had been more than offset by what he described as widespread rent gouging in the islands, and by Bermuda placing a head tax on American military officers travelling back and forth between there and the United States.

On September 26 Colonel Frank Knox, the secretary of the navy, arrived at Hamilton on board an American naval vessel. After he had completed an inspection of U.S. military facilities there, he attended a large dinner party given by Commandant James. It was around this time that the American government obtained a lease of the buildings and grounds of the Bermuda Biological Station for use as a temporary hospital. (The station's activities were transferred to the government aquarium at Flatts.) In January 1942 a delegation from Bermuda met informally with officials from the British and American governments in Washington; headed by Lord Knollys, the governor, it discussed such touchy questions as the need for additional land, roads, immigration, shipping, bridges, tariff concessions, and customs problems. Not only were household goods and personal belongings taxed by Bermuda, but also petroleum products and fuel oil.

On July 1 an anti-aircraft training center was established in the islands. As a result of the rapidity with which the military facilities on Bermuda had been built, on March 30, 1943, Commandant James presented the E pennant—the highest American award for excellence in war production—to Mr. L. E. Brownson, the president of the construction company. Then late in October the House of Assembly proposed to assume the cost of the land used for the U.S. bases, a sum totalling approximately £560,000, with the revenue to be raised by direct taxation, a property tax, and death duties. Another important development which took place during 1943 was the setting up of the DD-DE (destroyer and destroyer escort) Shakedown Task Force, which by November had readied ninety-nine destroyer escorts and twenty destroyers for active duty. The following January (1944) the Air Transport Command, the forerunner of the present Military Airlift Command, began operations in the islands.

Although a number of civilian construction workers quartered aboard the *Berkshire,* an old Hudson River steamboat, devoted their off-hours to drinking, gambling, and other forms of dissipation, by the time of their departure in 1943 perhaps no more than three or four really disagreeable incidents had taken place. Both Brigadier General Alden G. Strong and Admiral Ingram C. Sowell made a constant effort to iron out difficulties involving American military personnel and tighten up shore leave discipline.[50] Nevertheless, in December 1944 the House of Assembly placed a curfew on American sailors because of alleged misbehavior; it was charged during the debate by Morris A. Gibbons, the former president of the Bermuda Chamber of Commerce, that U.S. naval personnel on shore leave had been guilty of criminal misconduct. (The islands, one should note, had been lightly policed in time of peace by Bermudian authorities.) Several days later, however, the House of Assembly concluded that as a whole the conduct of the American military had been exemplary, after local merchants had vehemently protested the decline in free spending as a result of the curfew.

With respect to the status of tourists and businessmen from the mainland, Alan Jackson reported in the *Saturday Evening Post* on July 25, 1942, that "no visitors, even Americans who own Bermudian land, may come down here any more unless they come on official business."[51] Yet in the months ahead the Axis threat to Bermuda gradually lessened. By November 1943 the House of Assembly of the islands was voting £11,000 to the Trade and Development Board for advertising purposes in 1944; it was feared that prospective American and Canadian tourists might be repulsed by the impression that Bermuda was "a garrison place with the beaches full of barbed wire."[52] The ever-fickle House of Assembly only two weeks later drastically reduced the allotment to £650 for reasons not given.

While tourists and businessmen played a lesser role in Bermuda during World War 2 than they had before that conflict, another factor which had a disturbing impact on the islands' economy was the high wages which Americans paid to local labor. At the time when the Americans first landed, the ruling oligarchy set up the Bermuda Labor Board; when that body attempted to establish a prevailing wage, though, Admiral Sowell observed, "We just can't find people who will work for wages as low as they want us to pay labor."[53] Then on June 19, 1944, the Navy Department in Washington was asked to reduce naval base wages by from three to eight cents an hour, despite the gradual acceleration of the cost of living in the islands. The result was that local workers began organizing a labor union, the first such organization in Bermuda's history; to counter this move, the British brought in fifty natives from Barbados on a temporary basis, while the Bermudians imported fifty laborers from the Azores. But as is pointed out elsewhere in this volume, labor problems were not uncommon elsewhere in the British Atlantic islands during World War 2.[54]

During the final year of this conflict several members of Congress again expressed an interest in the United States acquiring Bermuda. These included Democratic Senators Kenneth McKellar of Tennessee and Robert Reynolds of North Carolina, as well as Democratic Representative Michael Bradley of Pennsylvania; the latter suggested that the islands might be obtained in exchange for wartime lend lease to Great Britain. Bradley had been a member of a subcommittee of the House Committee on Naval Affairs which had been detained in Bermuda for two days on its way to Europe shortly after VE-Day.[55] But on February 25, 1945, Rear Admiral Frank A. Braisted, the commandant of the U.S. naval operating base, openly took the position that only a tiny minority advocated the American occupation of Bermuda.

In January 1945 the submarine repair facility in the islands was placed in a caretaker status, and the DD-DE training facilities were moved to Guantanamo Bay, while in July the military base as a whole was placed in reduced status. That September the U.S. navy recommended that the Bermudian base be retained; in January 1946 there was a transfer of command to the air force. (The name "Fort Bell" was now dropped.) Assessing the American military presence in the islands during World War 2 retrospectively, Lord Burgley, the governor of Bermuda, observed that aside from a few incidents it had been "a model of what Anglo-American relationship can be."[56] Overlooked by Burgley in his remarks was the rather lukewarm attitude by his House of Assembly towards the American base.

But the U.S. occupation did bring to an end an era which in all likelihood will never return again, those three centuries when the automobile was absent from the islands.[57] Around 1890 it had been the Americans who had brought the bicycle to Bermuda, but horse-drawn carriages remained in wide use down to the time of World War 2, at which time the U.S. military obtained the right to drive automobiles on the grounds of its facilities. This right was eventually extended to off-base roads. By the latter part of the war Bermudian officials were complaining that the American trucks were pocking these highways, and requesting that the U.S. government pay for their repair. Under an agreement reached on April 18, 1945, the House of Assembly ratified a three-way arrangement providing for the asphalt resurfacing of 18½ miles of roads at a total estimated cost of $428,000; the American military was to execute the construction work, while Bermuda was to contribute $150,000 of the total cost. By this time, moreover, Bermudians were operating a considerable number of motor vehicles themselves,[58] so that the age of the horseless carriage had indeed arrived in the islands.

THE POSTWAR ERA

During the last three decades it has not always been easy to separate the U.S. military and non-military presence in the islands, if only because since January 1946 all commercial airlines flying into and out of Bermuda have used the military runways and air traffic control facilities there. One month later an air services agreement between England and America involving flights stopping in Bermuda was signed in the islands, entering into force immediately; extensions and amendments were added to this agreement in December 1946, January 1947, January 1948, February 1955, and May 1966. In addition, notes were exchanged at Washington during March and April 1951 with respect to the civil airport facilities at Kindley Field.[59]

Turning to the status of the military facilities in Bermuda during the post-World War 2 period, on July 1, 1950, the naval operating base was decommissioned, with a U.S. naval station taking its place. Operations at the naval station then were placed in reduced status until March 1951; at that time it was reactivated, and in the years which followed it functioned mainly as an anti-submarine base. As for aviation, during August 1952 a $1,707,198 contract was awarded to the Merritt Chapman & Scott Corporation, which was to build additional facilities at the Kindley Air Force Base, including bituminous paving for aircraft parking aprons and taxiways. A month afterwards this same firm won another contract for the construction of a 188,000-gallon-a-day plant which was to distill sea water into fresh water. Four years later, in December 1956, the American government asked its British counterpart for additional communication and housing facilities outside those areas then occupied by the U.S. forces, now that the last remnants of the British garrison had left the islands in mid-1953. Then in January 1957 the McDonough Construction Company of Florida obtained a $2 million contract for additional construction at Kindley Air Force Base.

Those laborers employed at the latter, moreover, were to be paid at the same rate as their counterparts in the United States, according to a controversial ruling of the circuit court of appeals in November 1947. Reversing a lower court order dismissing a suit for overtime compensation under the Fair Labor Standards Act, the court in effect held that the military base in Bermuda was a possession of America. Eleven employees and approximately $50,000 in overtime compensation claims were involved. On December 6, 1948, the U.S. Supreme Court upheld the circuit court of appeals ruling in a 5 to 4 vote; Justice Stanley Reed in a majority decision pointed out that it was not decisive that the military facilities had been acquired after the Fair Labor Standards Act had been passed. Critics of this ruling included the departments of State and Justice and the Wage-Hour Administration, along with Justice Robert Jackson of the U.S. Supreme Court, who stated that the decision reflected a philosophy of annexation. The legal adviser of the State Department, though, had taken the position on January 30, 1948, that the base lease did not involve a transfer of sovereignty. On March 8, 1949, the U.S. Supreme Court denied a rehearing of its December decision, thus allowing it to stand.

During these years there were other episodes that one might cite relative to American-Bermudian relations, although it is not always easy either to link them to each other or to the material above. First there was the status of the islands. Any possibility that Bermuda might be transferred to the United States was ruled out on May 8, 1947, by British Colonial Secretary Arthur Creech Jones; replying to a question before the House of Commons, Jones denied that the islands would be used to pay off England's World War 2 debt.[60] Then there was the matter of American extraterritorial rights in Bermuda, which came to the fore in 1952, when the House of Assembly debated a bill giving the American government exclusive jurisdiction over security offenses in the islands.[61] Despite an occasional controversy, however, relations between the two governments were generally friendly, as is evidenced by the $43,000 contribution which the government and people of Bermuda made towards the relief of the victims of Hurricane Diane in September 1955, after the latter had caused devastating floods throughout the eastern United States. A representative American goodwill gesture saw Dr. Edward M. Riley, director of research for Colonial Williamsburg, present 650 letters from the Tucker-Coleman and Blathywayt papers to the Bermudian government in July 1959.

Among the more prominent visitors to come to Bermuda in the aftermath of World War 2 was President Harry Truman, who arrived on the presidential yacht *Williamsburg* on August 22, 1946, for a week-long stay. This was basically an informal visit which did not involve any diplomatic talks; instead, the chief executive swam and fished, and toured the main island by automobile.[62] On the other hand, when President Dwight Eisenhower twice visited the islands during the 1950s, it was to engage in serious high level talks with the heads of state of foreign governments. In December 1953 "Ike" discussed international problems with Prime Minister Winston Churchill of Great Britain and Premier Joseph Laniel of France, while in March 1957 he held a Big Two summit meeting with Harold Macmillan, now the English prime minister.

Aside from these two presidents, by the mid-1950s American tourists visiting the islands were becoming on the average noticeably younger. To quote one contemporary observer, "In recent years Bermuda has become so indispensable an extension of the American university campus that the spring pilgrimage, a social requisite for every college boy or girl who can find the fare, almost seems deserving of some kind of academic recognition."[63] What once had been confined to Easter vacation now had become a common sight during a whole series of College Weeks. By 1961 there were around ten thousand U.S. servicemen and their dependents present, while the one television station was offering programs which were entirely canned and about 95 percent American, apart from the newscasts. Even the stalagmite figures in the caves of Hamilton Parish had acquired such names as Benjamin Franklin or New York Skyline; so pervasive had the American presence become that a Canadian magazine published an article at this time entitled "Crown Colony or U.S. Protectorate?" (This publication, *Saturday Night,* was not widely circulated in America.)

Although American and other foreign tourists continued to be the economic lifeblood of the islands, one might also cite a few instances of U.S. investment during the early post-war period. In August 1947, for example, a group including Pan American Airways and the Hilton Hotels Corporation obtained a 40 percent interest in the Mid-Ocean Club and three hotels: the Castle Harbour, the Bermudian, and the St. George. Since over £1 million supposedly changed hands in this transaction, it was perhaps the largest property deal to date in the islands' history. Then in January 1948 a Washington firm, R. and T. Electronics, bought the Bermuda Railway from the government, which had owned it for eighteen months. This electronics firm planned to dismantle 20 miles of track and ship it to South America; the coming of the automobile had rendered the railroad more or less obsolete. It was not until Hallowe'en 1931 that the first train in the islands' history had begun running from Hamilton to Somerset, following two decades of bitter opposition which saw a number of companies fail to complete the line.

During the 1960s and 1970s the American government continued its military operations in the islands, although in contrast with the days of John Smith three and a half centuries earlier the United States does not presently view Bermuda as a bit to rule a great horse (i.e., Spain). In 1963 modern, high speed land-based P-3 Orion aircraft replaced the seaplanes at the naval station. When drought stalked the islands in 1969, the U.S. navy shipped 4 million gallons of water there, a quarter of which went to the Bermudian government.[64] The following year an important administrative change occurred, since on July 1, 1970, Kindley Air Force Base was transferred from the air force to the navy. Representative happenings during a typical month in the mid-1970s (February 1974) included the role of a U.S. Navy tug in the freeing of the grain ship *Mount Julie* from a reef in Bermuda's main shipping channel, and the Legislative Council's approval of regulations "designed to allow American civilians employed at the Air Station to have the same on-base customs privileges as members of the U.S. Forces have."[65] One might also cite in this connection three agreements concerning Bermuda signed by America and England during this period: the space vehicle tracking and communication station one of 1961, the Kindley Base civil airport facilities one of 1968, and the U.S. naval air station one of 1971.

As for the economic front, in 1963 the *New York Times* observed that an increasing number of for rent advertisements were appearing in Bermudian newspapers; because of changes in the air force and navy organization there, many dependents were returning to the United States. Yet in 1966 and 1967 the tourist industry benefited the islands' economy to the amount of £14,477,000 and £18,420,000 respectively, while in 1972 421,000 visitors spent $120 million in Bermuda.[66] During the latter year there also was a revival of the export of lily flowers and lily bulbs to New York after a decade of inactivity. Yet while exports from the islands to America held constant at $2 million between 1955 and 1969, imports from America rose from 16 to 71 million, with food, textiles and clothing, and machinery predominating.

In September 1972 a U.S. Department of State publication noted that Bermuda had enjoyed steady economic prosperity since the end of World War 2. Two months earlier the islands had pegged their dollar to the American one, in the process breaking their link with the British pound sterling. As of 1972 Bermuda was receiving approximately $8 to $9 million annually from expenditures connected with the U.S. naval base; between 85 and 90 percent of the tourists were coming from America, while about 30 percent of the sixteen hundred "exempted" foreign companies were U.S. owned. (This percentage increased to over one-third of 2,300 by 1974.) America also provided the islands with 45 percent of their imports at this time, a figure which held quite steady for some recent years. Admittedly, U.S. land transportation equipment and petroleum products sales did lag, but only because of the peculiar Bermudian size and horsepower restrictions. By 1974 Americans had invested a total of $100 million in the islands' hotels, and were providing approximately 75 percent ($23.5 million in 1973) of the annual investment influx; thanks to the Bermudian restrictions on foreign investment in local businesses, much of this went into tourist complexes and property.

While the U.S. military and tourist presence remained strong, with ten thousand American citizens residing in the islands, the winds of change were beginning to blow through that country of which William Howard Taft once observed that no nation so small had ever played such a large role in world history. New trends were most in evidence in the social and political areas. The first blacks had been brought to Bermuda as early as 1616, three years before they arrived in the United States, but the desegregation of theaters and public rooms in hotels did not occur in the islands until 1959, five years after the landmark Supreme Court decision in America outlawing segregation in the public schools. Educational integration in Bermuda has progressed since 1964, while a law passed in early 1968 banned segregation in restaurants. Among the factors leading to these changes were post-war prosperity, the example of the West Indies, and the education of a growing number of colored Bermudians abroad. Yet as Kenneth McNaught points out, there is "a strong conservative feeling among Negro Bermudians" due to "the consciousness of Bermudians of all colors that what disrupts the tourist industry spells disaster for the colony."[67]

But the most serious challenge which the upper class has faced since the foundation of the colony has political ramifications as well. In 1968 a new constitution was put into operation providing for a crown-appointed governor with special responsibility for external affairs and security matters. He is to be assisted in the execution of his duties by a bicameral legislature composed of a Legislative Council whose eleven members are appointed by him, and by a House of Assembly whose forty members are elected by universal adult franchise. Elections must take place at least once every five years, although as in England the majority party is free to call one whenever it so desires.

When the United Bermuda Party defeated the Progressive Labour Party in the national election held the same year, it was the first election in the islands ever held under the party system. As a result of the returns, Sir Henry Tucker, whose party had won thirty seats, became Bermuda's first government leader. It is still too early, however, to determine whether these social and political developments will have any real impact on future American-Bermudian relations as the islands proceed into the last quarter of this century "Quo Fata Ferunt," as the islands' motto has it, whither the fates may carry. The assassination of the British governor there early in 1973 (during the investigation of which Scotland Yard asked the F.B.I. for assistance) indicates that an ill wind may have started to blow in Bermuda. When a 33-year-old black, Erskine Burrows, was hanged in December 1977 for the murder of Governor Richard Sharples, the subsequent rioting and firebombing on the part of Negro youths forced the islands' new governor to declare a state of emergency. Burrows had been a member of a now defunct revolutionary group, the Black Beret Cadres, and his execution was the first in Bermuda since the end of World War 2. But while many Negroes now favor independence for the islands as soon as possible, the white majority prefers a more leisurely timetable, especially since Great Britain did airlift in 250 troops to help quell the unrest.

5

ICELAND
Land of Ice and Fire

As early as the fourth century A.D. seafarers had become aware of the existence of Iceland, and by the ninth century Irish hermits had taken up residence there. But Icelandic history in the continuous sense did not begin until the arrival of Ingólfur Arnarson, who established a colony on the site of present-day Reykjavik in 874. Between then and the end of the tenth century, a number of other Norse pioneers came to the island, setting up homesteads upon their arrival, along with smaller groups of Scotch and Irish immigrants.

Perhaps the key date in early Icelandic history is 930 A.D. It was at this time that the first session of the "Althing" met at Thingvellir and the Commonwealth began. The Althing is widely looked upon today as the oldest functioning legislature in the world; as under the American Articles of Confederation of the 1780s, there originally was a legislature but no executive. Explorers from the island were active on the seas to the west during this period, the most famous being Leif Ericsson, who may have discovered the coast of America around 1000. (Henry Wadsworth Longfellow commemorated this possible event in his poem "The Skeleton in Armor.")

By 1220 six prominent families had gained control over the island, but after a local struggle for power among the chief settlers in 1262, the king of Norway seized it for his own. Another important administrative development took place in 1380, when Norway and Denmark became one nation following the death of Haakon VI, and authorities in Copenhagen assumed the responsibility for governing the island. During the following century, around 1477, Christopher Columbus may have come to Iceland fifteen years before his epoch-making

voyage to America; monks there may have given him his first information about the land to the west which their ancestors possibly visited
a half-millennium previously.

A century and a quarter later, in 1602, the Danish government established a total commercial monopoly over the island; this not only
crippled Iceland's trade, but also lowered its standard of living during
the seventeenth and eighteenth centuries. Then in 1662 the people
were forced to accept the absolute authority of the Danish king. In a
most significant constitutional development, the government of Denmark abolished the Althing in 1800 and transferred the seat of government to Reykjavik. During 1809, towards the end of the Napoleonic
Wars, the Danish adventurer Jörgen Jörgensen and the English merchant Samuel Phelps temporarily seized power in Iceland.

It was not until a generation after the abolition of the Althing
that King Frederick VI of Denmark set up a consultative assembly
at Copenhagen during 1834, nearly a decade before the Althing again
began to function in that capacity at Reykjavik in 1843. The trade of
the island also was opened to all nations in 1854, and the first steamship arrived in 1855; after 1870 Icelanders were granted more control
over this commerce, with Great Britain the leading market for their
sheep and horses. By this time Jón Sigurdsson had assumed leadership
over the nationalist movement, which he headed during the years from
1841 to 1879. Five years before his death, in 1864, the Althing re-
gained its legislative powers under a new constitution, as well as
control over domestic finances. Iceland was now a thousand years
old, if one dates its history from the arrival of Ingólfur Arnarson.

Then shortly after the turn of the twentieth century, Iceland obtained a constitutional amendment which gave it further control over
its internal affairs. The decade before the coming of World War 1 saw
further steps taken in the direction of progress; this series of events
culminated with the signing of a treaty with Denmark in 1918, under
which the government in Copenhagen recognized Iceland as an independent state under the Danish king. Similar in many respects to
the Statute of Westminster, this document provided that Denmark
was to conduct the island's foreign affairs, but that the former was
not to enter into agreements with other nations which affected the
latter, unless Iceland gave its consent.

U.S. INTEREST TO 1918

A century earlier the first commercial relations between America
and Iceland had begun. In 1809 the *Neptune* and the *Providence*
arrived at Reykjavik, loaded with a cargo of foodstuffs, brandy, and

tobacco, just before the War of 1812 disrupted Icelandic-American trade. Edward Cruft of Boston requested and obtained sole American trading rights in Iceland from the Danish government. The main reason that Cruft received these was that the governor general was of the opinion that his prices were low and the goods were valuable. Perhaps the first American both to visit the island and to write about it was Pliny Miles, who arrived in 1852. In evaluating the Icelanders Miles noted that "they possess a greater spirit of historical research and literary inquiry, have more scholars, poets and learned men, than can be found among an equal population on the face of the globe."[1] He was followed several years later by J. Ross Browne of California, who wrote three long articles for *Harper's* magazine which appeared during 1863.

In 1867 the southern expansionist Robert J. Walker suggested to Secretary of State William H. Seward, who was negotiating for the purchase of the Danish West Indies, "the propriety of obtaining from the same power Greenland, and probably Iceland also."[2] The report which Walker submitted to Seward several months later had been prepared by the U.S. Coast Guard Survey; it made reference to the superb fisheries of Iceland, as well as to its vast beds of lignite and its rich and extensive sulphur mountains. The ensuing congressional debate on the purchase of both Greenland and Iceland probably witnessed more criticism with respect to the former, although Republican Representative Thomas Williams of Pennsylvania did make a sarcastic reference to the valuable geysers of the latter.

In 1874 Icelanders celebrated the one thousandth anniversary of the Norse settlement of their homeland. At this time King Christian IX of Denmark visited the island, as did two Americans: Bayard Taylor, who was covering the ceremonies for the *New York Tribune,* and Samuel Kneeland, a M.I.T. professor of zoology and physiology who had come to study volcanic activity and to collect animal specimens. As he approached the shores of the island, Taylor composed a poem entitled "America to Iceland," which he began with the salutation "Welcome, the children of thy Vinland."[3] Significantly, there was some disagreement between Taylor and Kneeland as to the impact of the king's presence; the former felt that he made friends, while the latter was of the opinion that he aroused resentment. Here one might refer to Kneeland's additional observation that "my impression of this people . . . was that they are born republicans."[4]

Among those Americans most interested in the history and culture of the island was Theodore Roosevelt. T.R. liked to read the Icelandic sagas for relaxation, especially the *Njala;* given his heroic concept of life, this fascination was by no means surprising. By a strange coincidence, Lord James Bryce, the British ambassador to the United States, also was a devotee of this literature, and in its lighter moments the conversation between the two men sometimes turned to these glorious epics of the Far North.[5]

Around the turn of the twentieth century Icelandic trade with the United States reached a significant level. Writing from Copenhagen on December 20, 1904, American Consul Raymond R. Frazier pointed out that not only was there great interest in the establishment of a steamship line between the United States and Iceland but also Icelanders were consuming large quantities of American products. These imports, many of which entered Iceland by way of Scotland and England, included canned beef, Alaskan salmon, kerosene, and shoes. Conversely, Icelandic ponies were being shipped to the United States.

When the *Gullfoss* docked at New York City in May 1915, it became the first Icelandic-owned vessel to pay a visit to America in over nine hundred years, aside from being the first acquisition of the newly formed Icelandic Steamship Company. Captain Péturson and his crew were wined and dined at Peck's Restaurant on Fulton Street. By 1917 Iceland and the Faeroe Islands imported $2,400,000 worth of American goods annually, an increase of nearly $2,000,000 over 1916; the outbreak of World War 1 had cut off the usual supplies of items like flour from Denmark, Norway, and Great Britain, and thus the island had to turn elsewhere. Around this time there were a growing number of U.S. automobiles in Iceland, while American cotton goods had become more popular along the southern coast. Despite this increase in the volume of commerce, however, there were problems with respect to U.S.-Icelandic trade; these centered around island wool and American petroleum. In May 1918 Iceland agreed to sell its wool to the Allied governments rather than to Germany, while in September the Standard Oil Company of New Jersey won out over an originally designated British rival for the privilege of supplying petroleum to Iceland.

THE INTERWAR DECADES

The decades between the two world wars in Icelandic history featured progress in a number of areas, apart from the thrust towards final and complete separation from Denmark. Inland air transportation started as early as 1920, but local airlines did not operate on a fully organized basis until 1938. In addition, an increasing number of factories began processing fish and fish products after World War 1, many of them for export.

On June 8, 1925, President Calvin Coolidge delivered a speech before a Norwegian centennial celebration at the Minnesota Fair Grounds. In this speech the President gave Leif Ericsson rather than Columbus credit for discovering America; as one would expect, his address was highly laudatory in tone. Coolidge's claim that Leif Ericsson had found the mainland was challenged four years later on the floor of the House of Representatives by Democrat James O'Connor of Louisiana, who set forth the possibility that sixth-century Irish may have been the first Europeans to set eyes on the New World.

It was in 1929 and 1930 that the attention of Americans turned to Iceland as never before, thanks to the celebration there of the one thousandth anniversary of the first assembly of the Althing. On November 1 of the former year President Herbert Hoover had appointed a commission headed by Republican Senator Peter Norbeck of South Dakota to represent the United States and to present the people of Iceland with a statue of Leif Ericsson. Other members were Republican Representative O. B. Burtness of North Dakota, Detroit union executive Frederick H. Fljozdal, state official O. P. B. Jacobsen of Minnesota, and University of Illinois Professor Sveinbjorn Johnson. Congress appropriated $50,000 for the statue (to be executed by New York sculptor Sterling Calder) and $5,000 for the commission's expenses, after Republican Representative Fiorello La Guardia of New York had struck out a preamble to the resolution crediting Leif Ericsson with the discovery of America.[6] The states of Minnesota and North Dakota also sent delegations to the festivities held during the week of June 23, 1930, at Thingvellir, approximately thirty miles from Reykjavik.

One of the recommendations of the five-man Norbeck Commission was that permanent American representation in Iceland be established, if only because of the increased commercial ties. In this connection, Jay P. Moffat, the chief of the Division of Western European Affairs, declared on December 13, 1933, that ". . . the matter of sending a resident representative to Iceland has been given careful consideration for a number of years, but . . . it has not been found feasible to do so."[7] Iceland still maintained ties with Denmark through the king, and thus American diplomatic representation at Reykjavik was a touchy issue.

Following the close of World War 1, American trade with Iceland declined, although Great Britain continued to maintain her commerce with the island at the expense of Denmark. An economic survey of

Iceland conducted in 1928 for the U.S. Department of Commerce revealed that the island's main exports consisted of fish and fish products, shipped mainly to southern Europe; wool, sold principally to the United States; and mutton, sent largely to Norway and Great Britain. But as we have noted previously, much of American trade with Iceland went through such European nations as Denmark, Germany, Norway, and Great Britain, so that these statistics are misleading. At this time the bulk of Icelandic purchases from the United States consisted of foodstuffs, such as cereals and fresh and dried fruits; in addition, almost all the tires sold in the island were of American manufacture, as were about three-fourths of the 575 motor vehicles then in use there. Rubber footwear and canned milk from the United States also found a wide market in Iceland.

In 1931 Edward M. Groth, the American consul at Copenhagen, wrote a memorandum entitled "Possibility of Greater American Participation in Icelandic Trade," in which he examined the market for canned, fresh, and dried fruit. At this time a considerable number of apples and a limited quantity of oranges from the United States were reaching the island. Following 1934, American imports remained at the same relatively low level which had characterized the beginning of the inter-war period, but Icelandic exports to the United States increased significantly; by 1939 America had become as good a market as Germany, especially for cod liver oil. There also were changes in the trade of other nations with the island during the 1930s.

At the same time that merchants from numerous countries were active in the sea trade of Iceland, German and American airlines were trying to establish control over its air routes. Between 1928 and 1931 Lufthansa furnished the island with local service in conjunction with the Flugfjelag Islands (Flying Company of Iceland). This firm did go out of business, but the Premier granted to Germany most-favored–nation treatment with regard to any flying rights which Iceland might award to any other country up to 1940,[8] an action the denying of which was later to provoke ill feeling between the two nations. Then in 1932 Pan American Airlines acquired an Icelandic franchise, but this expired four years later without regular service having been established. Assessing the island in 1934 from the standpoint of aviation, Charles A. Lindbergh discounted the harbor at Reykjavik as "entirely unsuited for seaplane operation," but concluded that "there are many natural landing areas in Iceland and comparatively little difficulty would be encountered in constructing airports in almost any section."[9] As we will see, in the years which followed the aerial potentialities of the island became of great consequence to the United States, since a hostile German presence there might prove a threat to American security.

WORLD WAR 2: THE BRITISH PRESENCE

German designs on Iceland at the time of the outbreak of World War 2 were by no means limited to the previously chronicled expressions of interest in the island during the decade of the 1930s, extensive as these were. By 1939 Admiral Wilhelm Canaris's office had drawn up plans for the occupation of Iceland; another strategist had suggested using the island as a base for a possible invasion of Cape Cod and Rhode Island. While this military planning was going on, the takeover of Iceland was being prepared by Joachim von Ribbentrop and Horst von Pflugk-Burckhardt, both of whom had been building up a network of spies there for years.

Early in March 1939 a rumor began to circulate in Germany that another nation was preparing to establish a base in Iceland. Remembering the Icelandic promise earlier in the decade that Germany would be granted most-favored-nation treatment with regard to any flying rights awarded to any other country up to 1940, the Nazis sent the cruiser *Emden* and two other warships to Reykjavik to remind the Icelandic government of this prior commitment. For some reason, officials there were unable to find the document making this pledge; on the other hand, they did advise the Germans that the rumor that another country was getting ready to set up an airbase there was not true.

In Washington, too, there was a growing attention towards Iceland. The chief of the European Division, Jay Pierrepont Moffat, suggested to Secretary of State Cordell Hull on April 14, 1939 that the United States should establish a consular office in Reykjavik; Moffat quite correctly expressed concern that the Germans might attempt to set up submarine and airbases there. Moffat, though, failed to convert Hull, who observed that U.S. trade with Iceland was too limited to justify a consulate.

More general American interest in the island developed that summer following the opening of the Icelandic pavilion at the World's Fair in New York City. Isolationist Republican Senator Gerald P. Nye of North Dakota, speaking on this occasion, praised Iceland for not having an army; according to Nye, "America has had no better citizens than the Icelander, no migration that has so quickly and completely made itself American." Equally laudatory was Mayor Fiorello La Guardia of New

York City, who similarly took note of Iceland's lack of an army, as well as the absence of poverty and hunger there. In the opinion of the progressive Republican Mayor, "You have accomplished more per capita and per square mile than any other country in the whole world."[10]

On March 7, 1940, one month before the Germans invaded Denmark, Jesse M. Jones's Federal Loan Administration made public the allocation of $10 million to Denmark and $1 million to Iceland, mainly for the purchase of agricultural supplies in the United States. Two days after the Nazi takeover of Denmark, however, the Icelandic government released an official statement to the effect that it would not join any diplomatic alliance, and would protest any measures which might threaten its neutral stance. Then on April 16 the State Department announced that the United States would establish direct diplomatic relations with Iceland, in the wake of an invitation to this effect from the Icelandic Prime Minister. At the same time Secretary of the Treasury Henry Morgenthau, acting upon a suggestion from Secretary Hull, released the island from an earlier order freezing Danish credits.

But Iceland was not to remain free much longer from the shock waves which had been emanating from the continent since September 1939. On May 10, 1940, the same day that Sir Winston Churchill became prime minister, Great Britain occupied the island by force; the British eventually sent a large number of troops there and built two air bases. This marked the first time in its 1,000-year history that Iceland had been actively involved in a war. As one might expect, the German press looked upon the occupation of the island as an act of unprovoked aggression against a defenseless people, conveniently forgetting its own government's blatant takeover of Denmark the previous month. The *Deutsche Allgemeine Zeitung* even printed an editorial in which it argued that Iceland geographically is closer to Greenland than to Scotland; it thus lies within the Western Hemisphere, and falls under the protection of the Monroe Doctrine!

With British troops now occupying Iceland, Farmer-Labor Senator Ernest Lundeen of Minnesota delivered a lengthy address on the floor of the Senate on June 6. Adopting the position taken earlier by the *DAZ*, Lundeen opined in criticizing the English military presence that "Iceland is a part of the North American continent, of the Western Hemisphere—of the American Hemisphere, as I like to call it."[11] A month later, on July 12, Icelandic Consul General Vilhjalmur Thor asked Assistant Secretary of State Adolf A. Berle whether the United States would consider extending the Monroe Doctrine to Iceland, and whether the latter might be included in a customs union or given some special economic status. The American government did not act on the first request at this time, but in September President Franklin Roosevelt issued a proclamation suspending tonnage duties on Icelandic products imported into America.

Later that year an upgrading occurred in the rank of the diplomatic representatives exchanged by the United States and Iceland. On October 1 Lincoln MacVeagh became the American minister to Iceland, while on November 19 Thór Thórs presented to F.D.R. letters of credence as the Icelandic minister to the United States. A month later Bertel E. Kuniholm, the U.S. consul at Reykjavik, was approached informally by Stefán Stefánsson, the Icelandic foreign minister. Offering a gloomy assessment of the British chances of staving off a German invasion, Stefánsson opined that the military defeat of Great Britain would inevitably be followed by the withdrawal of the British garrison from Iceland. He therefore sought American assistance, but Secretary Hull informed Consul Kuniholm four days later that the United States was not prepared to send an American expeditionary force to the island, despite Stefánsson's request for assistance.

Developments in the North Atlantic were soon to alter this American reluctance. On March 25, 1941, the German government issued a new declaration which extended the Atlantic war zone to include Iceland; both Admiral Erich Raeder and Reichsmarschall Herman Göring favored the Nazi occupation of both it and the Azores. Throughout March and April there was extensive German submarine and airplane activity in the general vicinity of Iceland, and during the latter month the U.S.S. *Niblack* encountered and attacked a Nazi U-boat while on an armed reconnaissance mission. This episode marked the unofficial inception of hostilities between America and Germany.

Back in Washington British and American military officials agreed on the so-called ABC-1 Staff Agreement on March 27. This provided that the United States would take over the defense of Iceland from the British, probably in September. Three weeks later, on April 18, Admiral Ernest King's operations order defined the Western Hemisphere in such terms as to include at least the western part of Iceland.[12] Both the navy and the army, however, were quite unenthusiastic, with navy planners taking the position that the island had deficiencies as a strategic outpost to defend the Western Hemisphere.

Turning to the diplomatic front, the President instructed Harry Hopkins, his special assistant, to hold secret talks with Icelandic minister Thór Thórs in Washington concerning the future American role in the island. These discussions continued through the spring. Then on May 7 the British ambassador, Lord Halifax, informed Secretary Hull that the Germans were threatening to occupy Iceland; shortly after the middle of the month F.D.R. apparently reached the decision that America would have to defend the island, and he cabled Winston Churchill to this effect.

On June 2 Harry Hopkins, Secretary of War Henry Stimson, and Secretary of the Navy Frank Knox held a discussion on the British war effort, at which Knox endorsed American military action relative to Iceland and Stimson and Hopkins concurred. Stimson and Knox then met with Hull, and obtained at least his partial support for the Icelandic project. After the U.S. army was instructed two days later to prepare to take the place of the British forces in the island, it halted its preparations for an Azorean expedition. As for the marines, they were told on June 5 to be ready to leave for Iceland within fifteen days; on the next day F.D.R. tentatively decided to dispatch a part of the Pacific Fleet to the Atlantic.

Preparations moved one step further on June 16, when Admiral Harold Stark wrote Admiral Ernest King that the President had directed that United States troops relieve the British garrison in Iceland. At this time Stark placed both the marines and the U.S. navy on the alert. When the marine brigade left America on June 22, it was under instructions to carry out a one-sentence order: "TASK: IN COOPERATION WITH THE BRITISH GARRISON, DEFEND ICE—LAND AGAINST HOSTILE ATTACK."[13] Two days later the British minister to Reykjavik informed the Icelandic Prime Minister that his nation's troops were needed elsewhere. He also noted that the United States was prepared to send military forces to the island, but that President Roosevelt needed a prior invitation from the Icelandic government. Far from greeting this proposal warmly, Hermann Jónasson took the position that he could not invite American protection, despite the fact that many individuals in the Icelandic government favored it.[14] Another consideration which held up the negotiations was the rate of departure of the British forces. Undersecretary of State Sumner Welles pointed out in a memorandum dated June 28 that it should be made clear that these "would not necessarily be withdrawn and certainly not immediately."[15]

Despite these problems, on June 1 F.D.R. clarified matters in communication to the Icelandic Prime Minister in which he observed:

> The steps so taken by the Government of the United States are taken in full recognition of the sovereignty and independence of

Iceland and with the clear understanding that American military and naval forces sent to Iceland will in no way interfere in the slightest degree with the internal and domestic affairs of the Icelandic people and with the further understanding that immediately upon the termination of the present international emergency all such military and naval forces will be at once withdrawn, leaving the people of Iceland and their Government in full sovereign control of their own territory.[16]

On the same day Prime Minister Jónasson finally brought himself to issue a highly qualified invitation for the Americans to occupy the island, and a U.S. marine convoy arrived shortly thereafter to take up an eight months' residence. As Samuel Eliot Morison has summed it up, "Invitation, acceptance and execution had to be announced simultaneously."[17] In a brief message transmitted to Congress on July 7, the day of the occupation, F.D.R. justified this action on the grounds that a takeover by Germany would constitute a triple threat against Greenland and northern North America, against Atlantic shipping, and against the steady flow of munitions to Great Britain. The President also made the important point that, thanks to the use of American volunteer troops in occupying the island, there had been no violation of the statutory prohibition against the employment of draftees outside the Western Hemisphere.

If one accepts a Gallup poll of July 17 as an accurate mirror of American public opinion with respect to the Icelandic takeover, then 61 percent of the populace favored F.D.R.'s action, while only 20 percent opposed it. Among the more prominent journalistic critics was the *Christian Century,* which charged that "his intent to involve the United States in the shooting war is now clear."[18] Perhaps the earliest congressional opponent of the occupation was Democratic Senator Burton K. Wheeler of Montana, who informed the press of Roosevelt's actions as early as July 3; Nazi submarine commanders could have used this advance warning to launch an attack on the American expeditionary force on its way to Iceland. Other congressional critics included Republican Senator Robert Taft of Ohio, who opined that the President had no legal or constitutional right to send American troops to Iceland, and Republican Representative Frank C. Osmers of New Jersey, who declared that "President Roosevelt's order to the Navy to clear the Atlantic is a virtual declaration of war without the action of the Congress."[19]

On the other hand, Republican Representative John C. Kunkel of Pennsylvania looked upon the occupation as a wise move, while Republican Senator William Langer of North Dakota introduced a bill on July 24 permitting the unlimited entry of Icelandic immigrants down to July 1, 1946. A somewhat different concern was expressed by Republican Senator Arthur Vandenberg of Michigan, like Wheeler and Taft a pre-World War 2 isolationist. In quoting a recent statement by Winston Churchill in the House of Commons that the British still proposed to retain their army in Iceland Vandenberg took the position that America would have to occupy the island by itself, or otherwise it would risk U.S. involvement in the European war. Three months later Secretary Stimson informed Vandenberg that the relief of British troops in Iceland would be completed as soon as practicable.

WORLD WAR 2: THE AMERICAN PRESENCE

The arrival of American forces in Iceland came as no surprise, thanks to Wheeler, although many of the inhabitants were of the opinion that the first landing would not occur until approximately July 20. When the Althing met two days after the Americans arrived, it approved a defense agreement with the United States by the overwhelming margin of 39 to 3, with only Communists casting "nay" votes. To quote Foreign Minister Stefánsson, "It is not we who have changed but the world around us, and we must act accordingly."[20]

Nazi-occupied Denmark, moreover, was surprisingly sympathetic to the U.S. occupation, with newspaper editorials expressing the hope that Iceland would remain a member of the family of Nordic countries. In contrast, the German press was predictably hostile, engaging in personal attacks on F.D.R. The Vichy newspapers of France likewise took the position that President Roosevelt had committed an act of aggression, while even the officially neutral Madrid press editorialized that Europe would now have to formulate its own Monroe Doctrine.

In the middle of July American forces in the Atlantic received notice that "approach of any forces within fifty miles of Iceland will be deemed conclusive evidence of hostile intent and will justify attack on such Axis forces by the Armed Forces of the United States."[21] Then on July 19 a system went into effect for the convoying of American and Icelandic ships, "including shipping of any nationality which may join such United States or Iceland flag convoys."[22] Thanks to these and other developments, by the end of the month Admiral Harold Stark had concluded that the situation in Iceland might produce an incident.

Icelandic morale received an added boost in August from Winston Churchill, who reviewed both British and U.S. marine troops there on

his way back to England from the Atlantic Charter conference with
F.D.R. Shortly thereafter regular army units under the direction of
Major General C. H. Bonesteel started to arrive in Iceland. The protesting marines also served under his command, the only instance
during World War 2 where a Marine unit was detached for service with
the army.[23] Then on September 25, 1941, orders were given for the
construction of a fleet airbase near Reykjavik, which base was commissioned four months later on January 21, 1942. The army, too,
desired an air base of its own; it received authorization for the building
of one on November 7, 1941, but did not select the actual site until
February 1942. After the attack on Pearl Harbor construction was initiated on a naval operating base near Reykjavik, and on May 16, 1942,
this base was formally commissioned as Camp Knox. In the spring of
the latter year, too, work began on both Patterson Field near Keflavik,
but the U.S. military was unable to use either air base during 1942.

From the standpoint of administration, the command of military forces in Iceland passed into American control on April 22, 1942, long
after most of the British troops there had been withdrawn. Nevertheless, Great Britain did retain under its operational direction certain
British and Allied personnel. To quote a British diplomatic note, "These
personnel should not be regarded as being left over from the original
British force sent to defend the territory from invasion, but as perform-
ing special tasks of defending Iceland from attack by Germany's naval
forces and keeping open the sea routes for the trade of Iceland and of
the Allies."[24] A month later, on May 22, Secretary Hull approached the
Norwegian government-in-exile at London with respect to a War Department recommendation that the Independent Norwegian Company
stationed at Akureyri be transferred from the British command to the
American. The Norwegians accepted this proposal in principle on the
same day.

At the time that the supreme military command in Iceland came into
the possession of the Americans, Major General Bonesteel approached the
U.S. minister to Iceland, Lincoln MacVeagh. Bonesteel requested that
MacVeagh inform the Icelandic government that in the event of a serious attack on the island, he would set up a military government without
first clearing this action with the civilian authorities. Far from endorsing
this proposal, MacVeagh took the position that Bonesteel's approach
could only result in illwill and obstruction.[25] On May 4, moreover,
MacVeagh informed the Icelandic minister for Foreign Affairs that the
U.S. government had accepted the principle of reversion with all im-
movable installations, and that Iceland would not have to make any
payments in this connection. Highly acceptable to the Icelandic govern-

ment, this concession was predicated upon the condition that American nationals and aviation interests would then possess unconditional and unrestricted most-favored-nation rights concerning the use of former U.S. airfields. The question of landing rights in Iceland as a whole was postponed for discussion after the end of the war.

Returning to the navy, on July 7, 1942 the naval operating base and naval air facility at Reykjavik were established, while the fuel depot, salvage station, and recreation center at Hvalfjördur were set up on November 16. When the Ninth Construction Battalion composed of 704 enlisted men and 17 officers arrived on August 18, these Seabees quickly took over the construction work from the contractor's employees. By March 26, 1943, the first plane had landed at Meeks Field, although the paving was not totally completed there until July 1; the finishing touches on Patterson Field were executed on August 21. As of April 1 of that year there were 37,960 U.S. army personnel in Iceland, 4,428 navy personnel, and 262 marines.[26] Nevertheless, in August some British forces still remained in Iceland, mainly in the air and navy services.

In October Democratic Senator Richard Russell of Georgia, who was chairman of a special Senate Committee which toured the battlefronts, strongly urged that in the future the United States should retain its right to use the very extensive facilities in Iceland. But in the months which followed the American government began to reduce its military operations there, as it stepped up its war against Japan. Thus, on November 22 the transfer of the naval fuel depot to the British was authorized, while on December 20 the fleet air base was closed; then on January 21 and 31, 1944, respectively the air fuel depot was turned over to the British and the fleet airbase was evacuated. Finally, the chief of Naval Operations recommended on May 16 that U.S. naval personnel in Iceland be reduced to a skeleton crew of two hundred officers and men. It was on this day, too, that the naval facilities at Hvalfjördur were disestablished and turned over to the British.

While the U.S. military presence in Iceland waxed and waned during World War 2, there was a continuous flurry of activity on the diplomatic front. Despite an earlier flareup relative to the censoring of the mails in Bermuda, on November 21, 1941, Secretary Hull informed the Icelandic trade delegation that "this Government has agreed to the request of the Icelandic Government that during the present emergency United States Government personnel [will] undertake to maintain in Iceland censorship of telegrams and mail to and from Iceland."[27] Thus, a possibly troublesome confrontation was avoided in this specific case. Back in America, the Icelandic minister (Thór Thors) announced on

September 22, 1942, that his government would open consulates in Chicago, Boston, Minneapolis, Grand Forks, and Portland. This action was described by Thórs as a further step in Iceland's complete assumption of conduct of its foreign affairs.

Another important development which took place in November 1941 was the reaching of an understanding with a three-man Icelandic commission visiting the United States that the American government would pay for all the shipments of fish which Iceland sent Great Britain. Although there was no immediate economic impact, this U.S. financing proved to be of great consequence in both 1943 and 1944;[28] Iceland used the funds to purchase cereals, machinery, and coal in America which she formerly had obtained from Great Britain.[29] Thanks to the increased trade between the United States and the island, in March 1942 the Iceland Purchasing Commission commenced operations to facilitate the obtaining of critical materials. Between July of that year and July 1945 this new body purchased $7,281,245 worth of goods in America.

The increasing price charged in Iceland for petroleum products by the U.S. navy, however, became a key diplomatic issue during the first three months of 1943. For the last decade or so Great Britain had furnished the island with all its gasoline, oil, and kerosene. While the Icelandic government took the position that it must hold the lid on inflation, Secretary Hull noted that the American prices for petroleum products were the actual cost of delivery as determined by the War Shipping Administration, and that the lower prices charged by the British resulted from a subsidy. (It had been Great Britain which had suggested that the United States take over its Icelandic market.) Nevertheless, the American navy agreed in February to reduce these prices, leading the Icelandic foreign minister to observe the following month that this action had been of inestimable assistance to his government. That August 27 the United States and Iceland signed a new trade agreement.

Unlike Greenland, where social contacts between the U.S. military and the natives were relatively rare and in fact discouraged, Iceland experienced considerable mingling of soldier and citizen from the first. This led to a surprisingly wide variety of problems, as is evidenced from an October 4, 1941, report, "Relations between American Forces in Iceland and the Local Population." The twenty sources of irritation which this document cited were:

> (1) the cocky attitude of American soldiers and sailors in general; (2) non-payment of taxi fares; (3) appropriation of private cars; (4) disrespect for Icelandic authority; (5) carrying arms within city limits; (6) damage to civilian property; (7) use of

isolated army huts within the city limits for immoral purposes; (8) hazard caused to traffic by useless defenses at street corners; (9) consumption of alcohol on military reservations; (10) freedom of social contacts with girls under age; (11) noisy behavior in the streets; (12) lack of sufficient military police; (13) lack of cooperation between civilian police and military police; (14) lack of civilian authority to restrain military offenders; (15) absence of suitable guards at likely trouble centers; (16) confusion in regulation of street traffic; (17) omission of the military to inform the civilian police when trouble occurs in the latter's absence, particularly in outlying places; (18) disregard by the military of the necessary rules of the road; (19) military use of Icelandic buses already taxed to the maximum; and (20) the crowding of civilians off the sidewalks by groups of soldiers.[30]

By the end of October Major General Bonesteel was pointing out to American Minister MacVeagh that vigilante committees were being formed in Reykjavik to protect defenseless persons from the U.S. military; these groups as a rule were composed of local youths between 18 and 24 years of age armed with clubs. This movement apparently had originated with the support of the weekly publication *Thjódólfur*, which was critical of the Allies; Prime Minister Jónasson had seemed unaware of this vigilante activity, yet gave instructions that the chief of police was to stifle it at once, after he had learned of it. But when he was confronted with a series of complaints against American soldiers presented before the magistrate judge of Reykjavik between July 26 and September 27, Minister MacVeagh downgraded their significance with the observation that "the complaints listed, with one exception, have to do with cases of rowdyism, none the less regrettable for being minor in character."[31] Early in November a shooting episode did take place at a Hafnarfjördur dance hall; although the trigger-happy American soldier bore arms illegally and was absent without permission from his unit, the U.S. provost marshal, Lieutenant Colonel Kilgarif, took the position that the provocation on the part of the Icelanders was considerable.

As a result of episodes of this nature, Major General Bonesteel issued orders on October 28 which banned enlisted men's dances at U.S. army camps in the Reykjavik area, placed severe restrictions on those held elsewhere, and forbade the advertising of dances in local newspapers. According to the chief of police, though, even in the provinces Icelandic parents were opposed to their daughters associating with American soldiers. MacVeagh's response as usual was to look at the bright side; he noted that local complaints were generally directed against the British, who were still present in large numbers at Reykjavik.[32] When Prime Minister Jónasson submitted a new series of complaints six months later with respect to American military behavior, MacVeagh observed that Jónasson had made two categorical statements which were definitely incorrect, and that the situation had never justified the Prime Minister's use of the word "intolerable."[33]

Even as late as 1944 friction was still marring the relations between the Icelanders and the American military garrison. According to Major Thomas A. Glaze, the chief of the U.S. army's military police in the island, liquor and women caused most of the problems; as has been the case since the beginning of history, when soldiers are paid, many of them want to go out in search of a good time. Major Glaze noted, however, that far from experiencing any problems with the entire Icelandic population, most of the difficulties centered around a hardcore group of eight girls and fifteen men.[34]

The war years also were ones of constitutional change in Iceland. Ten months after the American occupation, on May 16, 1942, the Althing endorsed a resolution to the effect that it did not plan to renew the union with Denmark; with the Germans occupying Denmark, it was difficult, if not impossible, for the government in Copenhagen to implement the terms of the Danish treaty of 1918. Then when the Althing approved a new franchise bill reducing rural representation on May 22, the National Coalition Government came to an end, and Ólafur Thórs of the Independence Party formed a minority government in which he served as foreign minister.

A month later, on June 26, Harry Hopkins visited the island as a special envoy of President Franklin D. Roosevelt, and informed the regent and the Prime Minister that his government opposed the premature abrogation of the Act of Union between Iceland and Denmark. Such an action, wrote Secretary of State Cordell Hull to the American Chargé in Iceland, Warner, on July 22, "would be seized upon by the Germans to spread pernicious propaganda, at which they are adept, in Denmark and other Scandinavian countries which might react unfavorably on both Icelandic and American interests."[35] Thanks at least in part to this intervention, the Prime Minister of Iceland informed Warner on September 9 that although in normal times this proposed change in status would be a purely Icelandic concern, the government of the island had decided to postpone action for the present. He added that this step might well hurt his party in the upcoming elections, and in fact had already caused dissension within it. Later that month the United States government agreed not to object to the new Icelandic parliament passing a resolution declaring that Iceland would become a republic in 1944, since the Act of Union expired during that year in any event.

On February 25 of that year the Althing declared the treaty with Denmark terminated, and called for a plebiscite on both this act of separation and the new constitution. King Christian of Denmark naturally was quite displeased with this turn of events, and on May 2 he wrote the Icelandic Prime Minister that he hoped the union between the two countries would not be severed until foreign troops had been removed from both Iceland and Denmark. Nevertheless, at the May 20-23 plebiscite 98.6 percent of the total electorate of Iceland voted; of those who voted, 97.3 percent favored abrogation of the union and 95 percent a republican form of government. As a result, on June 16 the Althing declared that the treaty with Denmark was no longer in effect, and on the following day a new republic was proclaimed at the ancient parliamentary site of Thingvellir, with Sveinn Björnsson as president.

Early in June the United States Senate, with the House of Representatives concurring, passed a resolution expressing "to the Icelandic Althing, the oldest parliamentary body in the world, its congratulations on the establishment of the Republic of Iceland. . . ."[36] The Speaker of the Althing, who was greatly pleased by this action, noted that America had been the first country to favor the reestablishment of the Icelandic republic, and also had been the first nation to appoint a special ambassador to the island for the official celebration (Louis G. Dreyfus).[37] Perhaps the only negative voice was that of the Communists, whose members in the Althing not only cast blank ballots for president but also failed to rise in acknowledgment of the congressional joint resolution. As for their allies in the press, one editorial in the leftist *Thjódviljinn* bore the headlines: "Icelanders: The Battle against the American Incorporation Policy of the Coca Cola Power Must Now Begin in Earnest."[38]

During the last year of the war in Europe, there were a few additional developments of consequence relative to the United States and Iceland, the more important of them centering around the post-war American military role on the island. On August 21, 1944, Democratic Senators Tom Connally of Texas and Carl Hatch of New Mexico both suggested that the United States should acquire title to or lease a number of Pacific and Atlantic islands; in the opinion of the former, an Icelandic base would not only be vital but should be easily acquired through long-term lease. Five days later, however, President Björnsson and Foreign Minister Thórs held a news conference in which they declared that the island did not plan to grant America a permanent military base there. In the words of Björnsson, "We are a nation of individualists and we did not establish our republic in order to become less independent."[39] This news conference preceded a visit by Björnsson to the United States, where he was the guest at a White House dinner.

Early in 1945, following the Yalta conference, the Allies extended an invitation for unarmed Iceland to declare war on the Axis, but the Althing rejected this with only the Communists voting "aye"; Iceland, moreover, did not become a charter member of the United Nations later that year.[40] That June, with the war in Europe over, Brigadier General Martinius Stennett, the American commander in Iceland, stated that the island would be needed as a military base for only another four or five months, after which the only U.S. military personnel remaining on the island would be at the airfield near Reykjavik. At the end of the year, in November, the British returned control over the air station, the fuel depot, and the ammunition depot to the Americans.

In assessing the U.S. military presence in Iceland during World War 2 in its totality, Samuel Eliot Morison has suggested that the island's basic utility was as an escort and air base for covering convoys. Aside from the occasionally unpleasant contacts between the servicemen and the inhabitants, other problems included morale, labor employment, censorship, claims payments, defense, military government, trade, and Icelandic sovereignty. Sometimes these were solved by the U.S. military and the government of the island working together, sometimes by the governments of the two countries acting in unison, and sometimes by the joint efforts of all three. Among the claims cases were the ones involving Halldór's cow, which was electrocuted by an electric wire near Kjósarsýsla; the Hvalfjördur farmer, whose puffins (a variety of birds) stopped laying eggs due to machine gun practice; and a fox breeder of Kollafjördur, who complained because his white Arctics ate their cubs when airplanes flew overhead.[41]

It was pointed out earlier that there were a great many British soldiers present on the island at the time of the initial American landing, and that Icelanders frequently complained about various aspects of their behavior, too. According to Clifton Lisle, the inhabitants generally preferred the British Tommies to the American G.I.s, but the more formal British officer was less popular than his U.S. counterpart. However, despite a number of unpleasant incidents involving military personnel which led to earlier complaints, the Icelandic government sent the U.S. legation a diplomatic note on August 7, 1943, downplaying their significance. In evaluating the behavior of the British and American troops, its author frankly asserted: "In order to prevent any misunderstanding the Icelandic Government wish to point out that relations between Icelanders and Icelandic authorities and forces from other nations stationed here have been such that dissatisfaction in that respect has not in any way been the cause of this communication."[42]

One might suggest that one reason for the occasional misbehavior on the part of American as well as British soldiers was the widespread boredom and general unhappiness resulting from their being stationed on the island. According to Samuel Eliot Morison, U.S. sailors frequently referred to Reykjavik as Rinky Dink, while Richard W. Johnson noted relative to the marines the lack of female company, the presence of only two motion picture theatres in Reykjavik, and the generally inferior chow. One oasis in this desert was a recreation hut located at the naval base containing the longest bar in Iceland, motion picture equipment, and juke boxes. One of the few individuals to whom military life in the island apparently was fun and games was the late Commander Daniel V. Gallery, who in his memoirs relates a whole string of colorful stories, including that of the pushball which was mistaken by a British anti-aircraft battery for a mine.

From the overall standpoint World War 2—and the resulting American and British presence—led to social, cultural, material, political, and economic changes in Iceland. As Agnes Rothery has pointed out, U.S. soldiers "brought with them improved techniques and inventions. They left behind them road-building machinery, ten thousand Quonset huts, a fashion for ice cream sodas, and a most tremendous inflation."[43] Icelanders came to use such American words as "guy" and "crew cut," but Americans at times confused the Icelandic word *stúlka* (girl) for *Stuka* (the German dive bomber). Even President Björnsson himself admitted that commercial relations with the United States had grown as a result of the war, and that many young Icelanders now looked to America for further education and culture. Perhaps the most extreme claim with respect to the impact of the war and the occupation is that of John Joseph Hunt, who concludes that the two in conjunction "lifted the island out of 1,000 years of isolation and placed her in the stream of world affairs."[44] In any event, few would dispute the generalization that during these five years Iceland did indeed enter a new period in its history.

RECENT ICELANDIC POLITICAL AFFAIRS

Although we have attempted throughout this volume in the case of every nation to present enough background information to place

American relations with that country in their proper historical perspective, this is doubly necessary in the case of Iceland, if only because of the complex four-party system long in operation there. To make comprehension even more difficult, there never has been a truly definitive study of the Icelandic political system, at least in English. In the pages which follow we will attempt to isolate and identify some key features of the politics and government of Iceland.

Any understanding of modern Icelandic political developments must begin with the Constitution of 1944, which reaffirmed the parliamentary system of government. The president, who is popularly elected, serves for four years and is eligible for reelection. He not only summons the legislative Althing into session annually and calls extraordinary meetings of that body, but he also may dissolve the Althing. When that occurs, there must be a new general election within two months. The president, too, has the power to veto measures passed by the legislature, which are then submitted to the voters in a plebiscite.

Early in 1952 President Sveinn Björnsson, who had been titular head of Iceland since the reestablishment of the republic, died. As a result of the election held that June, Ásgeir Ásgeirsson became president; after being reelected in 1956, 1960, and 1964, Ásgeirsson retired in 1968. At this time Kristján Eldjárn won the presidency in a landslide vote, and he was returned to office unopposed four years later for another term.

While the Althing originally consisted of fifty-two members under the 1944 Constitution, in 1959 this number increased to sixty, with the towns gaining more than the rural areas proportionately. The legislature is a bicameral one, with one-third of its members serving in the upper house, and two-thirds in the lower house. Both houses are equally powerful in legislative matters, unlike the House of Commons and the House of Lords in Great Britain.

Long before the Constitution of 1944, though, a multi-party system had evolved in Iceland. Although each of the four major parties was national in scope, their strength varied by region; economic factors apparently played a more important role in shaping them than religious or social considerations did. In post–World War 2 Iceland these four parties were the Independence (Conservative), the Progressives, the Social Democrats, and the Communists (who sometimes attempted to conceal their identity). Each party had its Reykjavik daily, but the Independence Party was strongest in the towns, while the Progressive Party had its base in the rural areas. Fishing, industrial, and commercial interests, along with certain farm groups, dominated the basically liberal

Independence Party; the farmers, cooperative societies, intellectuals, and teachers were the backbone of the rather isolationist and nationalist Progressives. As for the anti-Communist Social Democrats, they were probably the weakest of the four major parties, while the Communists became the main labor party, although there was little, if any, poverty in Iceland for them to exploit politically. Unlike the Progressives, the Communists drew much of their strength from the Reykjavik area.

In a nation of limited size and limited population, it is not surprising that personalities frequently sway the voters more than issues. (This helps explain the relatively strong showing of various Communist candidates at different times and places.) As was the case in America before the one-man ruling over a decade ago, the rural areas enjoyed over-representation in the Icelandic legislature; as a result, the rural-oriented Progressives benefited at the expense of the other parties. No single party was able to win a majority of Althing seats in any election held in Iceland following 1934, with the result that one coalition government followed another on the island. Yet only the Independence Party and the Progressive Party contended for national leadership during these four decades, with the Social Democrats and the Communists playing a lesser role. To complicate matters further, party organization at times was relatively loose, while opportunism shaped party actions as much as ideology on occasion.

Looking at recent developments in a broader perspective, one might well generalize that modern Iceland has much of which to be proud, if only the fact that it enjoys the highest literacy rate in the entire world. Nevertheless—unlike Greenland—Iceland is in many ways a model Scandinavian welfare state, and this point is central to an appreciation of its politics and government. When President Ásgier Ásgiersson visited the United States in 1967, the then President Lyndon B. Johnson noted that the land of ice and fire had eliminated extreme poverty at the same time that it operated a free democratic government. L.B.J., of course, had his own ambitious Great Society program for America. But what has made the Icelandic welfare state so unique is, as we have pointed out above, the high cultural development of the people. This helps explain the late British poet W. H. Auden's summation: "Fortunate island, where all men are equal, but not vulgar—yet."[45]

TRADE, FISHING, AND INTERNATIONAL FRICTION

Any discussion of Icelandic commerce during the last three decades inevitably will center on the island's fisheries, and it is not possible to examine these without reference to both the prolonged attempt by the government of Iceland to extend its territorial limits and the resulting friction with Great Britain. It was on May 15, 1952, that the Icelandic government moved the outer limits of its fisheries to a point 4 miles from those lines connecting the island's longest promontories. At the same time it terminated a 1901 agreement between Denmark and Great Britain fixing the territorial limits of Iceland at 3 miles from the coast; angry British trawler owners at both Hull and Grimsby barred Icelandic vessels from their facilities in protest.

With the British market for its fish no longer available, in August 1953 Iceland turned to the Soviet Union, with which it signed a $12 million trade agreement. Under this Russia was to purchase Icelandic fish, and in return the island was to buy Soviet petroleum products, cereals, and cement. The two governments renewed this agreement in September 1955, to be effective through 1956; although Great Britain lifted its embargo against the island in November 1956, its commerce in Icelandic fish did not revert to the earlier pattern. As for the American reaction, in May 1954 the U.S. Tariff Commission had advocated the imposition of quotas on fish and an increase in tariff rates, thanks in part to pressure from the ever vigilant New England fishing interests. President Dwight Eisenhower, however, refused to go along with this recommendation.

A decade earlier, in 1946, the leading American imports into Iceland had been motor vehicles, machinery and non-electrical appliances, fuel oils, electrical machines and appliances, and sugar, while the main Icelandic exports to America had been cod liver oil, frozen fish, and herring meal. Total imports stood at $99,232,000, total exports at only $38,328,000. As of 1949 the leading importers of Icelandic products were, by percentage, Great Britain, 36; Germany, 23; United States, 6; Italy, 5; half the fish which the island shipped abroad went to England, while more was sent to Germany and to Czechoslovakia than to America. By 1952 the United States was purchasing a quarter of the total exports of Iceland, mostly various forms of fish, but within three years it was buying only one-eighth. Conversely, the Soviet Union had quadrupled its percentage share from 7 in 1952 to 28 in 1956, as the island's total output of frozen fish rose from 25,000 tons in 1953 to 50,000 in 1955.

Then on September 1, 1958, Iceland, following the precedent established previously by a number of other nations, extended its territorial limits to 12 miles. Belgian and German trawlers retreated further to sea on that date, but British vessels remained closer to shore, precipitating a series of minor incidents with Icelandic gunboats over the next few weeks. The Law of the Sea Conference, held at Geneva in

the spring of 1958 with over eighty nations in attendance, had drafted
four maritime pacts, but nevertheless had failed to reach an agreement
on this key issue;[46] here the American delegation headed by Arthur H.
Dean fought for the traditional 3-mile limit. Fortunately for Iceland,
relations with Great Britain improved somewhat during 1959, largely
for the reason that English fishermen found the disputed waters somewhat disappointing. This may have been a factor in Great Britain's acceptance of a treaty with Iceland on February 27, 1961, which included
a mutual acceptance of the 12-mile limit, but allowed English boats
to fish between 6 and 12 miles offshore for the next three years.

Two weeks before Iceland extended its territorial limits, on August 19,
1958, it obtained a large credit from the Soviet Union to buy fishing
vessels in East Germany, with repayment to take the form of Icelandic
goods. The island also continued to sell fish to the United States in the
years which followed, but there were a number of barriers to Icelandic-
American commerce in general; among these were relatively high prices
for U.S. goods, freight rates, and duties, and a lack of cooperation on
the part of many U.S. firms. In analyzing the evolution of American
trade with Iceland between 1960 and 1966, though, one discovers that
in at least several categories the United States increased its share of
imports into the island: transportation equipment, electrical machinery,
metal manufactures, and paper products. In addition, agricultural items
such as wheat, tobacco, and feed grains were brought in from America
under the PL 480 (Title 4) program. By 1965 the leading markets for
Icelandic goods were, in order, Great Britain, the United States, West
Germany, Denmark, and the Soviet Union, while the leading sources of
Icelandic imports were the same countries in the same order.

Thanks to the fact that similar goods could be obtained in Europe
at lower prices than in America, by 1968 the U.S. export level to
Iceland had begun to decline relative to that of West Germany and
Great Britain. America still furnished the island with 80 percent of
its tobacco and tobacco products, however, while both private and
public U.S. funds had become a key source of investment loan capital
and of short term financing. The most popular passenger car was Ford,
the most popular trucks Ford and Chevrolet; in 1973 one American
firm sold $1.5 million worth of earth-moving equipment for the Sigalda
hydro-electric project, while in 1975 Union Carbide agreed to build a
$75 million ferro-alloy plant at Hvalfjördur. With respect to Icelandic
exports to America, these quadrupled between 1955 and 1969 from
$7 million to $28 million. By 1970—the year during which Iceland
became a member of the European Free Trade Association—the United
States was the leading market for Icelandic exports, followed in order

by Great Britain and West Germany. Another source of income to the island was the growing number of American tourists, which rose sharply during the decade of the 1960s from 13,000 to 63,000.

In recent years the question of Iceland's fishing limits has continued to be a source of international friction, especially after the Icelandic government extended these from 12 to 50 nautical miles on September 1, 1972. The Faeroe Islands and Belgium then reached understandings with Iceland permitting temporary and limited fishing within these limits, but not Great Britain and West Germany. After fighting a brief, undeclared codfish war with its British counterpart, the Icelandic government reached an agreement with Prime Minister Edward Heath in October 1973 which restricted British fishing in the waters of Iceland.

The United States, though, was hardly in a position to criticize its northern neighbor for taking these steps. The governors of the six New England states, who were perhaps unusually sensitive to the problem of fish depletion, had resolved in September 1971 that "the New England Governors' Conference hereby urges the New England Congressional Delegation and the Executive Branch of the Federal Government to lend their full support to passage of emergency legislation which would extend fisheries jurisdiction 200 miles from our nation's shoreline."[47] A subsequent act passed by the Massachusetts legislature and signed into law by Republican Governor Francis W. Sargeant authorized the director of Marine Fisheries to adopt regulations protecting fisheries within 200 miles of the coast. Thus, it by no means has been only the Icelanders who have advocated more distant territorial limits and restricted fishermen of other nations.

THE KEFLAVIK BASE TO 1956

During this ten-year period following World War 2, the United States entered into an unusually large number of understandings with Iceland. Iceland received a total of $8.3 million in assistance under the European Recovery Program between April 1948 and June 1949, of which $2.3 million was a loan, $2.5 million a grant, and $3.5 million conditional aid. Four years later, on May 16, 1953, the Mutual Security Agency announced that it was suspending American financial help to Iceland; a final U.S. allotment of $5.45 million on May 13 brought the total advanced that nation for defense support and economic aid since April 1948 to $37 million. (The MSA was the successor of the ERP, or Marshall Plan.)

While the Russians may have been purchasing more fish from
Iceland than the United States by the end of the decade of the 1940s,
it was America rather than the Soviet Union which was operating a military base there. In both 1945 and 1947 Republican Representative
Bertrand Gearhart of California had suggested that the American
government offer statehood to Iceland, but this proposal offended
the Icelanders.[48] With U.S. troops still stationed in the island, early
in March 1947 the Soviet Union navy newspaper *Red Fleet* quoted
the Danish press to the effect that the presence of the American military there would endanger the neutral status of Denmark, or would
lead other powers to demand Icelandic bases.

Then on March 21 Secretary of Commerce Henry Wallace observed
in an interview with a Scandinavian correspondent that "the only
interpretation the Russians could place on continued occupancy of
bases in Iceland by American troops would be that it was aimed at
them."[49] The anti-cold warrior Wallace pointed out five years later
that he had been speaking off the record and as an individual, but
Joseph Alsop wrote a story published in *Life* on May 20 in which he
attacked Wallace, while President Harry Truman, Secretary of State
James Byrnes, and Republican Senator Arthur Vandenberg of Michigan also were critical of his remarks.[50] Democratic Senator Claude
Pepper of Florida likewise was attacked for his views on Iceland by
Secretary of Defense James Forrestal.

Several weeks prior to the appearance of Alsop's article, Prime
Minister Ólafur Thórs had informed the people of the island in a
broadcast that the United States had sought three bases there, but
that it would not obtain them.[51] That fall, on September 20, the
State Department announced that under a new accord with Iceland
all U.S. military and naval personnel would leave the island within
180 days; nevertheless, only several hundred of these had been stationed
in that country during recent months. America, however, did retain the
right to keep civilian personnel at the Keflavik airport, which was to
become an international terminal open to the entire world.[52] To the
Christian Century this five-year accord was "a move in the right direction," since "the recovery of morality in international relations re-
quires that nations keep their word, even when it is given to small and
helpless neighbors."[53] The following month the Althing ratified the
accord by a vote of 32 to 19.

When the U.S. army air force announced in March 1947 that it
would convert the temporary wartime installation at Harmon Field
in Newfoundland into peacetime permanency, it had provided earlier
for the transfer of the Keflavik airfield to a subsidiary of American

Overseas Airlines. On April 9 the last American soldiers remaining in Iceland departed, 20 of them by plane and the others on the transport *Edmund B. Alexander*. That fall the Inter-American Treaty of Reciprocal Assistance provided for the defense of Greenland, but failed to include Iceland.

With the outbreak of the Korean War in the summer of 1950, the Icelandic government began to reassess the desirability of American troops being stationed there. Earlier that year, in March, its police court had sentenced twenty Communists to jail terms of three to eighteen months for having instigated an anti-U.S. riot the previous year. With Iceland a member of NATO since 1949, the American government obtained permission in May 1951 to reestablish its military presence in the island, and the first U.S. troops arrived shortly thereafter; the Icelandic government polled the forty-three non-Communist members of the Althing, who were agreeable to this step, but formal approval by that body did not take place until after the American soldiers had actually landed. Then on July 6 the Iceland Defense Force officially was elevated to the level of a command. Under this Icelandic-American agreement the government of Iceland was to regulate the number of U.S. troops stationed there, as well as to supervise civil aviation at Keflavik.[54]

No sooner had the Korean War ground to a halt on June 26, 1953, than local opposition began to mount against the American military presence in Iceland. During that fall the Social Democrats introduced a resolution into the Althing calling for a revision of the 1951 treaty; in effect, this would have confined American troops to the Keflavik airfield and the Hvalfjördur fuel depot, required the U.S. to employ Icelandic laborers exclusively, and cut the time for serving notice relative to a treaty revision from six to three months. Even more hostile were the Communists, who wanted the treaty between Iceland and America abrogated. The U.S. reaction to these criticisms was in general a bitter one, for as one American national there put it, "If Icelanders think we are going to accept virtual imprisonment and then if war comes fight for our jailors they are crazy."[55] But the American government did agree to reopen negotiations relative to the future of the Keflavik facilities in January 1954, and on May 25 it reached an understanding with its Icelandic counterpart with respect to changes in the method of implementing the 1951 treaty. Highly technical in nature, these pertained chiefly to the role of construction work and the military areas in implementing NATO objectives, taking into account local conditions.

On July 16, 1955, President Dwight Eisenhower stopped off at Reykjavik on his way back to Washington from the Geneva Big Four conference. This was indeed a noteworthy occasion, since no other foreign head of state had visited the island since the reestablishment of the republic in 1944; the two presidents, American and Icelandic, drank a toast to the success of the conference at Geneva, after both had reviewed the honor guard. This meeting, it was hoped, would pave the way for the inauguration of a harmonious period in Icelandic-American relations, but instead it was simply a prelude to the storm which erupted the following year.

Early in 1956, on March 28, the Althing adopted a resolution calling for the withdrawal of the American military after the Progressive Party had broken with the coalition government on this issue. President Ásgeir Ásgeirsson then dissolved the Althing and called for a new election a year in advance. As for the reasons for this split, the leading authority on post-World War 2 Icelandic-American relations, Donald E. Nuechterlein, observed retrospectively in 1961 that "the record indicates clearly that domestic political considerations have played a major and perhaps decisive role in determining the Icelandic government's policy in defense affairs."[56] Of all the political parties, it was the Progressives who played the major role in altering Icelanders' attitude towards foreign relations between 1940 and 1956.

A number of arguments were advanced by critical Icelanders as to why it would be desirable to eliminate the American military presence. Perhaps the weakest of these was the possibility of incidents between U.S. soldiers and the native population; the chances of these occurring had been minimized, since the government of Iceland had placed restrictions on soldiers with passes visiting Reykjavik. A more serious problem was the high wages that Icelandic workers received at the Keflavik base. Not only did these laborers not want to seek employment elsewhere, but their generous pay fed the inflationary spiral which had pushed the cost of living index from 100 in 1950 to 178 in 1956. To make matters even worse, the Communists had assumed a leading voice in the direction of the unions, and they also encouraged Icelandic hostility to America by magnifying and distorting every incident that arose. Thus, stories were circulated that atom bombs supposedly would be stored in a domed structure housing electronic equipment, while a larger hanger at Keflavik was christened "Hell Hanger" because it allegedly was to be a future depository for hydrogen bombs.

Still another problem which arose for the first time in 1955 centered around the installation of a television station at the Keflavik base. The American government had offered to make the transmission strong enough so that Icelanders living in Reykjavik could receive the pictures on their sets, but Icelandic authorities refused to allow this increase in power when granting the permission to operate a station in March. Yet that nation which the nineteenth-century English poet, craftsman, and socialist William Morris once referred to as the Greece of the North was by no means totally hostile towards American culture. In the years preceding this crisis musicians and musical groups of the caliber of Isaac Stern, Blanche Thebom, E. Power Biggs, the Philadelphia Woodwind Quintet, and the U.S. Air Force Band had visited the island, while in October 1955 Nobel Prize winning author William Faulkner lectured at the University of Iceland to overflow crowds. Unfortunately for the Americans, however, the percentage of Icelanders who studied in the United States and Canada had declined sharply since the close of World War 2; higher educational costs in North America were causing them to enroll in European schools.

At this time the leader of the Progressive Party was the 60-year-old Hermann Jónasson, whose oldest son had married an American girl and worked in California. This was the same Hermann Jónasson who in July 1941 had invited U.S. troops to occupy Iceland,[57] but who fifteen years later assumed a key role in the movement to eliminate the American military presence from the island. In an interview published by *U.S. News and World Report* in July 1956, Jónasson commented that while the nationality of the occupying forces was irrelevant, "The stay for a long period of time of foreign forces in a country is a menace to the culture and independence of the people of that country."[58] Observing that there had been a decrease in cold war tensions during the last year or two, the Progressive Party leader took the position that Iceland did not want armed forces stationed there in peacetime.

When the voters went to the polls on June 24, 1956, the result was more confusing than clear-cut. The strongly pro-American Independence Party increased its share of the popular vote from 37.1 to 42.2 percent, but actually lost two seats in the Althing, its total dropping from 21 to 19. The other parties combined polled 47,000 votes to 35,000 for the Independence Party; as for the new anti-American Progressive Party, it saw its share of the popular vote fall from 21.9 to 15.6 percent, yet it nevertheless gained one seat in the Althing. It was highly significant that many Icelanders living in the vicinity of the Keflavik base voted for the Independence Party.

Three days after the election Secretary of State John Foster Dulles held a press conference in which he took the position that the Keflavik base had continuing importance from the standpoint of the security of the West and of the North Atlantic Community, and that the island was facing a greater danger than the Icelanders realized. Two days before the election, moreover, the Icelandic government had requested that the North Atlantic Council review the defense agreement between the United States and the island. (Iceland had joined NATO in 1949). In favoring its continuance, this council transmitted a report to both countries in which it noted that "it would be possible for an aggressor to seize control of Iceland with very small forces, either airborne or of the seaborne commando type, before effective assistance could be rendered."[59]

Elsewhere in the world developments were taking place which had as profound an impact on Icelandic attitudes as the outbreak of the Korean War a half-dozen years earlier. On October 29 the Israeli army invaded the Gaza Strip and the Sinai Peninsula, while on October 31 a joint Anglo-French armed force attacked Egypt; then on November 4 Soviet troops and tanks unleashed an onslaught against Hungarian dissidents and reformers in Budapest. This last action in particular disturbed Icelanders, who pelted and insulted Communists attending a reception held on the Bolshevik holiday of November 7 at the Soviet legation in Reykjavik.

By the end of that month American and Icelandic officials had reached an understanding which permitted U.S. troops to remain at the Keflavik facilities, in the process bypassing the North Atlantic Treaty Organization. The United States also committed itself to initiate new construction at the air base and at the nearby harbor at Njardvik, and to provide economic and financial aid to the island during the next four months.[60] But this was by no means the only positive development in Icelandic-American relations to occur at this time. Two weeks later, on December 10, President Dwight Eisenhower vetoed a recommendation made by the U.S. Tariff Commission that the duties on ground-fish fillets be raised.[61] Then on December 23 Vice President Richard Nixon met with President Ásgeir Ásgeirsson and Prime Minister Hermann Jónasson at Ásgeirsson's residence,[62] while on December 28 the International Cooperation Administration announced that it would make a $4 million loan to help finance Icelandic imports.[63] Considering the hostile political atmosphere existing in the island as late as that spring, this volte face in Icelandic-American relations at the close of the year was indeed remarkable.

THE KEFLAVIK BASE SINCE 1956

Between 1956 and the present the American and Icelandic governments have continued the pattern initiated during the first post-war decade by entering into a number of diplomatic agreements. The earliest of these included a $25,000 educational exchange agreement under the Fulbright Act (1957),[64] a $2,785,000 agricultural surplus commodity agreement under Public Law 480 (1957),[65] and a $1,760,000 ICA loan to help finance the construction of the Upper Sog hydro-electric project (1959).[66] Other understandings concluded during the later years of the Eisenhower administration included a $6 million grant for monetary stabilization which was to be employed to purchase various commodities (1961).[67]

As for the Kennedy-Johnson administration, it participated in the signing of a whole series of agricultural commodities agreements. During the J.F.K. era, too, the rector of the University of Iceland announced on October 6, 1961, that the American government had awarded the school a $198,000 grant on its fiftieth anniversary.[68]

By 1969 the total grants and credits extended to Iceland by the United States since 1945 had reached the $68 million mark, but only $3 million of this sum was committed between 1963 and 1969. Cumulative economic assistance under the foreign assistance and predecessor acts between 1948 and 1969 totalled $60.2 million. Of this figure, $24.7 million took the form of loans, $35.5 million that of grants.

Let us now return to our chronological survey of diplomatic, military, and other events in the chronology of Iceland-American relations. On December 20, 1957, two and a half years after his first visit, President Dwight Eisenhower stopped off at Reykjavik on his return to the United States from Paris. Meeting with President Ásgeir Ásgeirsson at the airport for an hour, he discussed the island's economy, but it was not revealed whether the base issue arose or not. During the next eighteen months Senators Theodore Green of Rhode Island and J. William Fulbright of Arkansas, and Majority Leader Lyndon Johnson of Texas (all Democrats) brought before the U.S. Senate a bill which would pay the Icelandic government $5,402,09 in final settlement of claims resulting from certain acts committed by U.S. military personnel during their residence in Iceland between 1941 and 1947. Arising out of the provisions contained in paragraph 5 of the 1941 agreement, 374 accident claims remained outstanding at the time that the Americans withdrew from the island; unfortunately, certain restrictions imposed by the Foreign Claims Act had blocked their settlement. On November 23, 1956, the American and Icelandic governments agreed to the sum mentioned above (the equivalent of 88,000 kroner) as the amount due the latter,[69] but the U.S. Congress did not pass the necessary legislation (which reduced the sum slightly to $5,378.98) until August 24, 1959.

This year also witnessed another series of unpleasant incidents involving Icelandic nationals and the American military. In mid-July the government of Iceland banned U.S. servicemen from the ancient parliamentary site of Thingvellir, after they had littered the place with cans and bottles during their Fourth of July celebration; prior to this holiday they frequently had held weekend parties there, which young Icelandic girls often attended.[70] Then in August a U.S. officer's wife was arrested for drunken driving, but was freed from the island police by American troops. Finally, in September a U.S. sentry ordered two Icelandic air control officers and two American pilots of a German airline to lie flat on the muddy ground for fifteen minutes until his superior arrived, after they had entered a restricted area at night and were unable to produce passes. (This area was open during the day, which caused the confusion.)[71] As a result, the axe fell at the very top of the U.S. military hierarchy in Iceland; Brigadier General Albert Pritchard, a combat pilot during World War 2 and a bomber wing commander in Korea, lost his Icelandic command. Lest this seem a drastic and even unfair step, it must be remembered that a parliamentary election was coming up in October, and the Communists were attempting to make political capital out of these and other incidents.[72]

The following year the U.S. army withdrew from Iceland, and the American defense force there eventually declined to three thousand men. An important administrative change occurred on July 1, when the U.S. navy took over the command of the defense force and shifted the base of its early warning squadrons to the island from Argentia, Newfoundland. Three months earlier the defense force had requested that the power of the television transmitter at Keflavik be increased from 50 to 250 watts, the latter being the wattage of the smallest available equipment. Although the Icelandic government granted permission for this without undue delay, in March 1964 sixty prominent Icelandic intellectuals petitioned the Althing in protest. In the words of this document, "It is dangerous, as well as dishonourable for the Icelanders as a civilized, independent nation, to permit a foreign state to operate a television station in this country, reaching more than half the population."[73] Fortunately, the introduction of six-day television programming weekly by Iceland State Radio in 1967 somewhat defused this issue, since the Armed Forces Radio and Television Service chose not to compete with a commercial station.

Back in Washington, on April 24, 1963, Republican Representative Frank J. Becker of New York protested the showing of the motion picture *Gogo,* the first movie ever made in Iceland. In this sad but amateurish epic a local taxicab driver commits suicide over a widow turned prostitute; other leading characters include two Americans, one a souse, the other a girl corrupter, portrayed by actual U.S. military personnel at Keflavik.[74] This episode proved to be a tempest in a teapot.

The following year Prime Minister Bjarni Benediktsson paid a call on President Lyndon Johnson, who had himself visited Iceland in 1963 as vice president, while President Ásgeir Ásgeirsson followed suit three years later, in 1967. (Mayor John Lindsay of New York City also entertained Ásgeirsson at the Cloisters.) At this time one of the leading boosters of the island in Congress was Democratic Senator Quentin Burdick of North Dakota, who commented on Icelandic Independence Day in June of 1965, 1966, and 1967 on the floor of the Senate. Burdick was playing the same role relative to Iceland that Adam Clayton Powell had assumed by this time vis-à-vis Jamaica, there being Icelanders in North Dakota as there are Jamaicans in New York City. Aside from Burdick's efforts on the floor of Congress, ex-soldier Dave Zinkoff of Philadelphia has served in recent years as the editor of the annual Icelandic veterans' newsletter *White Falcon Jr.,* complete with pictures and accounts and calls for periodic reunions in the island.[75]

The shifting political winds in Iceland again blew against the continued U.S. military presence at Keflavik when a coalition of Progressives, the Communist People's Alliance, and the liberal left came to power following the June 1971 elections. Although Prime Minister Ólafur Jóhannesson had earlier stated that his aim was to negotiate an American withdrawal before the next election in 1975, in April 1972 the government of Iceland did accept a U.S. offer to finance the lengthening of the second runway at Keflavik. But when Secretary of State William P. Rogers visited Reykjavik in May, two-hundred youths critical of American policy towards Vietnam prevented him from entering the Manuscript Institute, while still another group forced the secretary of state to take a detour after it had blocked the main highway. Confronted with a potentially explosive situation, the Icelandic government continued to maintain various restrictions on the American military; no less than three-quarters of the enlisted men did not leave the Keflavik base during their one-year tour of duty.

Nevertheless, by December 1973 the Progressive newspaper *Timinn* was publishing an editorial to the effect that the Americans could stay at Keflavik, provided that there was a gradual changeover to civilian operation, and the People's Alliance newspaper was reflecting the dissension within the ruling coalition by declaring this proposal unacceptable.

In his 1971 book *Iceland: From Neutrality to NATO Membership* Benedikt Gröndal observed relative to the American defense force that since 1961 "the Admirals in command have enjoyed excellent relations with the Icelandic Government, and years have passed without incidents like those which disturbed relations in the fifties."[76] Accordingly, in October 1974 the State Department announced that officials in Reykjavik had agreed to the continued operation of the Keflavik base by the United States, contingent upon a reduction in the 3,300 American military personnel stationed there. By this time the coalition government in power had resigned following an Icelandic national election, and a new coalition government led by the Progressives and the Independence Party had assumed power in July, with Geir Hallgrímmson as prime minister.

Although the usually perceptive Lord James Bryce observed of Iceland many years ago that it "had a glorious dawn and has lain in twilight ever since,"[77] developments over the last generation have demonstrated that the island continues to have a military and strategic importance for the United States. During World War 2 Sir Winston Churchill declared that "whoever holds Iceland holds a pistol at the head of North America and Europe;"[78] this assessment still holds true militarily in the age of the intercontinental ballistic missile. And as we have seen, Iceland remains of interest to the United States for other reasons as well, including the question of fishing rights and territorial limits.

6

THE AZORES
The Hesperides' Golden Apples

To different observers the Azores have presented different images. To the ancients these nine islands were probably the Hesperides, the source of the legendary golden apples, while to modern playwright Karel Capek they were the setting for his play *R.U.R.*, a nightmarish fantasy which culminates in robots taking over the world. The Portuguese called them the Islands of the Hawks from the time that they discovered them in 1427 and won permanent possession of them in 1432. But it was not until 1763, over three centuries later, that New England whalers began to visit the Azores for the first time.

Perhaps the first historically important figure to manifest an interest in the Azores was Prince Henry the Navigator of Portugal, who sent the explorer Gonçalo Velho Cabral on an exploratory expedition. Columbus later visited them on his way back from the West Indies, as did Vasco da Gama on his return from India. Although the first colonists were mostly Portuguese, a smaller number of Flemish settlers, as well as Bretons and Moors, also arrived during the fifteenth century. By 1500 all the islands were inhabited, and commerce with the mother country was flourishing.

During the Spanish takeover of Portugal in 1541 the Azores played a major role. The inhabitants of Terceira objected to this bold action on the part of Philip II of Spain; two years later the marquess of Santa Cruz stifled dissent there by leading a Spanish fleet against the rebellious inhabitants. For the next sixty years, down to 1640, the Azores remained a part of Spain, along with the rest of Portugal. There was an attempt to establish a central government in the Azores, but it was not until 1766—around the time of the first American

contacts—that the marquess of Pombal set up an office at Angra do
Heróismo for a governor and captain-general, who were to oversee
the entire group of islands.

EARLY AMERICAN RELATIONS AND THE WAR OF 1812

When the American whalers from such Massachusetts towns as
New Bedford and Nantucket stopped at Horta on Faial, they obtained
not only water but also fresh fruits. Records indicate that those Nantucket whaleships which cruised off the Azores in 1768 averaged approximately 150 barrels of whale oil per vessel. Probably the first
leader to emerge among the Americans was Thomas Hickling, an
inventive Yankee who introduced orange culture improvements before
the American Revolution; orange growing was the most important
Azorean agricultural pursuit during the eighteenth and nineteenth
centuries. At the time of the American Revolution itself, privateers
from the newly independent United States both watered and pro-
visioned in the Azores, and a temporary flareup occurred in which
inhabitants of Flores exchanged shots with them.

Unfortunately for the historian, early records of American contacts
with the Azores are limited, and deal largely with the relief and
protection of American seamen. Those files which still exist indicate
that John Street became the U.S. consul at Faial in 1790, his name
being the first which appears in the surviving records. Since Street
served from then until 1806, Thomas Hickling could not hold the
same position simultaneously; he thus became the U.S. vice consul
for São Miguel and Santa Maria on July 7, 1795. When Street retired in 1806, John Bass Dabney assumed his position. During the
years that followed the Dabney family dominated Azorean affairs;
the Bay State also monopolized the diplomatic representation at
Zanzibar during this period. But this concentration of Massachusetts
consuls in both places was only appropriate, given the extensive commercial ties then existing between the New England state and both
Zanzibar and the Azores.

In the years prior to the outbreak of the War of 1812, Faial in the
Azores became, in the words of Samuel Eliot Morison, "a new St.
Eustatius, a go-between for nations forbidden to trade with one another."[1] John Bass Dabney was not only the American consul at
Faial but also a leading merchant; during the course of the nineteenth
century the Dabney family continued to ship oil to Boston, in return
importing foodstuffs and notions. It must be remembered that in the

early national period the American consuls in the Azores were not highly paid, and they consequently were allowed to engage in business on the side, as did their counterparts in Zanzibar and elsewhere. During the War of 1812, moreover, a thriving enterprise developed in the Azores from the mere transfer of U.S. products from American to British ships, and vice versa. Key Azorean exports to the United States at this time included whale oil, as well as wines from Pico.

From a military standpoint, the Azorean highlight of this war was the confrontation between the American privateer *General Armstrong* and three British men-of-war in September 1814. The U.S. captain, Samuel Chester Reed, was surprised at anchor in the harbor at Faial by the *Plantagenet, Rota,* and *Carnation;* although Reed fought heroically, it eventually became necessary for him to scuttle the *General Armstrong* to prevent the British from seizing it. Because of the many casualties suffered in the skirmish, His Majesty's ships had to return to England instead of proceeding directly to New Orleans as had been originally planned. In the opinion of Theodore Roosevelt and various other military historians, the failure of these three vessels to follow their original course may well have contributed to General Andrew Jackson's victory over the British at New Orleans in January 1815.

Looking at the *General Armstrong* incident from the standpoint of international law, Consul Dabney had told Captain Reed that the neutrality of the port would be respected, which is one reason why the latter kept his vessel at anchor. Upon being informed about the details of the encounter, the State Department demanded reparations from the Portuguese. Fortunately for the British, upon signing the Treaty of Ghent in 1814 the United States renounced all such claims against the mother country; officially Great Britain argued that its naval officers had wanted only to inspect the American vessel, not to attack her. It was not until 1882 that Congress was to pass a bill recognizing the claims arising out of this case after every other attempt to obtain legal satisfaction had failed.[2] (We will examine these developments shortly.) One is reminded of the claims of Hamet Caramalli and his descendants arising out of Consul William Eaton's successful attack on Derna in Tripoli during 1805, claims which Caramalli and his descendants attempted to press against the American government down to the time of the Civil War.

THE DABNEY CONSULATE AND THE U.S. CIVIL WAR

In 1832 one of the more important political developments in the history of the islands occurred. At this time a new constitution was introduced, and the islands were grouped into three administrative districts: Ponta Delgada, Angra, and Horta. With a civil war raging in Portugal former Emperor Dom Pedro I of Brazil allied himself with revolutionary Azorean elements in an attempt to force his absolutist brother Dom Miguel from the Portuguese throne. It was in the Azores that Dom Pedro organized his army and navy in his successful attempt to invade Portugal, overthrow his brother, and replace the monarchy with a more liberal government; at this time England and France allied themselves with Portuguese and Spanish liberals against Dom Miguel.

Despite this revolutionary upheaval, Charles William Dabney, who had been consul since the death of his father in 1826, continued to represent the United States until 1869. This may well be the record for continuous service in a consular position; Dabney also had been assisting his father since 1817. Although both Dabneys devoted much of their time to the relief of destitute American seamen, they so endeared themselves to the people of the islands that they became known as the "Father of the Poor." Along with Portuguese entrepreneurs the younger Dabney also played a major role in expanding the shore whaling industry of Faial during the 1850s.

One troublesome issue which refused to go away during the pre-Civil War years was the *General Armstrong* claims. In 1850, during the presidency of Zachary Taylor, Secretary of State John Clayton sent instructions to James Clay, the American minister to Portugal, that a final demand for settlement be made. Shortly after Clay presented his note to the Portuguese government on June 21, the Russian minister offered to act as a mediator, but Clay refused to assent to either his intervention or an earlier Portuguese proposal that a third power arbitrate this case. Several days later Clay departed for home, seriously jeopardizing future U.S.-Portuguese relations.

But on July 9, 1850, Zachary Taylor died. Daniel Webster now took over as secretary of state, replacing Clayton, and quickly submitted the question to arbitration over the protests of the vessel's owners. Louis Napoleon agreed to serve as an arbitrator. When the French emperor later decided against America, the owners of the vessel took the position that the U.S. government had lost its claim against Portugal through its actions and thus should take upon itself the responsibility for making it good. There was some justification for the owners' discontent, since the State Department failed to submit to Louis Napoleon that portion of the diplomatic correspondence between America and Portugal in which the latter admitted its respon-

sibility. The case did go before Congress, but that body referred it
to the court of claims; a decade later, at the time of the outbreak
of the Civil War, it still remained a sensitive judicial issue.

During the American Civil War Consul Charles William Dabney
played an important role in handling the international aspects of this
conflict. The focal point of controversy in the Azores was the fitting
out and equipping for battle of the *Alabama* there in August 1862;
built in England for Confederate use, this vessel was to wreak havoc
on Union shipping. So severe were the depredations of the *Alabama*
that the Alabama Claims Commission later awarded the United States
$15,500,000 in compensation. While she was in the Azores, Dabney
made a valiant attempt to guide American war vessels into a confrontation with the hated raider, but to no avail. In fact, the *Alabama*
captured and burned the whaler *Ocean Rover* off Flores, and later
destroyed eight other vessels which had come to the latter's assistance.

DIPLOMATIC CONTACTS AND TRADE, 1867-1914

Five years later, in 1867, Thomas Hickling, Jr., who had succeeded
his 91-year-old father as vice consul at São Miguel in 1835, petitioned
against a recent action by the U.S. government which had reduced his
office to a consular agency. Stressing the vigorous export trade of
Ponta Delgada, Hickling mentioned that some wealthy American
citizens had visited the island recently, along with such notables as
Prince Jerome Napoleon and Dom Pedro of Portugal. Hickling also
pointed out that neither he nor his father had sought reimbursement
from the U.S. government for the expense of running the vice consulate, but Washington was unmoved by his pleas. Two years later, in
1869, Hickling resigned, turning the consular agency over to his
nephew, Thomas E. Ivens.

Although there was talk in America of annexing Santo Domingo
(the present-day Dominican Republic) during the Grant administration, and the U.S. consul at Tripoli, Michel Vidal, was lobbying for
the acquisition of a naval base there, a report appeared in the *New
York Times* on May 21, 1874, that Azorean newspapers were denying "the existence in those islands of a movement in favor of annexation to the United States."[3] Two years later the treatment of American seamen became an issue in the Azores. Nine destitute U.S. sailors
had sought passports from Azorean officials to enable them to leave
for Boston, whereupon the civil governor of São Miguel had sent
Ivens a bill for $13.50. No such charge apparently had ever been

made at Faial or at Lisbon before. The Portuguese government eventually refunded the passport fees, at the same time offering an apology; the amount at stake may have been trivial, but the principle was not.

Back at Washington, in 1882 the *General Armstrong* case finally ground to an unsatisfactory halt (at least in the eyes of the claimants) two decades after the death of Captain Reed. Two of the three judges on the court of claims ruled that the claim was indeed a valid one and ought to be paid by the American government, and set the amount due the vessel's owners at $70,739; then one of the judges reversed himself on technical grounds at the rehearing. As a result, the case again was placed in the hands of Congress, which obliged by passing a bill which the President allowed to become law without his signature; this measure was indefinite as to any specific settlement, since the secretary of state was instructed to adjust the claims on principles of justice and equity. At the time of the death of Reed's son in 1896, much of the original $70,739 remained unpaid. Whether justice was blind in this particular case is a matter of dispute; that it was pathetically slow is beyond controversy.

It was at this time (1895) that the Portuguese government granted the three administrative districts (Ponta Delgada, Angra, and Horta) autonomous administration within certain limits. In 1899 the American government converted the São Miguel office into a consulate and the Horta office into an agency.

A quarter of a century earlier, in 1876, the U.S. consul at Faial, Samuel Dabney, had joined forces with his brother-in-law George Oliver; together they entered into a partnership with Samuel Silva, a Portuguese American who once had captained a New Bedford whaling ship. Under this partnership Dabney furnished the ships (two fully equipped whaleships from New Bedford) and Silva the crews (most of whom had served previously on American whalers). Such a conflict of interest between diplomacy and commerce, of course, was nothing new for American officials in the Azores, cases in point being the orange growing activities of Thomas Hickling and the mercantile ones of John Bass Dabney.

Although Samuel Dabney engaged in the whaling business while also serving as the American consul, other U.S. citizens who did not hold diplomatic positions were participating in a rather limited import and export trade. During the 1890s Yankee sea captain Joshua Slocum observed on his arrival at Horta: "It was the season for fruit . . . and there was soon more of all kinds of it to put on board than I knew what to do with."[4] Consul Dabney's report on the "Trade and

Commerce of the Azores" for May 12, 1882, however, had noted that exports to the United States during 1881 were of little value. Statistics for the first half of 1883 reveal that aside from straw hats and braid the leading Azorean exports to the United States were old metal, fruit, oranges, embroideries, and wine. Thirteen years later, between mid-1895 and mid-1896, Faial exported ambergris and São Miguel pineapple plants to America. As for U.S. exports to the Azores, during the latter period they consisted of such items as dry goods, lumber, petroleum, and sugar.

More data is available on Azorean-American commerce for the first decade of the twentieth century than during any other comparable period in history, but this decade did not witness any striking change in long established trade patterns. During 1899 12 ships from the United States docked at Ponta Delgada, compared to 401 from Great Britain and 164 from Portugal. By the middle of 1901 wheat, coal, oil, lumber, corn, and cotton had become the leading American imports into the Azores, while the amount of the Azorean exports to the United States remained small. Six years later Consul John F. Jewell reported that American-made goods were popular in the Azores, but that a travelling salesman from the United States was rarely seen.

Factors contributing to the absence of a larger export trade were the Azores' relative geographical isolation compared with Europe, the unwillingness of U.S. exporters to fill small orders, the absence of regular freight steamers, and the high Portuguese tariff on American manufactured goods. During 1907 São Miguel exported salted fish to America, while Faial sent embroideries, straw hats, and yarn. But as Consul E. A. Creevey observed in 1908, since "there are no regular freight facilities between the United States and the Azores . . . imports from the United States must find their way here by way of England, Germany, or Portugal."[5] Between 1911 and 1912 American exports to the Azores declined a third, while those from Great Britain and Portugal fell off noticeably; Azorean exports in general also declined, thanks to reduced bean, corn, and sugar crops, with Faial exporting nothing to the United States.

As we have seen, down to World War 1 American trade with the Azores had been relatively limited, as had been U.S. involvement there. The islands, too, had yet to become a major tourist attraction for Americans. But as early as the years following the close of the War of 1812 the youthful historian William Hickling Prescott, the grandson of Thomas Hickling, had visited the islands; he here developed the mental discipline to overcome his damaged vision, which later allowed him to write such monumental epics as the history of the

Spanish conquest of the New World. A later but equally prominent arrival was Mark Twain. Although he is far more remembered for his vacations in Bermuda, Samuel L. Clemens did visit the Azores during 1900, and has left us with a memorable portrait of an islands street scene in his *The Innocents Abroad*.[6]

Of all those Americans of Portuguese ancestry who have committed their observations about the Azores to writing, perhaps none has been more articulate during the present century than John Dos Passos, author of *U.S.A.* The prolific author, best known in his later years for espousing conservative causes, received the Peter Francisco Award from the Portuguese Continental Union in New York City on June 17, 1961. As early as 1920 Dos Passos had described the islands as "extraordinarily beautiful, buff and pale green with violet cliffs and vast plumed clouds piled above them." Of all the nine, Pico with its "dark cone" seemingly made the greatest impression on him, although he also found Flores "handsome—all green and plowed fields and waterfalls coming over the cliffs."[7] Dos Passos's paternal grandfather, however, had been born on Madeira, and it was Funchal that the author-to-be first visited at the age of 8 in 1904.

WORLD WAR 1: THE PONTA DELGADA NAVAL BASE

While the various types of U.S. contacts with the Azores had perhaps not been of great significance prior to 1914, the islands had been of importance to Europe even before the discovery of America. "The very essence of Azorean history," writes James H. Guill, "has been the strategic location of the archipelago in respect to the world's shipping lanes."[8] Thus, in an age when modern navies frequently clash upon the ocean, and airplane squadrons fight above the waters, it was only natural that the U.S. military would turn its attention to the islands, especially as American involvement in the great European war which began in 1914 drew closer and closer.

By the end of this conflict the United States had acquired a temporary military base at Ponta Delgada, although as late as April 12, 1918, Secretary of the Navy Josephus Daniels denied that this event had occurred. "We have coal there," observed Daniels, "but we do not call a place where we have coal a naval base."[9] Assistant Secretary of the Navy Franklin D. Roosevelt also took a similar position at this time. Nevertheless, records at the National Archives in Washington demonstrate that as early as August 16, 1917, the Navy Department had come to the conclusion that the establishment of a base at Ponta

Delgada was necessary;[10] according to the German strategist General von Reuter, had Germany had possession of the Azores, she would have won World War 1. Reports had been circulating prior to this time that the Germans were using one of the islands as a submarine base, and German submarines did sink a number of vessels in the vicinity of the Azores.

Unfortunately for those American strategists favoring such a base, the Navy Department and the State Department worked at cross purposes in relation to the islands, partly for the reason that the former had not developed elaborate plans for their utilization. Following the close of the war, in 1921, Admiral William S. Sims used the Azores mixup as evidence to substantiate his general thesis that the Navy Department had not been prepared for war in 1917; he specifically charged that the navy had failed to make the necessary diplomatic arrangements in connection with the arrival of its forces in the islands. In addition, several changes of administration in Lisbon caused officials there during this period to alternate between militarism and pacifism, while the British government was apprehensive about the possible exporting of American coal to Portugal. To confuse matters further, the United States reached no formal agreement with Portugal relative to the Azores during the war.

Despite these complicating factors the Americans won the goodwill of the inhabitants of Ponta Delgada as early as July 4, 1917. On this date a German submarine raked the town there with its deck guns; the accidental presence of an American collier, however, prevented more extensive damage. It is little wonder, therefore, that the citizens of Ponta Delgada immediately adopted a pro-American stance, and a year later there was a gigantic celebration of the Fourth of July in the Azores. "These Islands," Rear Admiral Herbert O. Dunn wrote the secretary of the navy, "have caught the spark of patriotism so ably struck by our Commander-in-Chief, and on this Fourth of July they assisted most loyally and enthusiastically in celebrating the glorious day. Thousands of natives cheered the American flag as the High Commissioner hoisted it over the Palace."[11] By the time that the U.S. navy finally withdrew from the Azores during the following year (1919), there even was considerable support for the islands obtaining their independence under American protection, a development which did not escape the attention of edgy Portuguese officials back in Lisbon.

Although he may have been reluctant to label it a naval base, the fact remains that Franklin D. Roosevelt, acting in his capacity as assistant secretary of the navy, did review an American fleet at Ponta

Delgada during one of his two wartime trips to France.[12] Of more lasting impact was the presence of Admiral Dunn in the Azores during World War 1. So successfully did he deal with both the governmental authorities and the islands' population that a town square was named after him: Largo Almirante Dunn. This square, quite appropriately, was the one in front of the present-day Hotel de San Pedro, a building which Thomas Hickling originally constructed over a century before.

Three months before the Armistice, on August 18, Admiral Dunn and the high commissioner for the Azores drew up an agreement providing for naval air stations at Horta and Ponta Delgada. Under its provisions, Portugal was to furnish the land for the bases and the United States the supplies and the equipment. In another interdepartmental mixup the State Department failed to receive a copy of this agreement, while the supplies and the equipment did not reach the Azores until after the Armistice. But as we shall see shortly, the islands were on the verge of entering the air age.

One month later, on September 5, 1918, the Censorship Board in Washington passed a resolution advocating the establishment of a censorship station in the Azores under the joint auspices of the Americans, British, French, and Portuguese. Officials of the board were quite concerned at this time as to how to censor the flow of mail between Spain and the South American republics. Nothing apparently came of this proposal thanks to State Department inaction, but there was a precedent for it. According to Secretary of State Robert Lansing, for reasons of military security authorities in London had been intercepting not only cablegrams destined for neutral European countries, but also ones sent by American businessmen to South America via the Azores. As is pointed out in the chapter on Bermuda, this question later arose there at the time of the outbreak of World War 2.

Unlike certain U.S. overseas bases following the latter conflict, America abandoned its naval station in the Azores after World War 1 rather quickly, in September 1919. Although the State Department did manage to obtain bunkering facilities at Ponta Delgada for U.S. merchant vessels, the attempt to win landing rights and other privileges for commercial aircraft proved a failure. A year earlier, in 1918, U.S. officials had closed the consulate on São Miguel. One is reminded in this connection of such parallel occurrences on the African continent during this period as the wartime shutdown of the Ethiopian consulate in 1914 and the Zanzibari one in 1915.

THE INTER-WAR YEARS

The withdrawal of the American navy from Ponta Delgada was soon followed by the final departure of U.S. whalers from the islands. According to Consul E. A. Creevey in 1908, "seven American whaling vessels called at São Miguel for the purpose of reprovisioning; five years later eight others stopped at Horta on the island of Faial. The last American whaler to visit the Azores was probably the *Athlete,* which also docked at Horta in 1921. Four years later the last two whaling schooners, the *John R. Manta* and the *Margarett,* went into inactive status at New Bedford, Massachusetts.

But while the whalers were disappearing, the flyers were arriving. On May 17, 1919, the first airplane ever to cross the Atlantic Ocean, a U.S. navy-operated craft, landed at Horta; three days later it also touched down at Ponta Delgada, before finally landing at Lisbon a week later. Flown by the now forgotten Albert C. Read, this airplane was only one of four which had left New York City for England via the Azores and Portugal. Read was later followed to the islands by such prominent American pilots as Charles A. Lindbergh and Ruth Helder. Twenty years after the initial Read landing, in 1939, Pan American Clippers began regular stops at the Azores between Europe and America.

Although official U.S. interest in the islands between the two world wars was minimal, in 1933 "the people of the Azores" apparently sent a petition to the American government asking that President Franklin D. Roosevelt become their ruler. One of F.D.R.'s aides again called this to his attention on July 12, 1941. It is not clear whether this mysterious document came from private or governmental sources in the islands, and whether it was inspired by the economic collapse which seized the world in 1929 and the years which followed; it in any event does reveal that their inhabitants had not forgotten the United States between the two world wars.

In 1940, on the eve of American entry into World War 2, the chief U.S. exports to the Azores were fuels, hardware, electrical and radio appliances, tobacco, newsprint and cigarette paper, toilet articles, chemicals, and foodstuffs. While most imports into the islands continued to come from America, aside from British coal and Portuguese textiles, Portugal took the bulk of Azorean exports, the United States, Great Britain, and Canada the remainder. The main American imports from the islands at this time were embroideries, dasheens, and small quantities of hemp and pineapple.[13] Here there had been less of a change over the years than there had been in the case of the U.S. exports to the islands.

But even more important, the United States continued to enjoy the good will of the Azoreans, as it had during World War 1 and on other occasions. Writing from Ponta Delgada on May 17, 1940, a wealthy and prominent American citizen living in the Azores opined that "most of the people here love the United States and there is a very close friendship throughout São Miguel in regard to America." This individual, Jose Maria Bensaude, also concluded that "the United States gave so much help to people here in the past that it will be very difficult for the population here, especially the poor class, to change their attitude towards America."[14] As we shall see, this favorable opinion was to persist, not only during World War 2, but following that conflict as well.

WORLD WAR 2 NEGOTIATIONS

Although the United States did not sign an agreement with the Portuguese government for the construction of an airbase on Santa Maria until November 1944, only six months before the end of the war in Europe, the Azores had begun to play a role in American diplomatic maneuverings long before the Japanese attack on Pearl Harbor officially brought us into this conflict. In March 1940 President Franklin Roosevelt raised the question of future German actions against the Azores in a talk with the American minister to Portugal, Herbert C. Pell, then home on leave. Several months later, in July, the Department of State instructed its diplomatic representatives in both Portugal and Spain that the American government felt a deep concern for the future status of their Atlantic island possessions.

To the German Foreign Office, these negotiations between the United States and Portugal constituted evidence that a joint Anglo-American naval base in the Azores was a possibility. This assessment may have been a bit premature, but in September the American naval representative in London did hold a series of discussions with his British counterpart; here representatives of the two nations agreed that the United States would occupy the Atlantic Portuguese islands (both the Azores and the Cape Verdes) in the event of war. In October army and navy staff officers formulated a plan for American forces quickly to occupy the Azores, despite the fact that the army lacked the troops and the navy the ships for such an operation at

this time. By January 1941, however, the Army War Plans Division
had come to the conclusion that a U.S. occupation of the Azores was
not vital from the standpoint of hemispheric defense, and should take
place only in the event that America became an active participant in
the war. Army hostility to Azorean operations in general continued
to persist in the months to come, while Hanson Baldwin played down
the strategic importance of the islands in an article which appeared
in the *New York Times* during July.

Despite this behind-the-scenes coolness on the part of army planners,
at least several public figures and governmental officials took a more
positive stance on the Azores during this period. On December 29
President Franklin Roosevelt pointed out during the course of a radio
address that the Azores are closer to the Atlantic Coast than Hawaii
is to the Pacific Coast. A more surprising backer of a vigorous Azorean
policy was the isolationist editor and publisher of the *Chicago Tribune*,
Colonel Robert R. McCormick, who testified before the Senate Foreign
Relations Committee on February 6 that he would favor an American
occupation of the Azores in the event of a German takeover of Portugal. Then in an apparent volte face which reversed without explanation
McCormick's earlier stance, the *Tribune* editorialized on July 3 that
the suggestion that the United States occupy the Azores or Cape
Verde Islands as a defense measure had not been made in good faith.

At this stage of the war Portugal was still embracing neutrality, as
was its pro-Axis neighbor Spain, while both nations continued to pursue
internal policies with a decidedly fascistic tinge. The Germans, though,
were thinking at this time of a military occupation of the Iberian
peninsula, even readying a number of Panzer divisions for the planned
takeover; an added bonus would be the seizure of the Azores as an
air or submarine base. The Portuguese prime minister, António de
Oliveira Salazar, was so concerned about a possible Nazi occupation
of his country that he not only dispatched part of the Portuguese army
to the Azores, but also formulated a plan for the transfer of the Libson
regime there after a token display of military resistance against the
Germans. Salazar then asked Portugal's ancient ally, Great Britain, to
help him protect the Azores. But fortunately for Portugal, Adolf Hitler
abandoned his scheme to occupy the islands; he did this with great regret, since the Azores would afford him the best air facility for
attacking America if she should enter the war. Prior to reaching this
painful decision Admiral Erich Raeder had informed the German dictator that the Nazis lacked the military capacity to defend the Atlantic
islands should Germany take them over.

Nazi intentions at this time remained unclear to the Allies, but the Portuguese Prime Minister did not want U.S. troops in the Azores, either. First of all, as J. K. Sweeney has noted, the Portuguese were almost pathologically suspicious concerning their empire; second, Salazar was disturbed by what he regarded as the materialism of Wall Street and the immorality of California. In April it had become necessary for Secretary of State Cordell Hull to reassure him that America was not about to occupy the islands. During the same month the British prime minister, Winston Churchill, advocated an American naval visit to the Azores and to Lisbon, but on May 1 Hull wrote our ambassador to Great Britain, John G. Winant, that ". . . we received strong protest from Portuguese Government in regard to a proposed friendly visit to Azores and Cape Verde Islands at this time. In view of this we deferred proposed visit."[15]

Despite this Portuguese reluctance the liberal internationalist Senator Claude Pepper of Florida delivered an address on May 6 in which he advocated the U.S. occupation of those "points of vantage from which [the] monsters are preparing to attack us. In that category I include Greenland, Iceland, the Azores, the Cape Verde Islands, the Canary Islands, [and] Dakar."[16] Three days later the American government informed its Portuguese counterpart that the senator's remarks did not necessarily represent the official policy of this country. Another advocate of an aggressive policy was the Committee to Defend America by Aiding the Allies, which urged that, in the event of a German takeover of Dakar, the Canary Islands, the Cape Verde Islands, and the Azores, the U.S. in cooperation with the British should occupy them first on a temporary basis. Of course, not every American spokesman favored the occupation of the islands; Democratic Senators Bennett Champ Clark of Missouri and Patrick McCarran of Nevada are cases in point.

While Pepper was arousing a furor with his utterances, the American military continued to debate what the United States should do with respect to the Azores. Under the ABC-1 Staff Agreement of March 27, planners gave operations in Europe preference over those in the Pacific, should America enter the war. The Azores and the other Atlantic islands, however, were to remain the basic responsibility of the British, although U.S. forces might assist in the occupation of both the Azores and Cape Verdes. Despite this staff agreement, the War Plans Division on May 7 did rank the Azores second only to Dakar as an area of urgency, with Iceland far down the list in sixteenth place; the sending of American troops to the Azores was considered as more justifiable from the standpoint of national defense than the dispatching of ones to Iceland. Accordingly, on May 22, 1941, Admiral Harold Stark received word from the President that he should have the navy ready on thirty days' notice to occupy the Azores,[17] while two days later the Joint Chiefs of Staff obtained instructions from Roosevelt to prepare an Azorean occupation force of U.S. marines.

Only three weeks after Senator Claude Pepper's address—which the Roosevelt administration had so quickly disavowed—Franklin Roosevelt made his unlimited emergency speech on May 27, 1941. In this fireside chat F.D.R. declared that "the island outposts of the New World, if occupied or controlled by Germany, would directly endanger the freedom of the Atlantic and our physical safety."[18] This was four days after the British Foreign Office had cabled Lord Halifax, the British ambassador to the United States, on May 23 in relation to the Azores that it would be preferable to hold American assistance in reserve at the moment; two days after the President's address, on May 29, Roosevelt received word from British Prime Minister Winston Churchill that the British were preparing to offer Portugal anti-aircraft and other equipment, with which to defend the Azores and the Cape Verde Islands.

The Portuguese themselves were by no means reassured by Roosevelt's speech. On May 30 Prime Minister Salazar, fearful of both German reprisals and local unrest, protested that his government had been pursuing a policy of strict neutrality, and had gone to great lengths to fortify the Azores against attack. During the first few days of June, partly as a result of this protest, partly as a result of the rumored German invasion of Russia, F.D.R. reached an agreement with Winston Churchill that an Allied occupation of Iceland would be substituted for that of the Azores. Rumor became fact on June 22, when Hitler attacked the Soviet Union.

On June 7 the U.S. army had placed in reserve, at least for the time being, its plan for an Azorean expedition, while on June 10 Secretary of State Cordell Hull gave officials in Lisbon categorical assurances that America had no aggressive intentions towards the Azores or Cape Verde Islands.[19] Nevertheless, three days later the Portuguese minister in Washington informed Undersecretary of State Sumner Welles that "many newspaper articles and editorials which the Germans took pains to see were republished in the Portuguese press, were beginning to make the Portuguese people suspicious that the Government of the United States was going to seize the present opportunity of taking possession of their overseas colonies."[20] Such a rumor had already appeared in the Italian *Popolo di Roma* on April 29, but with the variation that the British would handle the takeover and the Americans support this action. Hull's assurances notwithstanding, the Portuguese press remained unconvinced as to the sincerity of American intentions. An editorial which appeared in the semi-official *Diário da Manha* of Lisbon on July 11 took exception to the continued references to the Atlantic islands by U.S. senators and American newspapers in the wake of the dispatch of American troops to Iceland. As a reassuring gesture, President Roosevelt wrote Prime Minister Salazar that Portugal should retain control of the Azores and Cape Verde Islands. In his reply, dated July 29, Salazar observed that the Portuguese military was not apprehensive about a German attack on the Azores, but that if he was unable to obtain the necessary munitions and equipment from Great Britain, he would welcome American assistance. The door, it would seem, was now ajar for the United States, and both the British and the Brazilians encouraged Portugal to keep it open.

By August the revived threat of a German drive into southwestern Europe led to a reconsideration of the Azorean project, with the U.S. army as unenthusiastic as ever. On August 5 Hull denied a rumor that the American government was supporting a Brazilian takeover of the Azores if only because Brazil lacked the equipment, but elsewhere Roosevelt was about to make a commitment relative to the islands. Meeting with Churchill at their Atlantic Charter conference off the Newfoundland coast on August 11, F.D.R. and the British Prime Minister reached four basic understandings. One of these called for U.S. armed forces to occupy the Azores, while Great Britain would take over the Cape Verde Islands; a token Brazilian contingent would accompany the Americans, for the sake of appearances.[21]

Despite this understanding, the proposed Anglo-American takeover of the Azores, the (Spanish) Canaries, and the Cape Verde Islands did not materialize in September as planned. The German threat had diminished by that time, while the Portuguese remained cool to an Allied occupation. In pursuing this matter Myron C. Taylor stopped off to see Salazar on his way back to the United States from talks at the Vatican in September, but received little, if any, encouragement. Back at home Secretary of War Henry Stimson noted in his diary that he was opposed to any military operations which would "bog down" the army in such "side issues" as the Azores and Dakar. During the autumn President Roosevelt wrote the naval historian

Samuel Eliot Morison to the effect that he regretfully could not include the Azores in the Western Hemisphere, for the reason that this was a strategic impossibility; although it probably did not influence F.D.R., a public opinion poll conducted in October revealed that only 45.9 percent of the interviewees favored the United States helping to defend them, if Germany threatened to take them. Although the newly activated operational staff of General Headquarters did draw up a new joint expeditionary force plan for the occupation of the islands by the U.S. army and marines in September and October, the service chiefs advised F.D.R. in December that it would be impossible to undertake an occupation of the Azores unless American troops were shifted there from Iceland.

During the following year the Azores did not appear frequently as a news item in U.S. newspapers, nor did military planners develop any new projects of consequence relative to them. But the Portuguese diplomatic correspondence with the United States for the first six months of 1942 does reveal that behind the scenes American-Azorean relations were not all sweetness and light. Thus, on March 28 the civil governor of Ponta Delgada created a furor with his proclamation that "all foreigners without exception are required to concentrate themselves on the football field of the local high school following any rifle firing a signal of 3 shots. . . ."[22] Those not cooperating were to be regarded as traitors and executed without trial. In addition, all foreigners who lived on the island of São Miguel outside the city of Ponta Delgada were expected to move into that town by April 5; meanwhile the U.S. consul received orders from the Portuguese government to furnish it with the names of those American citizens who were residing on this island.

When the U.S. minister to Portugal, Bert Fish, called upon the chief of the political section of the Portuguese Foreign Ministry, Costa Carneiro, on April 9, that official refrained from defending the football field order, but pointed out relative to the concentration of all foreign residents in Ponta Delgada that Germans and Italians would be affected as well as Americans. Eleven days later Costa Carneiro went further, characterizing the football field order as absurd and a mistake, but Fish cabled Hull at the beginning of May that the military had refused to cancel the order that foreigners in São Miguel move into Ponta Delgada. In this connection, the U.S. legation complained that most of the Americans of Portuguese extraction were so poor that they could not afford to leave their Azorean farms. Although these differences were not resolved to the satisfaction of the American government, there were fewer of them during the second part of the year; it was probably too much to hope that they could be settled entirely to Washington's satisfaction.

In January 1943 President Franklin Roosevelt held a meeting with President Getúlio Vargas of Brazil at Natal; on the twenty-ninth F.D.R. asked Vargas to propose to Salazar that troops from Brazil be transported to the Azores to relieve their Portuguese counterparts. By this time an Azorean airbase for Allied use had become a priority, since the Germans were employing their submarine wolf packs to destroy Allied shipping in the mid-Atlantic. To counteract this problem, the U.S. navy did dispatch a number of small aircraft carriers there, but this move by no means eliminated the menace.

As a result, during the same month as the Roosevelt-Vargas meeting the Air Transport Command of the army air forces requested that Pan American Airways investigate the possibility of obtaining land airport facilities in the Azores, ostensibly for commercial purposes, but actually for military reasons. There was a need for improved, as well as additional landing facilities in the islands, and by May construction was proceeding on airports on both Terceira and São Miguel. While the Portuguese Prime Minister would not agree to admit military forces other than those of Great Britain into the Azores, he would grant fueling facilities to American warships and merchant vessels.

WORLD WAR 2 AGREEMENTS

On August 17, 1943, the British and Portuguese governments reached an agreement setting forth permissible military activities in the Azores on the part of Great Britain. Under this Great Britain obtained the use of Lajes Field on Terceira, as well as the port of Horta; the main British objective in acquiring these facilities was to engage in anti-submarine warfare maneuvers. With respect to the American military presence, Franklin Roosevelt pointed out later to Winston Churchill that "it was not practicable . . . to have included in that agreement adequate provision for U.S. Navy facilities in [the] Azores, or any provision whatever for facilities for U.S. air transport and air ferrying operations."[23]

Now that negotiations between the British and the Portuguese had been completed, it was possible for the American government to approach the Portuguese regime with a freer hand relative to the U.S. obtaining various military facilities in the Azores, including a naval base, an aircraft base, a cable system, radar installations, and observation posts. A leading figure in these discussions was the theoretician of the cold war George Kennan, then a chargé in Portugal who was acting for the first time as a negotiator rather than merely as an observer, in the aftermath of Minister Fish's death. The rising young diplomat, who was instructed to approach Salazar on October 16, showed an initial reluctance to press American demands. In this connection he wrote Secretary of State Hull on October 20 that "our existing program advanced at this time would confirm Salazar's fears that we want nothing less than the whole archipelago, lock, stock and barrel. . . ,"[24] a little over a month later Kennan again protested to Hull that "I enter into these conversations with misgivings in view of our failure to reach complete agreement with the British in advance as to our joint military and strategic requirements."[25]

Kennan, who regarded Salazar as one of the most notable men in Europe, and a man of high moral principles, received permission from F.D.R. to handle matters as he saw fit. He then suddenly was recalled to Washington and admonished by both Secretary of War Henry Stimson and the Joint Chiefs of Staff at the Pentagon. Kennan next saw Roosevelt who reassured him, thus soothing to a degree Kennan's damaged ego, about which no one else seemed overly concerned.

Viewed retrospectively, Kennan's failure to press Salazar for as much as possible as quickly as possible was justified. The Portuguese Prime Minister was quite concerned with the impact on Spain of the presence of the United States in the Azores; he also was fearful of compromising what was left of Portuguese neutrality, and hence was hesitant to grant any additional facilities even to the British. With respect to possible American bases, Salazar tended to be the most favorably disposed towards Terceira, least amenable towards São Miguel, and open-minded towards Santa Maria. São Miguel, of course, was the only open port in the islands and the center of Portuguese administration.

While the Portuguese Prime Minister procrastinated, on December 1 military representatives of the United States signed a joint agreement with their British counterparts; a restricted number of ferried and transport aircraft from America could now land at Lajes airport. Thanks to this arrangement, U.S. pilots were able to reach North Africa via the Azores from Newfoundland or Bermuda. On December 31 the Portuguese government through Salazar gave its consent to this agreement, provided that the operation remained under British control. The numerous attempts to disguise American activities in the Azores led one U.S. naval officer to comment to another: "Now do you understand the Azores situation? If you do, you are the only one in the Navy who does!"[26]

In the months which followed American negotiations with Salazar continued. Although he did object to a U.S. navy squadron based in the islands engaging in anti-submarine patrol work, he looked with more favor upon the suggestion that Pan American Airways conduct a survey of possible Azorean airfields. At this time the Portuguese Prime Minister remained unconvinced that a second field would be necessary, even though the Americans had to extend the one at Lajes. While these talks were going on, on January 6, 1944, Admiral Ernest J. King took a major administrative step when he set up the United States Naval Forces Azores Command, or ComNavZor. Three days later the first contingent of Seabees, of the Ninety-sixth Construction Battalion, arrived in the islands; the acting military governor was hesitant at first to permit these to land, and a nasty incident was averted only when he finally gave them permission to disembark. Despite this confrontation, by February American Airlines and Trans World Airlines as contract carriers had begun to operate regularly scheduled flights through the islands. Although they originally flew from the Lajes base to Scotland, later on there was an airlift into North Africa, featuring Pan American Airways.

On February 26 Raymond Henry Norweb, the new minister to Portugal, informed Salazar that to permit the American military to build a second airfield in the Azores "constituted the greatest single contribution Portugal could make to [the] liberation of Timor in particular and our operations in [the] Far East in general."[27] The Japanese had overrun Timor in early 1942, but a statement of Portuguese belligerency with respect to its liberation might lead the Japanese also to seize Macao, which the Chinese in turn might take and not return to Portugal. Moved by troubleshooter Norweb's arguments, on April 7 Salazar authorized the immediate expansion of the Lajes airport, and then in May he communicated with Pan American Airways relative to the surveying of Santa Maria Island.

Construction of an airfield, built and paid for by the Portuguese with a view to postwar communications, would begin immediately upon the completion of this survey. But Salazar refused to resolve the question of the eventual use of Santa Maria in these talks, as he apparently felt that he needed negotiating leverage relative to other diplomatic issues. It was around this time (May) that Pan American Airways began to fly from Miami through Bermuda and the Azores to Casablanca, even though a meeting of minds had yet to occur on a second airbase.

On June 15 Secretary Hull warned Ambassador Winant in London to avoid making any connection in diplomatic discussions between the

Anglo-Portuguese agreement on the Azores and Portuguese-American negotiations relative to Santa Maria. But in July, when the Portuguese government gave U.S. aircraft permission to operate from Lajes airbase under the R.A.F. Coastal Command, it did so on the condition that the American planes also display British insignia. Another complicating factor, according to Hull, was the widespread hostility in Congress to Pan American Airways being granted a monopoly over U.S. overseas aviation; he was of the opinion that a majority of both houses was against this concession at that time.

Meanwhile Ambassador Norweb wrote Hull from Lisbon on July 7 that Prime Minister Salazar had "received our favorable response to Portugal's desire for voluntary participation in the eventual liberation of Timor with evident satisfaction. . . ."[28] Hull, though, chided Norweb for not having brought up the Santa Maria question, and on July 18 F.D.R. wrote Salazar that because of the weather hazard the airport there would either have to be constructed immediately or the project abandoned. Upon receiving this message, the Portuguese Prime Minister complained to the U.S. ambassador that he "was very much put out" by Roosevelt pressing him on this matter, since he had to take into account "the unalterable fact of Portugal's neutrality vis-à-vis Japan."[29] Salazar also declared, over the objections of Norweb, that the United States and Portugal were still involved with the question of construction, and that he would deal with the use and control of the airport later. While this wrangling was still going on, in mid-July Pan American Airways submitted a total tender of $3,130,000 for the construction of an airport on Santa Maria. On the twenty-seventh Salazar notified F.D.R.: "It appears to me that the fundamental accord with the construction company has been satisfactorily made so that work can commence immediately and continue at the rate considered proper."[30]

Diplomatic negotiations with the Portuguese continued in September, after a lull in August, with the turning point occurring in a series of conversations which Norweb had with Salazar on October 9-10-11. By this time the Portuguese embargo on the export of wolfram to Germany was four months old, while the U.S. military continued to push across the Pacific. Yet at this late date Salazar still remained hesitant, and the American ambassador wrote Hull that "it was only upon my earnest and persistent personal appeal that he said 'Yes' and drafted a telegram to the Azores authorizing immediate construction on the major project."[31] The Portuguese Prime Minister complained that he was being asked to approve a blank check, and Norweb in fact was of the opinion that the Americans received better terms from the Portuguese than the British had. Despite this breakthrough in the negotiations, it was not until November 28 that the governments of the United States and Portugal signed the final agreement vis-à-vis the Santa Maria airbase, with the latter expecting still another understanding relative to Timor with the former.[32]

Having examined Portuguese-American diplomacy at great length, there remains for consideration the question of the day-to-day relations of American military personnel in the Azores with the British forces stationed there. At first these appear to have been a bit strained, according to the *Report on Establishing U.S. Naval Activities in the Azores, January to August, 1944.* Quoting this document, those American officers "who gave advice rather consistently suggested that the British would 'try to pull the wool over our eyes' and to be on guard." Yet there was to be no confrontation with them, since U.S. military personnel "were instructed to keep all conversation on a light level and to smile broadly at anyone who tried to open an argument that might become heated."[33]

Portuguese authorities in the Azores at first did not display any official knowledge of the American presence, but U.S. officials eventually broke the ice by inviting them to a cocktail party. By August 1944 conversations with the Portuguese authorities had grown more friendly. One problem which did arise was that the well-paid American personnel might inflate the Azorean economy beyond control by spending too freely. An attempt was made to solve this dilemma by restricting each soldier to a limited amount of escudos per month, and by encouraging him to save part of his salary. U.S. officials, too, refrained from acting in too humanitarian a manner when a military truck hit a pole, knocking down a live wire and electrocuting a donkey. This was for the reason that Portuguese authorities generally took the position that the owner should lose a little should such an accident occur, and that American generosity might lead some Azoreans to push their beasts of burden under the wheels of U.S. trucks.

Fortunately, there was not so much friction over the soldiers fraternizing with the local girls as there was in Iceland during World War 2. To quote the *ComNavZor* report, ". . . the American enlisted men (the British competed a little) gained a reputation for gallantry and his company was sought to the exclusion of the Portuguese soldier."[34] In summing up the overall American impact on the islands during this conflict, one might conjecture that it perhaps was less than it had been on Iceland and Greenland, where the U.S. military had arrived in full force at a far earlier date; the war in Europe, moreover, was to end less than six months after the signing of the November 28, 1944, agreement.

LAJES FIELD IN THE POST-WAR YEARS

On May 30, 1946, a little more than a year after the termination of the war in Europe, the U.S. government transferred the American base at Santa Maria to the Portuguese government, which in turn authorized for eighteen months the passage in transit through Lajes Field of American and British aircraft serving the forces of occupation in Germany and Japan. (The British simultaneously abandoned control over Lajes Field to the Portuguese.) In 1947 the former American airbase on Santa Maria became a commercial field. After the abovementioned May 1946 agreement expired, there was a lapse of several months before American and Portuguese officials reached an agreement on February 2, 1948, which permitted U.S. military aircraft to continue using Lajes. Portugal, of course, was by no means averse to America granting it favors in return. As C. L. Sulzberger observed that November, "Unlike Spain, Portugal is in the Marshall Plan. This country plans to ask for about $640 million for a four-year period."[35]

The following year, 1949, the United States broke with its isolationist stance towards Europe by signing the North Atlantic Treaty, a permanent entangling alliance against which Thomas Jefferson and other Founding Fathers had cautioned. One result of this action was that the American government also signed a defense agreement with Portugal on September 6, 1951; under this the United States received a grant of Azorean base rights in the event of war, with the Americans and the Portuguese jointly constructing the facilities. Once completed, these were to be turned over to Portugal for maintenance.

Unfortunately for the United States, by the time that negotiators for both countries were considering the renewal of this agreement in 1956, the question of Portuguese colonialism had become a complicating factor. India, which had been independent for a decade, was casting its eyes on the Portuguese enclave of Goa at this time, and only the illness of President Dwight Eisenhower led to the postponement of a scheduled visit by Indian Prime Minister Jawaharlal Nehru to the United States. Although there was no meeting of minds at this time over the political aspects of the American airbase in the Azores, Portuguese and U.S. authorities did agree that the facilities there should be enlarged. It was not until November 15, 1957, however, that the foreign minister of Portugal, Dr. Paulo Cunha, and the American ambassador, James C. H. Bonbright, signed an agreement which extended the 1951 Azores Common Defense Pact until December 31, 1962.

In assessing the U.S. military presence in the Azores since World War 2, one might examine conditions at Lajes at time intervals of several years. In 1957 there were approximately eighteen hundred Americans resident at the airbase, then valued at $200 million; at this time transient flights averaged around 1,200 departures each month. But in the years ahead flights through the Azores were by no means always of a routine character. Thus, in 1958 a number of American marines passed through Lajes on their way to Lebanon, while in 1961 the U.S. air force routed its transports through the islands at the time of the Congo crisis. During the Berlin flareup of the same year 2,000 plane departures from the Azores were recorded during a peak month; the average number was perhaps half of this, totalling approximately 14,000 takeoffs during a year. Aside from the Air Force operations there, the navy was standing guard over a new, secret installation which was to be used for the storage of undersea weapons for Polaris-armed nuclear submarines.

As the expiration date for the 1951 Azores Common Defense Pact neared, a series of incidents arose which complicated negotiations. The seizure of the liner *Santa Maria* by a former colonial official and others in January 1961 was one of these; reports circulated at this time (which were denied by the State Department) that the Portuguese government would not renew the Azores airbase lease unless the United States treated the seizure as piracy on the high seas. Far more serious in the long run, though, was the American vote in the Security Council of the United Nations in June, which urged Portugal to cease repressive measures in her fight against the rebels in Angola, who had launched a war for independence several months earlier. Because of this stance, complained Portuguese officials, the government of India felt less hesitant to execute its scheme to seize and annex Goa, and in fact did so later that same year.

By the end of 1961 the *New York Times* had concluded that in the age of the long-range missile and the nuclear-powered submarine and surface ship ". . . the Azores are not strategically indispensable. Both the United States and NATO can get along without them if they have to."[36] This was not the sentiment of former Secretary of State Dean Acheson, who described the bases there in the *Yale Review* as those most important to America. Nevertheless, when the agreement providing for U.S. use of military facilities in the Azores expired in 1962, Portugal refused to renew it; instead, it invited the American government to stay in the islands on an ad hoc basis—a move that heightened rather than lessened tension between the two nations. One of the most prominent individuals who did not wish to see

U.S. base rights in the Azores lapse was Republican Senator Barry Goldwater of Arizona, a noted hard-liner on the cold war.

More successful in dealing with the Portuguese were the French, who in April 1964 obtained permission to establish a missile tracking base in the Azores, and to land planes and dock ships carrying measuring equipment. The French ballistic launching center was at Biscarosse in southwest France. France in return promised to assist Portugal with its naval construction program; it was to supply the latter with eight warships, including four new Dauphine class submarines. Since its treaty with Lisbon had expired, the United States rejected a similar request for naval vessels.

But treaty or no treaty, in the words of the *New York Times*, "the United States and Portugal have settled into an uneasy but mutually acceptable arrangement on continuing American air base rights in the Azores."[37] Portuguese-American relations in the islands, moreover, remained quite friendly, although there was some apprehension among the local Portuguese in the months after the treaty expired. One circumstance which did have a detrimental effect on these relations was the lack of jobs because of contract cancellations, but this was more than balanced by the veterinarian and earthquake relief programs, both of which we will examine in detail. A level of rapport had developed between Americans and Portuguese in the Azores which led "visitors from the mainland [to] express great surprise at the friendship, trust, and spirit of cooperation that existed here."[38] This contrasted with the attitude of Prime Minister Salazar back in Lisbon, who bitterly denounced American policy towards Africa in a March 1966 interview with correspondent Tad Szulc.

By the late 1960s, though, the *New York Times* was reporting a noticeable drop in United States military activity and personnel at Lajes Field. In the spring of 1968 there generally were less than a dozen aircraft on the ground at the one-time "crossroads of the Atlantic"; perhaps fifteen hundred military personnel remained, about half the number present during the peak of operations during the early 1960s. During November of this year Secretary of State Dean Rusk held talks with Portuguese leaders, at which officials of both nations agreed to resume negotiations over the American military base in the Azores. At this time, of course, there was a French guided-missile tracking base on Flores, which had not been there when the 1951 agreement between the United States and Portugal expired in 1962; according to Walter Hackett, who visited the islands in 1969,

"No one of the American military at Lajes will speak about this new base. The same holds true of the Portuguese in the Azores."[39]

In the spring of 1970 the American secretary of state, who was now William Rogers, reached an agreement in principle with the Portuguese foreign minister, Rui Patricio, to resume discussions over the Azores base. But as Rogers advised Patricio, the United States first would have to concentrate on negotiations with Spain about a military agreement signed in 1953 and due to expire in September 1970, so as to prevent our rights there from lapsing. In December 1971 the American and Portuguese governments finally did sign a five-year Azorean pact, retroactive to 1969; under this agreement, unlike past ones, the United States was to furnish $1 million in cash, $5 million in surplus equipment, $30 million in agricultural goods, and $400 million in export credit.[40] The Senate Foreign Relations Committee objected to this agreement on the grounds that it should have taken the form of a treaty,[41] while critics of U.S. foreign policy charged that the economic aid would assist the Portuguese in combating the African insurgents.

During the same year, in December, there was a meeting between President Richard Nixon and French President Georges Pompidou on Terceira, hosted by Prime Minister Marcello Caetano of Portugal;[42] here the United States agreed to devalue the dollar in return for the revaluation of other key world currencies. Then in 1973 the American government used the islands as a base to supply Israel in its war with Egypt. More recently, in June 1974, the soon-to-resign Nixon conferred with Portuguese President António de Spínola, again on Terceira, and promised Lisbon economic aid. The former agreement between Portugal and America had expired in February, but the U.S. soon was operating again in the Azores on an informal basis.

Writing in the summer of 1975 from Lajes, James Reston noted that about fifteen hundred American servicemen remained in the islands, aside from their families. The U.S. military, which received a $13.8 million annual payroll from Washington, much of which was spent for local services, shared its bases on Terceira and Santa Maria with the Portuguese armed forces. Significantly, in justifying the American military presence there from the standpoint of anti-submarine surveillance and aircraft refueling, Reston echoed the arguments set forth by Undersecretary of State for Political Affairs U. Alexis Johnson, testifying on behalf of the 1971 Portuguese-American agreement before the Senate Committee on

Foreign Relations on February 1, 1972.[43] By the mid-1970s the anti-submarine warfare network in the Azores had come to consist of a vast system of underwater sonar surveillance devices connected to the naval listening station at Ponta Delgada, together with a group of Terceira-based anti-submarine planes carrying both detection and destruction equipment. Thanks to this vast apparatus, it currently is possible for the U.S. military to track any Russian submarine in the Atlantic or western Mediterranean within 1,000 miles.

Paralleling the well publicized military activities since World War 2 which we have examined here, there have been other, lesser known efforts designed to keep American-Azorean relations on a friendly basis. The first of these involved island cattle. According to Angelo J. Cerchione, "As late as January of 1950, there still was no veterinarian assigned to Lajes," while "almost all of the food used at the base was imported at considerable expense to palate and pocketbook."[44] But during that year U.S. veterinarians began testing the entire Terceiran cattle population for tuberculosis, and they eventually extended their efforts to all nine islands. Beginning in 1959, too, Captain Anton Kammerlocker, who was also a doctor, used President Dwight Eisenhower's "People-to-People" program as a vehicle for improving the Azorean food supply. At this time there was a shortage of lard, but the importation of the Duroc-Jersey pig helped to solve this problem. Among the other animals, vegetables, and fruits involved in supportive projects were sheep, goats, turkeys, chickens, hybrid corn, pasture grasses, alfalfa, apples, and oranges. Catfish were even imported and stocked in Azorean lakes to supplement the slimness of the winter ocean catch resulting from frequently severe storms. "If the decade of the Sixties can be characterized as one of exuberant experimentation and progress," concludes Cerchione, "the Seventies has made its start as one of program analysis and refinement."[45]

RECENT DEVELOPMENTS

Although whalers from the United States no longer stop in the Azores, other American vessels still do so. Naval ships occasionally dock at Ponta Delgada to refuel and to take on supplies, while American yachtsmen generally prefer the facilities at Horta. In 1971 the roster of U.S.-owned vessels which visited Ponta Delgada included 29 naval ships, 19 commercial craft, and 15 pleasure boats. There has been no serious incident resulting from these contacts, but this absence of friction has been the general pattern throughout the history of Azorean-American relations.

Trade between the United States and the Azores also has continued since World War 2, but on its usual modest scale. In 1950 the chief Azorean exports to the United States included handmade embroideries, canned fish, sperm oil, casein, and dasheens, with a total value of approximately $800,000. On the other hand, during this year America exported to the Azores leaf tobacco, embroidery material, and a few automobile parts.[46] Nearly two decades later, in 1969, American exports to the Azores totalled 24 million escudos ($850,000 U.S.), Azorean exports to America 29 million escudos ($1 million U.S.).

Trans World Airlines still services the islands from the air, and there are Transportes Aeroes Portugueses flights from Lisbon to Boston and New York City, but relatively few Americans come to the Azores today either as tourists or on business. The main exception to this generalization is the large number of immigrant Azoreans to the United States who return to their families in the islands on holidays. American private investment in the Azores remains limited, largely because of the limited resources of the islands, although some U.S. private firms have contemplated buying into the Azorean cattle industry.

The most pronounced American economic impact on the islands, of course, has resulted from the existence of the military base. We have noted that during World War 2 U.S. officials feared that excessive spending by American soldiers might have an inflationary effect on the Azorean economy, but in more recent years local authorities have come to welcome American spending. By 1962 the Lajes airbase was contributing $9 million a year to the economic life of the islands, especially Terceira, where the level of prosperity was higher than on the other eight. Six years later, in 1968, the *New York Times* reported that the United States was injecting $12 million annually into the Terceiran economy. Tad Szulc found more recently that the airbase was Terceira's principal industry, and "I haven't met anyone in the Azores who is agitating for the removal of Lajes."[47]

Despite the increased level of prosperity in the islands, Azoreans continue to emigrate to the United States. A part of this influx was triggered by a series of volcanic eruptions between 1958 and 1964 which displaced approximately 25,000 people from their homes. There had been a major eruption in 1926, as well as earthquakes on Terceira in 1951 and in the city of Ponta Delgada in 1952. Then a submarine volcano coughed up an island near Faial in the fall of 1957, and earthquakes continued for the remainder of the year, with occurrences of volcanic activity in March and August of 1958.

As late as the summer of 1958 Portugal had yet to request aid from any other government, although CARE did fly in food from the United States and blankets from Rome. At that time Democratic Senators John Pastore of Rhode Island and John Kennedy of Massachusetts co-sponsored a bill permitting a number of the surviving victims to enter the United States as non-quota immigrants. In the words of Senator Pastore, whose state like Massachusetts had attracted thousands of Portuguese immigrants, "The bill would make available 1,500 special non-quota immigrant visas for issuance to certain distressed aliens in the Azores and their spouses and minor children, including stepchildren and children adopted prior to July 1, 1953."[48] While Senator Pastore was describing the terrors of Pico Gordo volcano, Senator Kennedy was pointing out that American long had provided asylum for victims of both political persecution and natural disasters. Despite some criticisms, the Azorean relief measure passed Congress on September 2, 1958.

By 1960, though, Senator Pastore was taking the position that the extra Azorean quota of 1,500 was too low, since there were still some 500 families who met the disaster qualifications for admittance. Congress then passed a bill increasing the Azorean quota, which became law on July 14, 1960. Nevertheless, when an earthquake hit São Jorge with full force in February 1964, it became necessary for 20,000 persons to evacuate their homes; at this time Senator Edward Kennedy of Massachusetts took up the cause of Azorean relief earlier advocated by his brother, the late President. The generally cooperative attitude with which the Azoreans received these American expressions of concern over a period of a half-dozen years stands in sharp contrast to the hostile reaction of the Governor of Jamaica a half century earlier when the United States offered assistance in the wake of the great earthquake of 1907.[49] Of course, a number of congressmen from Massachusetts and Rhode Island had praised the Salazar regime year after year on its April anniversary.

With Portuguese emigration to America in recent years on the upswing, Lisbon's hold over its African empire has ended since the coup of 1974. At the time of this writing the Azores remain affiliated with Portugal, where complex revolutionary forces are at work. Whether a Communist takeover on the mainland would lead to the islands declaring their independence is indeed a critical concern of the United

States; many conservative Azoreans are deeply troubled by possible reforms in the islands which might affect their traditional lifestyles. From the American standpoint, with Salazar dead and Caetano no longer prime minister, the future of U.S. military operations in the Azores has become uncertain, contingent upon future developments in Lisbon.

During June 1975 Governor Countinho of the Azores was forced to resign after protestors had accused him of being a Communist sympathizer. Countinho, who was replaced by the civil military commander, charged that the demonstrators were separatists who wished to switch the allegiance of the islands from Portugal to the United States; of the two dozen persons arrested following this demonstration, one (Vitor Cruz) was an employee at the American consulate. That November *Time* reported that the Central Intelligence Agency had established links between the Azorean Liberation Front and the U.S. Department of State, the type of accusation which critics of American foreign policy on more than one occasion have seized upon as proof of U.S. meddling in the internal affairs of other countries. Perhaps moved by independence sentiment in its Atlantic possessions, by the end of the year the Portuguese cabinet had decreed provisional regional autonomy for both the Azores and Madeira. It would seem, therefore, that the harmonious quality which has characterized American relations with the former since the age of the whaler has been tempered with an element of discord.

Further evidence of this growing friction was the cancellation of a proposed trip by the leaders of the new regional government of the Azores to the United States in October 1976, a trip which was to have been financed by a group of American businessmen who had been lobbying in the islands. Disturbed by this "unfriendly intervention," President Ramalho Eanes of Portugal himself reportedly discouraged this abortive visit. It remains to be seen how much more interference of this sort from Portugal the Azoreans will tolerate, since over the centuries they have shown themselves to be a proud and non-subservient people.

7

GREENLAND
The Home of the Weather

"From Greenland's icy mountains to India's coral strands"—
innumerable Americans have sung the hymn, but precious few have
experienced in person the forbidding terrain of the world's largest
island. It was over a millennium ago that ships from Iceland first
sighted Greenland; beginning in 982, Eric the Red spent three years
on the island's southern coast near Julianehaab. It was Eric who
named the island "Greenland" in an attempt to attract prospective
settlers. In 986 fourteen ships with colonists arrived, and a republic was established shortly thereafter. Three centuries later, in
1261, the republic swore its allegiance to the king of Norway, eight
decades before the latter nation united with Denmark.

A series of developments, however, brought the European colonization of Greenland to an end during the fifteenth century. Among
these were the trading policies forced upon the kings of Norway by
the merchants of the Hanseatic League, and the deterioration in climate of Greenland itself which made cattle breeding more difficult.
In 1410 the last boat of settlers returned to Norway from the island. Although Icelandic fishermen may have continued to visit it
for the remainder of the century, Greenland remained unsettled by
Europeans for over two hundred years. But it was by no means
totally forgotten by them.

The history of modern Greenland began in 1721, when the Danish-
Norwegian missionary Hans Egede founded a settlement near Godthaab,
on the southwestern coast. (Godthaab itself was founded seven years

later, in 1728.) A half-century later, in 1774, the state took over the island's trade. But when Norway and Denmark dissolved their union in 1805, the latter kept Greenland. At this time knowledge of this icy domain remained almost totally limited to the southern half of the island.

EARLY U.S. INTEREST

American contacts with Greenland apparently began as early as 1732, at which time whaling ships visited Davis Strait in search of whales. Unfortunately for the whalers, after 1741 they were molested by French and Spanish privateers. Then during the following century explorers from the United States were active in the area. Between 1853 and 1855 Dr. Elisha Kane visited northwestern Greenland and Grinnell Land, reaching the highest latitude attained to that date by a sailing ship. On the island itself, in 1860-61 Dr. Isaac Hayes penetrated the interior ice to a depth of 40 miles at Port Foulke.

Back in Washington the first prominent Americans to take a real interest in Greenland were two expansionists, Secretary of State William Henry Seward and Robert J. Walker. The latter had previously advocated the annexation of Texas, Mexico, Alaska, St. Thomas, and Canada; when Seward was making an abortive attempt to purchase the Danish West Indies, Walker suggested to him that he might also try to obtain Iceland and Greenland. (Denmark, it might be noted, never has wanted even to discuss the possible sale of the latter.) When asked by Seward for further information, Walker turned to Professor Benjamin Pierce, the superintendent of the United States Coast Survey, who drafted a 72-page report. In his cover letter Walker made reference to Greenland's fisheries, coal, "inexhaustible" cryolite deposits, and harbors, as well as its possible role as a link in an independent line of interoceanic telegraph. From the standpoint of expansion, he also noted that were Greenland to become American, the likelihood of Canada joining the United States would increase.

Congress, which failed to approve the purchase of the Danish West Indies at this time, was far less enthusiastic. When Republican Representative C. C. Washburn of Wisconsin opposed an appropriation for the purchase of Alaska in 1868, his remark that a treaty was then being negotiated with Denmark for the purchase of Greenland brought laughter from some of the other members. The nay-sayers included Republican Representative Benjamin Butler of Massachusetts, who made a sneering reference to "one insane enough to buy the earthquakes in St. Thomas and icefields in Greenland," and Republican Representative Thomas Williams of Pennsylvania, who sarcastically referred to the great need for acquiring the glaciers of Greenland and geysers of Iceland.[1] Republican Representative Shelby M. Cullom of Illinois was a bit more sympathetic, but even he suggested that the national debt should be reduced before additional territory was added to the Union.

At the time of the Spanish-American War and the acquisition of an overseas empire, there was no revival of the drive to annex Greenland, but Republican Senator Henry Cabot Lodge of Massachusetts did propose to President Theodore Roosevelt in 1905 that he might reopen negotiations with Denmark relative to the island. T.R., however, was concerned at the time with numerous other questions which he regarded as more important.[2] Then in 1910 Maurice Francis Egan, the American minister to Denmark, proposed to the State Department on September 20 a complicated transaction which featured a swap of the Danish West Indies and Greenland for Mindanao, which Denmark in turn would trade to Germany for Northern Schleswig.[3] In writing departmental officials in Washington five years later, Egan noted that three days after he had sent his original letter he had received a memorial from a number of distinguished Danes endorsing this project. Although nothing came of his fanciful scheme, the Germans doubtless would have welcomed the opportunity to establish a foothold in the Philippines.

Still another prominent American to advocate the annexation of Greenland by the United States was the explorer Robert E. Peary, some of whose feats we shall examine shortly. In 1916 Peary wrote an article in which he observed that "geographically, Greenland belongs to North America and the Western Hemisphere, over which we have formally declared a sphere of influence by our Monroe Doctrine. Its possession by us will be in line with the Monroe Doctrine. . . ."[4] Elsewhere in the article Peary referred to such mineral resources of the island as cryolite, coal, graphite, and mica, as well as to the glacial streams which might be employed to produce electrical energy; comparing it with Alaska, he suggested that the island might indeed prove a sound and valuable investment.

The mining of low grade coal had begun on Disko Island as early as 1774, but it was the extraction of cryolite which eventually became the focal point of Greenland's mining industry. Cryolite is a sodium-aluminum fluoride which looks like hard-packed snow, and which first came to the attention of Danish officials just before 1800.

When the Danish government held an exhibition of Eskimo tools and artifacts from Greenland at Copenhagen in 1850, scientists noted that some of the stone sinkers for their nets were made from a white, translucent mineral: cryolite. The following year an investigating team from Denmark found a large deposit of the rare and valuable mineral at Ivigtut in southern Greenland; Eskimo fishermen long had been using blocks of cryolite for the foundation of their tents. By 1856 the first shipment of the mineral from Greenland to Denmark had taken place, and a plant for the production of soda was set up in Copenhagen. Then in 1865 the Pennsylvania Salt Manufacturing Company of Natrona signed a contract for the delivery of two-thirds of all the cryolite produced on the island. It was also in that year that the newly founded Kryolith Mine-og Handelsselskabet obtained a monopoly over the mining of the rare and valuable mineral in Greenland.

Between 1882 and 1903 more cryolite was transported to the United States each year than to Denmark, but between the latter date and the end of the first World War the reverse was true. The highest total production for any year during this period was in 1897, when over 13,000 tons of the mineral were mined. In that year over 10,000 tons were shipped to America, but in 1910 none was sent there at all; during World War 1, however, there was a marked increase in shipments to the United States. By this time cryolite was being used in making the opaque glaze for enameling glassware, and also was being employed in fluxes for reducing aluminum and in making white cement.[5]

PEARY'S EXPLORATIONS

Long before the close of the nineteenth century explorers from a number of countries had been active in Greenland. During the decade of the 1880s, for example, Baron Adolf Erik Nordenskiöld penetrated the interior of the island from Disko Island in the west, while in 1888 Fridtjof Nansen crossed the southern part of Greenland from the east coast.[6] But unquestionably the leading American explorer of the island was Robert E. Peary, who climaxed his career by becoming the first man to reach the North Pole on April 6, 1909. It was in tropical Nicaragua that Peary first read Nordenskiöld's book *Greenland;* his imagination fired, he made eight trips to the Arctic between 1886 and 1908. In attempting to account for Peary's successes, the writer Jeannette Mirsky has observed that "among Arctic explorers his is a unique nature, a paradoxical combination of forethought and prudence with dash and recklessness, of organizing ability with tremendous physical endurance and patience."[7] Of especial significance, too, is the fact that Peary not only employed Eskimos whenever possible but also copied their life and methods.

It was in 1886 that Peary first penetrated the interior of Greenland, starting inland just south of Disko Island. Fearful of supernatural beings, the natives refused to accompany him out on the ice cap, as they had also refused to accompany Nordenskiöld in 1870, but with one companion he was able to cross it for 110 miles, attaining an elevation of 7,500 feet above sea level. No other explorer had penetrated the interior to such a depth; to Peary the great white expanse was an imperial highway to the eastern coast.

In 1892 and 1895 Peary made double transections of North Greenland, becoming the first man ever to cross the island north of the Arctic Circle. Independence Bay was his eastern terminus on both occasions. Only a single European, Eivind Astrup, accompanied Peary on his first crossing by sledge; apart from delineating the northern limits of the main ice cap, Peary observed the rapid convergence of Greenland's shores north of the 78th parallel, as well as noting those wind patterns technically known as the glacial anticyclone. Peary's defiance of his environment was further manifested by the birth of a daughter, the "Snow Baby," at his headquarters on the island during the fall of 1893. An attempted expedition into the interior which departed in March 1894 had to turn back after a month, but in April 1895 Peary set out on his second successful double transection of North Greenland. It was only through forced marches and a fortunate absence of protracted storms on the great ice cap that Peary, two companions, and one surviving dog managed to stagger back to the home moraine on June 25. This feat brings to mind a remark by Christiansen, one of Nansen's men: "Good Lord, to think of people being so cruel to themselves as to go in for this sort of thing."[8]

Although Peary hardly was able to bring back to the United States fragments of the great ice cap as souvenirs, he did excavate the world's largest known meteorite, Ahnighito, and transport it to America. Europeans first learned of the existence of an "iron mountain" in Greenland during 1818 when John Ross came upon the Eskimos of Smith Sound. Subsequent Danish, Swedish, and British expeditions failed in their attempt to find it, but Peary and Hugh J. Lee located the "iron mountain" with the assistance of an Eskimo guide on May 27, 1894.

Having made two double transections of Greenland and having brought the largest meteorite known to man back to America, in 1898 Peary announced his law of the slope winds which he had arrived at some years earlier. The general thesis underlying this law was that the winds above the inland ice invariably blow in the same general direction as the slope. Two years later Peary thought that he had proved the insularity of Greenland by making a 600-mile sledge journey around the polar end; he called the northernmost point Cape Morris K. Jesup in honor of his chief patron.[9] It was also at this time that Peary concluded that the way to the North Pole was not via Greenland, since ice fields constantly sweep around the northern end of the island.

If Peary was the greatest Arctic explorer, he was not without his faults, and other (including Knud Rasmussen and Lauge Koch) have more recently added to our knowledge of Greenland. To quote Jeannette Mirsky, "No other great Arctic explorer was guilty of such inaccuracies as Peary. He was not inaccurate on purpose; it is rather that he failed to distinguish between ice-covered water and ice-covered land, rather than misjudged what he saw."[10] But Peary did survive, while other gifted explorers met their death in the frozen North.

Nevertheless, there were those of lesser caliber who blundered and lived to tell about it, including Professor Chamberlain of Chicago and Dr. Cook of Brooklyn. In June 1894 Chamberlain and Cook departed for Greenland on the steamer *Miranda* without receiving the prior approval of the Danish government, only to have their vessel spring a leak when leaving the colony of Sukkertoppen near Godthaab with fifty persons aboard. This incident led to an exchange of correspondence between Washington and Copenhagen; Danish officials pointed out that a royal ordinance of March 18, 1776, had forbidden all persons, whether Danes or foreigners, to dock at Greenland without advance permission except in the case of an emergency.[11] Despite Chamberlain and Cook's near disaster, Peary was able to obtain permission for his summer 1895 expedition with little difficulty.

DANISH SOVEREIGNTY FROM 1916

Successful as he was in charting the icy wastes of this island, Peary failed to prevent the United States from surrendering all possible rights in Greenland in 1916 at the time when America finally obtained the Danish West Indies. (It will be recalled that a century before the

United States had abandoned its far more substantial claims to Texas in connection with the purchase of Florida from Spain.) Another critic of the surrender of possible American rights in Greenland was the *Outlook,* which observed on September 27, 1916, that Greenland should be of great value to the United States.

During the early stages of the 1916 negotiations, Secretary of State Robert Lansing was willing to recognize Danish sovereignty over the island, provided that Denmark admitted "the principle of equal opportunity in whatever concerns the commerce and industry of all nations."[12] Nevertheless, the Danish negotiators demanded that the United States agree not to object to Denmark extending its political and economic interests over the entire island; thus there was to be no economic Open Door for America there. When Acting Secretary of State Frank Polk placed the Danish West Indies convention before President Woodrow Wilson for his approval on August 7, 1916, he included a separate declaration from Secretary of State Robert Lansing recognizing total Danish political and economic sovereignty over Greenland. The government of Denmark also requested that the terms of the convention be withheld from the public until both U.S. and Danish officials agreed to promulgate them.

The question of total Danish control over Greenland was complicated further four years later by the British request that, in return for their recognition of this, Denmark grant to England the right of preemption in the event that Denmark should decide to dispose of the frigid island. British authorities brought up the proximity of Greenland to Canada in this connection. But in the meanwhile the U.S. Department of State had informed London that owing to the importance of its geographical position, America was not disposed to recognize the right of preemption of a third party to Greenland. When Secretary of State Charles Evans Hughes advised Danish authorities to this effect on August 3, 1921, the Danish minister told him that Denmark neither had any desire to transfer the island to another nation nor had extended the right of preemption to a third party.

Denmark also asserted its sovereignty over all of Greenland during the same year. As late as 1916 it had only governed the western coast between Cape Farewell and 74° 30' north, and the trading station of Angmagssalik on the eastern coast, although in 1910 Knud Rasmussen did set up a private station at Thule. One result of this extension of authority was a dispute with Norway, with which Denmark had been united until 1814, over hunting and sealing rights in the uncolonized areas along the eastern coast. This protracted argument reached its climax in 1931, when Norwegian hunters acting on their own occupied the area between 71° and 75° in the name of the king. Authorities back in Oslo later approved this seizure after much soul searching. Two years later, however, the International Court of Justice at the Hague found the Norwegian occupation invalid; among those testifying on behalf of Denmark was the noted Greenland explorer Robert A. Bartlett, who cabled the Hague questioning whether modern Norwegians had ever been in Greenland.

During the decades between the two world wars an important change took place in the economy of the island which had a significant impact on its international trade. Prior to World War 1 seal hunting was a leading pursuit of many Greenlanders, but a change in climate accompanied by overintensive hunting led to its eventual decline. Instead, more and more of the inhabitants turned their attention to fishing for cod, which soon became a major export of the island as their number increased with the change in climate. Cryolite mining, too, continued as before, thriving in the decade following World War 1.

At late as 1936 Greenlandic exports to the United States totalled only $572,000, while imports from America amounted to a mere $1,476. Most of the former consisted of cryolite; the black cryolite went to the United States and Canada, and the white to Denmark. Then in 1939 the government of Denmark and private interests jointly set up a stock company to operate the mine at Ivigtut when the concession ran out. This proved to be a fundamental change, since the government took over half the shares and appointed the president of the company; from that time on half the yearly dividend went to the government to help cover the deficit incurred in administering the remainder of Greenland.

FLYERS AND SCIENTISTS

The airplane came to Greenland during the inter-war years. Contrary to what one might suppose, flying conditions are good on the average for the entire year in the northern two-thirds of Greenland, but progressively deteriorate as one approaches the southern tip. In addition, the presence of icebergs and ice fragments in the surrounding waters makes the use of flying boats anywhere difficult. Thus, it was in a land-based plane that Commander Richard Byrd flew 40 miles inland over the ice cap in 1925; his report that the ice field was as level and smooth as a ballroom floor stimulated further efforts. Three years later, in 1928, Bert R. J. Hassell and Parker Cramer received permission to fly over Greenland by linking their efforts with those of the third University of Michigan expedition. Plagued by a lack of fuel, they were forced to make a landing on the inland ice 75 miles from the airfield near Camp Lloyd, where they were rescued thanks to information provided by Eskimos.

A second attempt by Cramer, Robert Wood, and Robert Gast to cross the island in the summer of 1929 failed before the aviators had even reached Greenland, but finally in 1931 Cramer and Oliver L. Paquette of the Canadian government radio service flew across the island, landing at Angmassalik. But triumph was to turn to tragedy shortly thereafter; following stops at Reykjavik in Iceland and Lerwick in the Orkneys, their plane went down in the North Sea during a bad storm, with both men losing their lives.[13] More fortunate was the German flyer Wolfgang von Gronau, who during the same year crossed Greenland from Scoresby Sound on the east central coast to Sukkertoppen, surviving his aerial transection of the island.

As early as the abortive Hassell-Cramer flight of 1928, Pan American Airways had begun investigating a possible northern route to Europe, in the process hiring Dr. Vilhjalmur Stefansson as its advisor for northern operations. In 1939 its exploratory permit for Greenland aviation lapsed, but during the prior decade it had contributed to four land expeditions, as well as financed a flight by Charles and Anne Morrow Lindbergh in 1933. The land expedition of 1935–36 maintained an aeronautical observer at Godthaab, who noted that flying boats could have landed on the surrounding water on any day of the winter.[14] Turning to the Lindberghs, in 1933 they discovered by flying along the western and eastern coats and crossing the interior ice twice that the mountains at Scoresby Sound extended 100 miles into the interior, not 30 as was previously thought.

While Cramer, von Gronau, and Lindbergh were charting the island's icy wastes from the skies, a series of expeditions sponsored by the University of Michigan, and later by the Smithsonian Institution, were active on both land and sea. Among the achievements of the five University of Michigan expeditions of 1926–33 was the discovery that the ceiling of the outblowing winds near the western border of the inland ice was approximately 2 miles. In this connection, scientists erected four aerological stations at various points in West Greenland: Ivigtut (61° N), Mount Evans ($67^\circ 30'$), Camp Scott (73°), and Peary Lodge ($74^\circ 15'$); each of these stations operated for at least a year, with that at Mount Evans functioning for two. A wireless station also was set up at the latter location, and on May 6, 1929, clear and loud radio communication was established between Mount Evans and Little America in Antarctica.[15] Then in the summer of 1932

Professor Ralph L. Belknap erected a memorial shaft in honor of Robert E. Peary at Cape York.

In contrast, the six Smithsonian Institution expeditions which visited Greenland between 1935 and 1940 focused their efforts on bringing back specimens of wild life. Typically productive was number six, which sailed within 578 miles of the North Pole and brought back four walrus pups for the New York Zoo, a polar bear named Carmichael for the Philadelphia Zoo, and a collection of mosses for Vassar College. With World War 2 now underway, Danish authorities nevertheless granted to the expedition permission to land in Greenland.

THE DANISH-AMERICAN AGREEMENT

In September 1939 the German dictator Adolf Hitler unleashed the onslaught on Poland which began World War 2. The Germans had already begun to display an interest in Greenland, and meteorologists from there had visited the island in 1938. Prior to their seizure of Norway, moreover, the Nazis had dangled Greenland, Iceland, and the Faeroes before collaborationist Vidkun Quisling as a tradeoff for Norse non-resistance to a German occupation.

American interest in Greenland was most openly evident during 1939 in the efforts of Farmer-Labor Senator Ernest Lundeen of Minnesota, who introduced resolutions on April 19 of that year calling for the annexation of Greenland, Curaçao, and Netherlands Guiana. Lundeen followed up this action by making a long speech on the floor of the Senate on June 15 advocating the purchase of Greenland. A leading critic of this scheme was Secretary of War Harry Woodring, who took the position that the island was too far from any practicable sea or air routes to the United States. That August the Danish minister for foreign affairs, in response to an American inquiry, asserted that the jurisdiction of the U.S. consul general at Copenhagen did not extend over Greenland.

Woodring's opinion to the contrary, there is little question but that the coming of the air age had enhanced the strategic importance of Greenland for the United States, as well as for the other World War 2 combatants. Although the island is often looked upon as a part of the Western Hemisphere, it is in fact only 130 miles distant from Iceland at one point; not only does it lie in the path of the shortest air route between North America and Europe, but it also is situated immediately north of the shortest steamship lanes between the two hemispheres.

Equally important, meteorological stations there are able to forecast weather conditions for both Europe and North America, which data is vital to both strategic military planning and to air and sea transportation. Thus, Greenland on the eve of World War 2 was by no means of interest to the United States only because it produced cryolite.

On March 17, 1940, a study group of the Council on Foreign Relations warned that Germany might overrun Denmark and acquire Greenland. On April 9 the possibility became a reality, as the Nazi military juggernaut moved north. When Danish Foreign Minister Henrik de Kauffmann met with President Franklin Roosevelt on the day following the German invasion, on leaving the conference de Kauffmann observed that he and F.D.R. were of the opinion that the island was a part of the American continent. Roosevelt confirmed this at a later press conference, but became evasive when queried as to the relationship of the Monroe Doctrine to Greenland. Then on April 12 Secretary of State Cordell Hull met with the British ambassador, Lord Lothian, who was reported later to have stated publicly that Great Britain or Canada would not occupy Greenland unless the latter was threatened by Germany. Hidden from public view at the time was the fact that on the day that the Germans had occupied Denmark, Undersecretary of State Sumner Welles had received a memorandum prepared in the State Department; this paper had concluded that geographically the island was a part of the Western Hemisphere.

The following day, April 13, the *Washington Times-Herald* published an editorial "Greenland, Denmark, and the United States: Our 'Keep Out' Sign," in which it observed that ". . . the United States had better lay plans for assuming protection of Greenland until and unless Denmark regains enough independence to claim it back."[16] On the floor of Congress five days later isolationist Republican Representative Hamilton Fish of New York introduced a resolution calling for the purchase of Greenland for $40 million, but in an accompanying speech adopted a hands-off approach towards Iceland. F.D.R. declined to comment on Fish's proposal, but did announce to a press conference that the American Red Cross would take care of the inhabitants of Greenland in the event that supplies were cut off as a result of war.

Despite Lord Lothian's April 12 conversation with Secretary of State Hull, on April 19 James Clement Dunn, the adviser on political relations to the secretary of state, saw fit to inform the Canadian foreign minister that the American government was not favorably disposed to its Canadian counterpart's sending a small defense force to Greenland. Yet the United States was not considering an American occupation of the island, as Secretary of State Cordell Hull informed Danish Foreign Minister de Kauffmann on the same day. In the words of the former, "The Government has been opposing protectorates generally, chiefly because nations engaged in military conquest are seizing smaller nations under the pretext that they are merely protecting them, whereas their real purpose is permanent domination."[17]

On April 24 Hugh S. Cumming, Jr., of the State Department's Division of European Affairs wrote a memorandum, in which he concluded that the director of the Greenland Administration residing in Copenhagen was no longer able to function properly as a result of the German military occupation of Denmark. As a result, he took the position that de facto authority over the island now rested with the resident commissioners (or governors) of North Greenland and South Greenland. Two days later Cordell Hull notified Henrik de Kauffmann that the United States temporarily wished to set up a consulate in Greenland, and de Kauffmann replied on the twenty-eighth that he was amenable to this proposal, having consulted the two governors.

Within a week, on May 3, the local government of Greenland requested American protection, making a temporary declaration of independence at this time. By May 18 the Navy Department had begun to formulate a minimum defense program for Ivigtut, and to investigate the possibility of selling guns and equipment to the authorities in Greenland at a nominal cost. Governor Aksel Svane of South Greenland, however, was not satisfied with the mere acquisition of military equipment from the United States. He thus queried American Consul James K. Penfield at Godthaab on May 24 as to whether it would be feasible to station an American military detachment at Ivigtut, or possibly have an armed Coast Guard vessel patrol the waters. (The new central administration had been placed at Godthaab, because ships could use the port facilities there all year round.)

The American consulate at Godthaab was officially opened on May 25.[18] On May 27 the governor of North Greenland, Eske Brun, authorized Penfield and Vice Consul George L. West to perform consular services there, although his abovementioned counterpart in South Greenland did not follow suit until July 1. By this time a Canadian consulate also had been established on the island. Shortly after Penfield's arrival, on June 3, the defense-conscious Brun and Svane requested the American government to land U.S. troops at Ivigtut as soon as possible. Cordell Hull's reply dated June 5 noted the American reluctance as a neutral to station military personnel in Greenland, except under exceptional circumstances.

On July 9 the governor of North Greenland and a number of other Danish officials arrived in the United States to discuss economic matters, while during the same month the U.S. Coast Guard vessel *Campbell* landed at Ivigtut with a shipment of guns and ammunition. During the following month the American government sent a military officer on a fruitless reconnaissance flight to identify possible airfield sites; on August 17 the Danish government in Copenhagen thanked its U.S. counterpart for aiding the population of the island by providing it with foodstuffs and other necessities.[19] Then on September 23 officials in the State Department reaffirmed to the British, Canadian, and Norwegian governments that the United States "could not acquiesce in any political, military, or naval steps which constituted a permanent occupation or change in the status of Greenland."[20]

While the American government was warning other countries to keep "hands off" with respect to Greenland, it could hardly be said that it was arming the islanders to the teeth. When the Coast Guard vessel *Northland* visited Ivigtut in October, it discovered that a three-inch anti-aircraft gun which the American government had sent there earlier still lay unassembled, since the Greenlanders lacked the technical knowledge to put it together. Back in Washington, on October 29, 1940, President Franklin Roosevelt issued a proclamation suspending tonnage duties with respect to the island. The following month Governor Aksel Svane of South Greenland arrived for talks, accompanied by the American Consul Penfield, while Governor Eske Brun of North Greenland took up residence in Godthaab, the new capital. Adopting a posture of neutrality for the island, Svane came out against the formal censorship of mail, but advocated the monitoring of radio messages.[21] Neither censorship nor immigration, though, proved to be much of a problem during the war years that followed, at least as far as Greenlandic-American relations were concerned.

Although American troops had yet to arrive on the scene, by December 18 a total of fifteen U.S. citizens had been employed by the Ivigtut Mine Company to perform ordinary police duties. The following month the Canadian government asked officials in Washington either to clarify their plans or else to allow Canada to take over the defense of Greenland; the United States, however, would not go along. Then on January 7, 1941 at a news conference F.D.R. laughed off a Reuters report out of Stockholm that American troops were in the process of occupying Greenland: "New one on me! must have been while I was asleep."[22]

Nevertheless, it was becoming apparent to the U.S. government by this time that it was necessary to act with respect to Greenland in the immediate future. Assistant Secretary of State Adolf A. Berle had adopted the position by February 1 that the island, as a part of the Western Hemisphere, was under the protective umbrella of the Monroe Doctrine; as a result, America could not permit belligerent activity in and around Greenland. (As noted above, F.D.R. took an evasive stance on the Monroe Doctrine and Greenland as late as April.) By mid-February the United States had begun to negotiate with the Danish foreign minister, Henrik de Kauffmann. Then on March 5 Berle completed the basis for a Danish-American understanding on the island, under which the American government would finance and construct the base facilities there itself. Three weeks later, on March 28, Berle presented de Kauffmann with the completed draft of an agreement, which the latter substantially accepted on April 4 before communicating its contents to the governors of North and South Greenland.

Even before then, in late March, the South Greenland Survey Party had arrived on March 31 from the United States on the Coast Guard vessel *Cayuaga*. To quote the report of Commander William Sinton, "The Greenland Government made available boats and radio facilities as well as local knowledge, and local Greenland officials in every place visited were both hospitable and helpful."[23] Among the major tasks of this expedition were to locate appropriate sites for air bases, radio facilities, and meteorological stations, as well as gather hydrographic information on the east coast. It arrived none too soon, since on March 25 the German government had issued a new decree which extended the war zone as far as the east coast of Greenland.

After allocating $5 million for the construction of aviation bases in Greenland on April 5, on April 9 President Franklin Roosevelt joined Danish Minister de Kauffmann in signing the final version of the joint agreement.[24] This action was made public on the following day, the same day that Congress approved as Public Law 32 the Pittman-Bloom Joint Resolution which had been introduced in June 1940. This measure forbade the recognition by the United States of the transfer of parts of the Western Hemisphere from one non-American power to another, thus opposing in advance the possible seizure of Greenland by the Nazis. Also on the same day there was a lengthy conference at the White House attended by the war cabinet and Harry Hopkins, at which F.D.R. extended the neutrality zone boundaries to longitude 25° west; this new line encompassed within its protective walls most of Greenland, which those present agreed to defend in its entirety.

The reaction from Copenhagen to the signing of this understanding was prompt and negative. On April 12 Danish Foreign Minister Eric Scavenius protested to Washington, in the process recalling Minister de Kauffmann who after all had perhaps acted arbitrarily in assuming so much authority with respect to Greenland. This, however, was only the response of the Nazi-dominated government; on April 13 Chargé Perkins reported from Copenhagen that the reaction of the Danish people in general was one of relief and satisfaction. It later was brought out at the post-war Nuremberg war crimes trials that Adolf Hitler and Foreign Minister Joachim von Ribbentrop were so incensed by the agreement that they demanded that de Kauffmann be tried for high treason.[25] On the other hand, Latin America remained complacent, even though the move might siphon off U.S. troops from the Southern Hemisphere. As for Greenland itself, Consul Penfield reported on April 12 that "neither Governor appears to find serious fault with the substance of the agreement," but that "both Governors were understandably greatly disturbed and resentful over the ultimatum-like manner in which the agreement was presented to them." Svane, who had been less favorably disposed than Brun to the landing of American troops at Ivigtut the previous June, was highly critical of de Kauffmann, who felt that the understanding was the only alternative to the occupation of the island by a belligerent power, Great Britain. It might be added that the governors of Greenland had the authority to act in emergencies under the 1925 law for the administering of the island.

Numerous other aspects of this understanding also merit commentary. In the first place, it took the form of an executive agreement rather than that of a treaty, not to preserve secrecy or to bypass the Senate, but because the Danish parliament never would have approved it. Second, the 1940 Act of Havana is referred to in both the preamble and article 1, although there was no consultation during the formulation of the agreement with any of the Latin American republics. It also differs from its companion agreement with Iceland, in that Franklin Roosevelt informed Congress on July 7, 1941, that following the termination of the present international emergency all American military forces would be withdrawn from that island, while the agreement with Greenland left the door open for future negotiations. But perhaps most important of all, there was some doubt raised in scholarly quarters as to the legal validity of the Greenland understanding. To quote Herbert W. Briggs:

> There is no evidence that the Danish Government was repudiating a validly binding international agreement. Their position (as soon

as they learned of it) was that the agreement was void *ab initio* because it was made by their acknowledged representative in Washington "without authorization" and "contrary to the constitution." The Danish Government may very well have been acting under duress in pointing out that the agreement was invalid *ab initio*, but this duress would not make an invalid agreement valid.[26]

THE U.S. IN GREENLAND DURING WORLD WAR 2

In signing this understanding the United States took a serious risk, in that it established a precedent for the Japanese to undertake a protective occupation of the Dutch East Indies.[27] But apart from its side effects, the agreement almost at once began to pose problems for Danish and American officials; one of the most serious of these was the extent to which there would be contacts between Greenlanders and U.S. military personnel. On April 26 Governor Svane informed the American consulate that natives could not be employed as workers on U.S. defense projects. Then two days later Cordell Hull pointed out to Secretary of the Navy Frank Knox that there was a dread in Greenland of contacts of any kind, since not only were the natives not immunized against European and American diseases but they also were inexperienced in even ordinary trading operations.[28] It was under such trying conditions that the American government successfully attempted during April to discourage a German lodgment at Scoresby Sound halfway up the eastern coast of Greenland.

On April 19 the American government had sent a message to the king of Denmark in which it pointed out that since the island was a part of the Western Hemisphere, the United States could not permit Denmark to transfer control of it to another European power. It, moreover, was obliged "to take steps which are tantamount to holding Greenland in trust for Denmark until such time as the Royal Danish Government ceases to be subject to decrees on the part of an occupying nation and full Danish control over Greenland may be restored."[29] On May 17 Danish officials in Copenhagen suggested that another neutral state having diplomatic representatives in Washington might represent Danish interests there, should a Danish chargé be inacceptable, only to have Cordell Hull reject this scheme on June 3. From that time onwards nothing could halt the disintegration of formal Danish-American relations, since the American government continued to deal with de Kauffmann. Finally on June 27 the chargé in Denmark, Perkins, notified Hull that the minister for foreign affairs had requested that all American consular officials leave Denmark by July 15.[30]

Although the diplomatic impasse between the United States and Denmark was reaching the point of no return, American military activity in Greenland was on the increase. Since the navy lacked vessels suited for use in its icy waters, on May 7 President Franklin Roosevelt orally authorized the transfer of the oceanic functions of the Coast Guard to the navy. Then at the beginning of June he endorsed a plan for the defense of Greenland; by the middle of the month American troops had begun to occupy the island. On June 19 an army engineer construction force departed from the United States to begin work on military airfields there. This force upon its arrival on July 6 proceeded to Narssarssuaq, 775 miles from both Goose Bay in Labrador and Reykjavik in Iceland. Narssarssuaq, which in Greenlandic means the great plain, lies directly across the fjord from the site of Eric the Red's old farm "Brattahlid," and the ruins of the oldest Catholic church in the Western Hemisphere.

While the work which had commenced on the Narssarssuaq base (Bluie West 1) proceeded on through the fall and winter, in late September construction began on another base, at Søndre Strømfjord (Bluie West 8) further up the west coast just north of the Arctic Circle. This was commanded by the colorful Norse-born Bernt Balchen, who at an earlier date had been Admiral Richard Byrd's chief South Pole pilot. During 1941 Captain Elliot Roosevelt and others had attempted without success to locate a site for a landing field on the eastern coast of the island, but on September 14 the Coast Guard cutter *Northland* did destroy a German radio station on the shores of a small bay in northeastern Greenland. Two days earlier Task Force 2 had captured the little Norwegian sealer *Buskø* in Mackenzie Bay, loaded with modern radio equipment for the Nazis; the *Bear* escorted the *Buskø* back to the United States afterwards. Since the Japanese attack on Pearl Harbor did not take place for another two months, it might be said that these now largely forgotten episodes marked the first American military action during World War 2.

The U.S. navy also became increasingly active in Greenland during this period. On November 28, 1941, a Chief of Naval Operations basic objective authorized various types of construction at Narssarssuaq and in the vicinity of Ivigtut. Among the major projects were a naval operating facility at Grønnedal, a naval facility at Narssarssuaq, a naval radio station at Gamatron, and a loran project at Frederiksdal. Although perhaps overshadowed by the more publicized airbases, these naval facilities also made a significant contribution to the war effort.

During the summer of 1942 a satisfactory site for an east coast airbase was finally located at Angmagssalik, and the construction of a landing strip (Bluie East 2) was finished in the fall. With the increasing number of flights across the island as a result of the war, it was inevitable that a plane would crash on the icecap sooner or later. Sometimes the rescues were successful, as the one which *Time* wrote up on August 17 under the caption "Balchen at Work"; other less publicized attempts at times resulted in the deaths of the rescuers themselves.

Then on June 23 Headquarters AAF issued a directive which provided for the setting up of an expedition to establish weather stations in the interior of Greenland. Task Force 4998-A began operations that month in the Comanche Bay area, continuing these until August 1, 1944; it later returned to the United States in January 1945. Admittedly, there was no wide-scale exploration of the ice cap, and not one of the three projected inland stations was set up, but the task force did make an extensive analysis of the problems connected with exploration, as well as pave the way for Project Snowman (1947) and Mint Julep (1953).[31] (These will be described in detail later.)

From July 1942 through October 1943 the focal point of Greenlandic-American diplomatic relations was the degree of contact to be permitted between the natives and the U.S. military. On July 11, 1942, Eske Brun requested that shore leaves be restricted to the colonies, and on November 21, 1942, Headquarters Greenland Base Command issued general order number 39 placing all native settlements except colonies off limits to army and navy personnel. The thirteen colonies were Julianehaab, Frederikshaab, Godthaab, Sukkertoppen, Holsteinsborg, Egedesminde, Godhavn, Christianshaab, Jakobshavn, Umanak, Upernavik, Angmagssalik, and Scoresby Sound. This order was formally communicated to the Greenland Administration on January 6, 1943 for its information.

Between that date and September 21 the U.S. consulate at Godthaab received a mere dozen complaints of alleged violations of no. 39. A typical incident occurred during the summer of 1943, when the U.S.S. *Arundel* admitted some natives aboard at Holsteinsborg and traded cigarettes with them. Despite this general adherence, on September 21 Eske Brun wrote a letter to the American consul, John B. Ocheltree, in which he referred to smuggling on a large scale and the apparent existence of prostitution. Ocheltree's retort was that he could not accept such sweeping assertions as accurate, but in mid-October the Greenland base commander, Colonel A. D. Smith, issued orders placing all settlements on the island off limits to U.S. military personnel, while the commander of the Greenland patrol, Admiral Edward H. Smith, prohibited future shore leave at Greenland settlements.[32]

One of the happier episodes in Greenlandic-American relations during this period took place in February 1943, when two hundred natives who had been isolated for two years were visited by a U.S. Coast Guard relief mission. They expressed their appreciation by sending a haunch of muskox to F.D.R. Back in the United States, at the American Bar Association convention at Chicago, Democratic Representative Jennings Randolph of West Virginia recommended on August 25 that America should acquire Greenland from Denmark for its strategic value and for its importance in global aviation. (Randolph was the national councillor of the National Aeronautic Association.)[33] Then three days later the Danish government resigned, and German troops entered Copenhagen and took over the most important administrative posts of the city.

The Nazis in Greenland fared less well than their Danish counterparts, thanks to the efforts of Bernt Balchen and others. On March 24 a German task force attacked Danish radio facilities on the eastern coast north of Scoresby Sound, later capturing two Danes on its way back to a Sabine Island hideout. But one of the prisoners managed to escape, reaching the U.S. patrol station at Scoresby Sound in May with a German captive; by the middle of the month a counterattack against the Nazis had been mounted by the American military. When a U.S. air force contingent led by Balchen reached Eskimonaes on May 14, the attackers found that it already had been gutted by the Germans, but Balchen ordered that additional bombs be dropped anyway.

Sabine Island was a different story. It was the northernmost bombing mission yet undertaken by the United States, as well as Balchen's first personal confrontation with the Nazis. When his unit attacked Sabine Island on May 25, there was fierce resistance on the part of the Germans, but Balchen nevertheless knocked out both the buildings and a ship with its anti-aircraft defenses.[34] Captain Carl C. von Paulsen later entered the Sabine Island hideout by sea, capturing a phonograph-playing, hand-grenade-carrying Nazi doctor without a struggle.

As of October 1943 there were 5,608 U.S. military personnel in Greenland. By December all the contractor's work on the American military facilities was finished; the construction there was done entirely by private firms, working under U.S. army supervision. But it was not until June 1944 that there was an official public announcement that the Greenland base was now complete. Never before in American history had so many men labored so far north on projects of this type. During the summer an average of 1,500 bombers a month and an equal number of transports passed through Greenland over the Great Circle route; at Narssarssuaq alone there was an all-time record of 130 aircraft landings on July 4.

Another military confrontation between the Germans and Americans occurred on September 1, 1944, when the *Northland* encountered an armed German trawler off Great Koldewey Island. After a 70-mile chase the crew of the *Kehdingen* scuttled their vessel and surrendered to the pursuers. Then on October 4 the Americans stormed Little Koldewey Island, capturing a dozen Germans, radio and meteorological equipment, and five hundred land mines. Finally, on October 15 the *Eastwind* and *Southwind* seized another Nazi trawler off Cape Borgen; the *Exsternstein,* afterwards renamed the *South Breeze,* had on board advanced radio and communication systems. On this occassion twenty Germans were captured. This episode marked the end of the struggle for weather observation stations in Greenland, since in its aftermath no Nazis remained in the area.

On the diplomatic front, on July 4 of this year Carl Brun, the councillor of the Danish legation in Washington, sent a copy of a letter which he had just received from his cousin Eske to Assistant Secretary of State Adolf A. Berle. In this letter Brun reaffirmed his policy of segregating the native Greenlanders from contact with Americans as far as it was possible to do so. The following year, after the Nazis had left Copenhagen, the Landsraad (the Assembly of Greenland) held a meeting at which the island's future status was discussed. As for its Danish counterpart, on May 16 the Rigsdag retroactively gave its approval to the April 9, 1941, agreement. That October the restored government of Denmark expressed a desire not to be paid for the use by the U.S. military of defense areas in Greenland, but Councillor Brun later informed the American government that the Danish Foreign Office was horrified at the possibility that the United States might seek post-war bases there. Denmark apparently feared that such an arrangement might lead to Russian demands for bases on the island of Bornholm.

In retrospect, there were aspects of the American military occupation of Greenland during World War 2 that make one wonder if a pre-Hitlerian German scientists's description of the island as an enormous bowl ranged by mountains and filled with a cake of ice did not accurately establish the limits of Greenland's usefulness. Military authorities did not decide upon the airport ferry until a full year after orders had been given to construct the bases; only a quarter of the planes that flew the North Atlantic route to Europe stopped on the island during the war. (In fact, Greenlandic landing fields proved of greater value following World War 2, when strong western headwinds severely limited the range of returning aircraft.) On the other hand, the American presence denied the Germans the use of the island, and the water and land patrols remained constantly vigilant in their attempt to keep away the Nazis. During the latter part of the war the Germans were especially interested in Greenland from the standpoint of meteorological information; the data which allowed General Dwight Eisenhower to plan the D-Day invasion of Europe in June 1944 came largely from the island.[35]

Although contacts between the American military personnel and the natives were discouraged, it could not be said with justification that there was no permanent U.S. impact on Greenland as a result of the war. As was the case with Bermuda, it was the Americans who introduced the automobile; prior to its arrival there was no stretch of paved road for these vehicles to drive on. During World War 2, also, an airplane landed on dry land for the first time in the island's history. The radical character of this technological revolution is accentuated by the fact that it was not until 1940 that paraffin lamps began taking the place of the traditional train-oil ones.

Greenland, however, was not looked upon by the average U.S. soldier as the nearest place on earth to paradise. Many a homesick G.I. referred to it as "Groanland." Even Bernt Balchen was moved to comment, "I don't suppose the full realization of how utterly isolated we were was borne in on the men until the last ship sailed back to the States." But there were new experiences to share in the frozen North; instead of hamburgers and fried chicken to eat, there were codfish liver and roe, seal meat, reindeer, ptarmigan, and arctic hare. Leisure time was devoted to such activities as skiing, outdoor boxing bouts, and indoor vaudeville shows. If anything, it was much easier during the long Arctic winter to forget the pressing domestic problems back home.[36]

On October 17, 1945, Eske Brun delivered a speech before the Greenland Society in Copenhagen in which he discussed wartime American activities in the Danish colony. Far from lambasting the United States, he observed: "I am convinced that during the present war there has been no greater miracle than the American contribution," and "Relations between the Danish authorities and the American military officials were always good."[37] Nor were the latter criticized for not prosecuting violations of the non-fraternization with natives rule, since in his opinion the necessary steps were taken at the proper time. Brun also pointed out the often overlooked fact that during the war the United States took the place of Denmark in supplying the island with oil, kerosene, cigarettes, and pipe tobacco.

But when Brun answered the query "What do the Greenlanders think of the Americans?" with the assessment that practically speaking they had not seen them, he overlooked the fact that contacts did take place on occasion. Primitive but representative was the assessment made by a native to U.S. Consul James K. Penfield: "They O.K. Absolute O.K. We know Americaner protect us from Germans so we go back to Denmark. See all this chew gummy the soldiers give me for my childs; such people is O.K."[38] Of course, far fewer Americans knew Greenlandic than knew Danish, and thus they had difficulty in really understanding the natives; nor did they always appreciate the Danish policy of protecting the indigenous people from influences harmful to their development.

THE MODERN AGE COMES TO GREENLAND

During the three decades since the close of World War 2, the movement of Greenland towards modernization has accelerated. As a first step, there was the meeting of the Council of Native Eskimos held in September 1945. A number of resolutions were passed at this gathering, including ones to the effect that Greenland should be administered from the island, and that there should be only one governor; there also was a call for the repeal of the measure adopted in 1925 protecting the Greenlanders from laws which actually were not as applicable to them as to the Danes. Officials back in Copenhagen were somewhat reluctant to implement all these reform demands, but they did inaugurate a five-year plan for the development of the island's economy, which was immediately criticized by some as inadequate. Then during the following year a special committee of Greenlanders and Danes began to investigate additional ways of modernizing the political, social, and economic life of Greenland. As a result, laws were passed beginning in 1950 to bring the island more and more into the twentieth century. Still another key development occurred in 1953, when Denmark agreed to permit the island to send two delegates to the Danish parliament.

Among the changes which were taking place in the economic area following World War 2 was the increasing exploitation of the lead deposits found in the Mesteravig region of the eastern coast, beginning in 1948. Four years later a Danish-Swedish-Canadian company was created to mine both these and the zinc deposits there; unfortunately, the original ore body was eventually exhausted, as were the cryolite deposits at Ivigtut. From the standpoint of fishing and agriculture, one might cite the discovery of shrimp fields in 1948 off Disko Island halfway up the western coast, as well as the introduction of domestic reindeer in 1952 into the Godthaab area. But even more important, in 1951 the Royal Greenland Trading Company lost its monopoly, and in the years since private Danish enterprise has been free to operate there. Since 1951 the island has been open for settlement to Danish subjects, and some Faeroese and Danish fishermen have taken up residence there, along with a growing number of small businessmen, artisans and laborers, and even bankers.

In post-war Greenland commercial planes also have become more and more numerous, not counting those American military aircraft using Thule. On November 15, 1954, a new route was inaugurated between Scandinavia and the Pacific Coast by way of Søndre Strømfjord, while six years later, on February 27, 1960, a new civil airport was opened across from the U.S. airbase there by Eske Brun. This facility included a new Scandinavian Airlines System hotel with room for 240 persons. The Americans had turned over the base at Narssarssuaq to the Danes in the fall of 1958; its chief user became the Danish military aircraft of the Greenland Command. Then two years later, in 1960, American and Danish officials signed an agreement at Copenhagen concerning the establishment of certain aeronautical facilities and services in Greenland.[39] With respect to possible landing sites on the northern coast of the island, it was reported in 1962 that the air force had discovered over fifty promising locations.[40] Still another step forward in commercial aviation took place in 1965, when Greenlandair, the world's longest helicopter line, inaugurated service along the western coast; in that year alone it carried thirteen thousand passengers—a total equal to one-third of the population of the island. This firm is owned by the Scandinavian Airlines System (50 percent of the shares) and by Greenlandic interests (the other 50 percent).

OVER AND UNDER THE ICE

Turning to U. S. activities in Greenland since World War 2, one might divide these into those which occurred during the years between 1945 and the signing of the 1951 Danish-American pact and the building of Thule during the early 1950s, and those which have taken place during the quarter-century since. Following World War 2, proponents of the U.S. annexing Greenland included Republican Representative Bertrand Gearhart of California, who introduced resolutions advocating this step in both 1945 and 1947, and Republican Senator Owen Brewster of Maine, who contributed a statement to *Collier's* during the latter year. (To Brewster, "Greenland's icy mountains are the ramparts of America.")[41] In the accompanying article Charles J. Hubbard suggested with respect to the purchase price that the figure should not be very high, perhaps $50 million; this was indeed a low figure, in view of the island's significance as an aviation facility and weather station during World War 2.

Three decades later, in 1977, the historian to the Danish royal court, Tage Kaarsted, was to make the claim that Secretary of State James F. Byrnes had approached Danish Foreign Minister Gustav Rasmussen at the United Nations in 1946 with an offer to buy Greenland for an unspecified amount. The government of Denmark, though, never gave serious consideration to this American offer. Kaarsted's claim was based in part on hitherto secret government files.

In 1946 Ikateq Airbase near Angmagssalik (Bluie East 2) was abandoned, but a Danish Greenland Command was established, with headquarters at Godthaab. During the following year the United States signed the Inter-American Treaty of Reciprocal Assistance at Rio de Janeiro; the security zone defined by this document, in article 4, omitted Iceland but included Greenland. Officials back in Copenhagen, however, were somewhat edgy about the American presence on the island. Thus, on March 13, 1947, Foreign Minister Rasmussen informed the Danish parliament that he was convinced that Denmark had no intention of selling Greenland to the United States or to any other nation, and that he was preparing to negotiate for the termination of those American military bases established under the 1941 agreement. At this time the Communists were especially vigorous in their attempts to end the U.S. role on the island, demanding that the mother country's parliament reestablish Denmark's full sovereignty over Greenland.[42]

As of 1947 there were perhaps 1,500 American military personnel remaining there. The three Coast Guard cutters assigned to the Greenland Patrol were based at Argentia in Newfoundland, while the navy was maintaining a small refuelling base with 150 men; the only radio beacon then operating was the one at Frederiksdal. While at one time the AAF had had eighteen weather stations, now there were only six, in addition to the jointly operated Danish-American one at Thule. Yet the American consulate at Godthaab remained open as it had during the war, and the U.S. consul was in fact the only representative of another nation active in Greenland.

Unquestionably, the most controversial aspect of the American military presence on the island at this time was the landing of a U.S. marine detachment at Egedesminde in 1947. It later was maintained by Washington that this unit was simply correcting maps, and thus that in reality this operation was only a very minor matter. During the same year the Americans landed on the icecap by ski-plane approximately 100 miles east of the semi-abandoned base at Søndre Strømfjord, afterwards pitching camp and carrying on scientific research for twenty-six days. The official report of Project Snowman concluded: "It is now possible to say that the Greenland ice cap has been rendered accessible to virtually unlimited military and scientific exploration."[43]

Despite Foreign Minister Rasmussen's 1947 statement opposing the American annexation of the island, in June 1950 he declared that Denmark had never thought that all United States troops would leave Greenland. At the same time he announced the willingness of the Danish government to take over the Sondrestrom Air Base (Bluie West 8) in the wake of rumors that the American government planned to evacuate its Greenland bases. Denmark could use it for mapmaking, fisheries, and as a weather station, as well as for communication with the mainland. Two months later, in August, Danish authorities did take over the Sondrestrom base, only to return it on September 11, 1951, to the Americans, who extended the runway.

At the same time that Rasmussen was expressing his interest in Bluie West 8, Colonel Robert B. Sykes talked with Danish authorities about the possibility of establishing a weather station in northern Greenland. Late in 1950 he and Eske Brun, now Denmark's undersecretary for Greenland affairs, conducted an aerial survey on the northern coast, during which they discovered an ice-free area on

Princess Dagmar's Peninsula. By March 1952 Operation Nord (or Operation Parkway) was underway, and after a difficult beginning a Danish weather station and a permanent landing strip were constructed there.[44]

A new development in Danish-American relations occurred on April 27, 1951, when the United States and Denmark signed a vitally important agreement calling for the joint defense of Greenland in the event that the latter was attacked or invaded. It replaced the 1941 pact. This document also provided for the mutual use by NATO members of the island's defense facilities; it was to remain in effect during the lifespan of that organization, with the door being left open to future changes in the terms of the agreement. Another key feature was that American troops were to be exempt from customs duties and taxes. Other agreements dating from this decade included a 1952 one relating to the registration with the International Telecommunication Union of frequencies used by U.S. authorities in Greenland, and a 1954 one concerning the establishment of an air route between Scandinavia and the United States by way of the island.

Even before the signing of the Danish-American agreement of 1951, though, the Supreme Air Command issued a directive in December 1950 calling for the construction of an advance heavy bomber base in Greenland. The Corps of Engineers built this at Thule on North Star Bay, well to the north of Sondrestrom. As we noted earlier, Thule had originally been founded as a trading post early in the twentieth century by Knud Rasmussen; the Eskimo village which was there at the time that construction began was moved sixty miles to the north. (The seals and the walruses departed with them.)

Supervising the construction of Thule—which was substantially complete by the summer of 1954—was Colonel Bernt Balchen, the World War 2 hero who had suggested the site to Air Secretary Thomas Finletter. Early in 1951 a convoy of 120 transport ships arrived on the scene with supplies, but in the months that followed the military transport service airlifted in much of the equipment, including a giant shovel. Initially Operation Blue Jay remained a secret operation; the 7,500 Thule-bound Americans who left from Norfolk in June were not told their final destination.

Built in the shadow of mesa-like Mount Dundas, Thule also possesses a harbor which is blocked by ice nine or ten months each year. Fogs sometimes close the airfield down in the summer, but at other times it enjoys some of the best flying weather in the

world. (Curiously, Thule is actually drier than the Sahara Desert.) As
for the adjacent town—which is as large as any of the Danish-
Greenlandic ones elsewhere in the island—it has been described
as an architect's nightmare, in that the buildings were designed to
be functional rather than aesthetic. The presence of permafrost
required that these be built on stilts, lest the buildings' heat melt
the permafrost and cause the foundations to sink; it also was necessary to weight them down with heavy concrete blocks.

Almost immediately following the inception of work on the base,
Thule came under the scrutiny of congressional investigators. A witness testified before the Senate Preparedness Investigating Committee on January 12, 1952, that 2,500 workers waiting to be sent
to Greenland had received $317,000 in stand-by pay the previous
year. (It was explained that otherwise the men would not wait, and
that it was not possible to fly them to the island until weather conditions cleared up.) Later that month senatorial investigators complained about the secrecy enveloping the base. Then General Lewis A.
Pick, chief of the Army Corps of Engineers, in testimony during a
senatorial hearing on February 21 set the total stand-by pay at
$3 million, including wages accumulated in the course of a forty-two-
day voyage; Pick added that the men were working under hazardous
conditions which were beyond anything ever encountered previously.
Bill Brinkley later observed in *Life* that ". . . before the taxpayer
starts writing indignant letters to his Congressman he would do
well to recall that for most of the brawny men of Blue Jay this
pay lasts for only the summer work season—about five months in
all, including transportation time. On the job they work 10-hour
days, seven days a week."[45]

The total cost of the base itself also became an object of controversy at this time. On March 29, 1952, Colonel Harry E. Reed,
chief of the Army Audit Bureau, told Senate investigators that Thule
would cost $1 billion, not $300 million as had been earlier reported.
To make matters worse, $40 million worth of materials which had
been shipped to Greenland remained unaccounted for. It was such
testimony that led Democratic Senator Lyndon Johnson of Texas to
comment that the inquiry had "just scratched the surface." The
following day, though, E. V. Huggins, the assistant secretary of the
Air Force, denied that the Thule airbase would cost a billion dollars,
placing the figure instead at under $250 million. Huggins also stated
that reports which he had received from air force personnel showed
that the construction work had been of high quality and well executed.

While the U.S. air force was entrenching itself at Thule, the navy was withdrawing from Greenland. NAF Narssarssuaq was inactivated on February 5, 1951, while NOB Greenland and Naval Station Grønnedal were disestablished on August 10; the latter was then transferred to the Danish government as part of the April agreement, and the Greenland Command moved there from Godthaab. By January 1952 there were no American naval personnel remaining on the island.

During the years that followed, U.S. military scientists also became more active in Greenland. Thus, in 1952 an eleven-man party from the Army Transportation Corps conducted the first mechanized expedition across the ice cap, a 1,330-mile round trip between Thule and Crown Prince Christians Land. Then during the following year the Research Studies Institute of the Air University in what became known as Project Mint Julep examined a patch of bare ice discovered in 1947 during Project Snowman. The main objective of Operation Mint Julep was to determine whether heavy wheeled aircraft could land on this ice strip. Still another expedition to Crown Prince Christians Land took place in the summer of 1955, when the Army Transportation Arctic Group conducted Project Eastwind, progressing over the frozen waste with caterpillar tractors, wanigans (insulated boxlike trailers), and ten-ton sleds. Finally, late in 1955 thirty-one men from the army's Trans-Arctic Group undertook an unprecedented sixty-day, 1,350-mile expedition which traversed the middle of the icecap from North to South and back; christened Operation Southwind, it was the first attempt ever made in the winter to cross this in a continuous movement.[46]

During the mid-1950s, too, army engineers had begun to dig tunnels into the Greenland ice cap. The first of these was constructed 200 miles east of Thule in 1955; gouged out by gigantic snow diggers, this was covered over with snow afterwards. By the winter of 1957–58 the army people had set up buildings inside the tunnel at this Site 2 (named "Fist Clench"), and sixty scientists and military men were living underground there conducting research. Still another project dating from this period was a 65-foot-square and 25-foot-high chamber which engineers hollowed out deep inside a glacier near Thule. This was indeed the ultimate refrigerated warehouse.[47]

To return to surface operations, around this time the Army Transportation Environmental Operations Group undertook a complete reconnaissance of Peary Land and Crown Prince Christians Land. This project, Operation Lead Dog, originally was conceived to extend over a period of several years. Of more limited duration was an expedition

which took place in March and April of 1958; here the Transportation
Arctic Group moved eight vehicles over the ice cap east of Søndre
Strømfjord. Employing a modified crevasse detector and modified
weasels on land, Operation King Dog had air support from H-19
helicopters. To sum up the military projects of the decade of the
1950s, one might quote from an orientation brochure handed to new
arrivals: "While [the ice cap] is an awesome and formidable sight,
it should be always respected, but never feared. . . . It is a challenge,
a frontier which must be conquered. American ingenuity, determina-
tion and scientific skill are dedicated to this task."[48]

Looking at scientific activities during the next decade, we find that
still another installation beneath the surface was begun on May 12,
1959, at Camp Century, 138 miles east of Thule and 6,200 feet above
sea level. Here army engineers constructed an underground city in
twenty-one tunnels—including a Main Street 1,100 feet long—that
featured twenty-eight prefabricated plywood buildings. Camp Century
originally was conceived strictly as a research base, where scientists
could monitor the weather constantly throughout the entire year.
Because of the high cost of diesel fuel to power and heat Camp
Century, in March 1960 the American and Danish governments
approved the installation of an atomic reactor there. Tested in an
elaborate dress rehearsal at Bristol, Virginia, in May, the $3,250,000
plant was shipped by sea during the summer on the *Marine Fiddler;*[49]
by October the army had turned on its reactor beneath the Greenland
icecap. Then on May 27, 1961, the Corps of Engineers accepted title
to the power plant.

Back closer to Thule, at Camp Tuto 18 miles to the east of the
air base, the army gouged a tunnel 1,100 feet into the glacier with
coal mining machinery, and filled the galleries radiating from this with
experimental buildings of various types. Its initial—if unplanned—
testing occurred on October 7, 1961, when a blizzard led to the maroon-
ing there of forty military personnel and polar specialists. As for later
developments at Camp Century, in the summer of 1963 army scientists laid plans to drill a 6,600-foot hole in the ice cap; prior to this
time their deepest probe in Greenland had bottomed out at 1,355
feet.[50] They hoped through the testing of the central core of ice
removed by the drilling to investigate snowfalls which had taken place
tens of thousands or even hundreds of thousands of years ago.[51] It was
not until July 4, 1966, however, that the drillers reached a depth of
4,562 feet at Camp Century and struck the bottom of the ice sheet.
In celebrating this feat the army served Coca Colas filled with two-
thousand-year-old ice cubes from the 1,800-foot level. By this time

the power plant had been removed to the United States and destroyed, since the pressure of the ice had begun to shrink the reactor tunnel at Camp Century.[52] In 1966 the army abandoned the doomed underground installation.[53]

Then in 1968 a diplomatically as well as scientifically explosive incident occurred in January when an air force B-52 crashed on the ice of North Star Bay 7 miles from Thule with an undetonated hydrogen bomb aboard. Fortunately, the radiation damage was limited to a few Eskimos picking up alpha particles on their boots. Nevertheless, the Danish government demanded that the U.S. air force spend millions of dollars in cleaning up the mess, although only a few bits and pieces of the B-52 remained.[54]

GREENLAND DURING THE 1970s

In an assessment of the U.S. presence in southwestern Greenland published in 1966, *U.S. News and World Report* observed that one rarely saw an American, since U.S. military officials were still discouraging contacts between the servicemen and the natives. Anyone wishing to pursue the common American habit of watching television in periods of leisure time, could only do it at the U.S. airbases at Søndre Strømfjord and Thule, where 500 and 1,700 air force personnel were stationed, respectively. By this time autos had become a common sight in Godthaab, but Eskimo dogs still roamed the streets of Egedesminde in search of food. With fish exports amounting to nearly $9 million in 1964, Norwegian, Portuguese, and French fishing fleets were active off the island in the summer. Even though the cryolite mine at Ivigtut had been exhausted, enough stockpiles were left to permit the sale of $3 million of this mineral yearly. Frontier life remained harsh in the Greenland of the mid-1960s, but even with the increased American and European presence there was little crime, and the racial tensions which frequently marked the decline of colonialism elsewhere were largely absent.

The quarter-century following the close of World War 2, as we have seen, did witness some exciting moments with respect to American operations in Greenland, but the reminiscences of some of the individuals who served as U.S. ambassador to Denmark during this period do not indicate that the island was constantly a source of friction, or even a focal point of attention, in Danish-American relations. A representative statement reflecting this generalization is William McC. Blair's comment: "The American military presence in Greenland was something we watched very carefully but happily it was never an issue and caused us no real problems."[55] In fact, the two topics most emphasized by those former ambassadors who expressed their views to the author were the colonial status of the Danish possession and the segregation of the natives.

Despite the coverage which they lavished on Greenland on earlier occasions, the *New York Times* and contemporary magazines have tended to neglect the island during the 1970s, although the U.S. military continue to be active there, maintaining with a limited number of troops its Distant Early Warning line against transpolar aircraft attacks, and the Ballistic Missile Early Warning System as a safeguard against Soviet missiles. One exception to this journalistic neglect has been the *Los Angeles Times,* which published an article in 1972 entitled "Danish Territory Faces Many Problems, Strives to Join Modern Society." According to its anonymous author, Greenland had yet to become a twentieth-century Scandinavian welfare state, thanks largely to the basically conservative orientation of those natives still belonging to a hunting and fishing culture. During 1974 the lead and zinc mine did earn over $12 million, but Greenlanders nevertheless obtained an equal amount from the age-old fishing industry. It remains to be seen what production, if any, will result from the oil concessions which such American companies as Chevron, Gulf, Mobil, Arco, and Murphy Oil—along with a number of foreign concerns—recently have acquired off the southwestern coast near Holsteinsborg and Sukkertoppen.[56]

Spending an average of $100 million a year on the island, the Danish government could perhaps point to its greatest achievement in the establishment of an effective health service and a successful campaign against tuberculosis. Also notable have been the expansion of the schools, the building of plants for the processing of fish, more roads and houses, and the growing use of electrical power. The result has been a veritable technological revolution which has posed a severe threat to the traditional Eskimo-hunter culture.

But despite these accomplishments, an awareness was growing in Denmark that Greenland sooner or later should be extended home rule. Thus on November 17, 1978 the Danish parliament voted to grant this right, with the Greenlanders expressing their approval in an election held during the following January. Then in April the citizens of Greenland elected their own parliament. Future plans, though, call for Denmark to provide an annual subsidy of $200 million or more to the Greenlanders, who now under home rule will have a greater voice in determining how these funds should be spent. The American military bases, it should be noted, were not an issue in the home rule debate.

Unfortunately, by the summer of 1978 it had become apparent to the international petroleum firms engaged in drilling operations that there was not going to be an oil boom in the Davis Strait off the western coast of Greenland. This shattered the hope of the islanders that they might become independent economically in the near future, although there are coal, uranium, iron, copper, nickel, and chronium deposits in Greenland. In addition, the modernization of the island has been accompanied by large-scale urban unemployment, as well as various psychological problems caused by the difficult adjustment from a primitive way of life to a more advanced one; alcoholism, violent crime, divorce, and promiscuity are far more common than they once were. Since most of the crime there is drink-related, Greenlanders agreed to ration alcoholic beverages beginning in January 1979, after rejecting prohibition in a national referendum held in June 1978. Depressed by these chronic problems, many young Greenlanders have drifted to Copenhagen, only to find that they lack the education for a better paying job there.

Finally, there remains the grim possibility that the island's climate may fluctuate over the centuries. While the present era may be warmer than past ones, colder weather may return and the great ice sheet engulf Greenland. Should this occur, there will be no future for Eskimo, Dane, or American there; instead, eternal nature will reclaim the island for her own.

8

CONCLUSION
A Pattern of Diversity

Having treated each of our six nations separately on a chronological basis, with some topical coverage, we turn in closing to an overall examination of various comparisons and contrasts. To facilitate this investigation, the entire span of American history down to World War 2 will be dealt with first, then that conflict itself, and then finally the three decades since World War 2. As we shall see, the major dissimilarities are not always between the three British base nations as a group and the three non-British ones as a unit; in fact some rather striking cross-group parallels emerge from a comprehensive analysis.

To begin with the diplomatic aspects, one generally equates the Monroe Doctrine with Latin America. Nevertheless, after the outbreak of World War 2 in Europe American officials attempted to justify an American military presence in the three British islands—and even Greenland—on the grounds that these islands lie within the geographical perimeters of that area covered by the doctrine. Fitting in Iceland, though, proved far more difficult, while the Azores are an impossibility.

As for the 1904 Roosevelt Corollary to the Monroe Doctrine—under which the American government assumed responsibility for customs collections in the Dominican Republic—one should note that this was a specific manifestation of the more general American hostility to European nations intervening anywhere in Latin America on behalf of the threatened investments of their nationals there. Yet a fact which many diplomatic historians have chosen to ignore is that the Roosevelt Corollary hardly acted as a restraint on American investments in such non-U.S. colonial areas in the Western Hemisphere as Jamaica, the Bahamas, or Bermuda. The present volume has attempted to trace these investments in detail.

A key building block of American foreign policy, of course, has been dollar diplomacy; and this is generally seen as a dominant aspect of U.S. relations with Latin America and China. Thomas A. Bailey has nevertheless observed that "the use of foreign policy to protect and promote American commercial interests dates from the earliest years of the republic, when the State Department strove to reopen trade with the British West Indies." This monograph has shown that while U.S. merchants have actively sought a varied commerce with these islands, the American government, rather than reciprocating has at times erected barriers against imports from the British colonial areas. This is especially true of Bermuda around the time of the Great Depression.

With respect to the American military presence in Iceland, Greenland, the Azores, the Bahamas, Jamaica, and Bermuda during and after World War 2, it would be a most profitable exercise to compare and contrast the results of this presence there with the results elsewhere in the world, but this is a most difficult task. Pertinent studies such as Leon B. Blair's excellent 1970 volume on Morocco *(Western Window in the Arab World)* are rare indeed. George Marion did publish a book in 1948 entitled *Bases and Empire: A Chart of American Expansion,* but his other works appear to be preoccupied with Communism; there are at most a few pages on each island in George Stambuk's 1963 opus *American Military Forces Abroad: Their Impact on the Western States,* and in Roland A. Paul's 1973 volume *American Military Commitments Abroad.*

Over the years the American government has looked with considerable suspicion upon foreign military activity—or even plans or preparations for such activity—throughout the New World, especially within the Caribbean Basin following the acquisition of the Canal Zone at the beginning of the twentieth century. This hostility probably has been directed against the Germany of the Teutonic Menace Hypothesis more than at any other nation, but the British also have been victimized at times; many Americans have resented the long-standing (if now passé) British naval supremacy. Yet this suspicion of foreign military activity did not prevent the American government from intervening militarily during the first third of the twentieth century in Mexico, Nicaragua, Honduras, Cuba, Haiti, and the Dominican Republic.

No volume such as this would be complete without some sort of a comparative analysis of the impact of the U.S. military interventions before the era of the Good Neighbor on the three insular nations mentioned above (Cuba, Haiti, and the Dominican Republic) and the corresponding American impact during World War 2 and afterwards on Iceland, Greenland, the Azores, the Bahamas, Jamaica, and Bermuda. Since the three independent countries were backward in many ways and needed to be brought into the twentieth century, one might suggest that the U.S. presence was more deeply felt there than it was in the six Atlantic outposts featured in this monograph, although certainly the latter impact was highly significant, especially in the economic and cultural areas. We have already cited Harold Sutphen's findings with respect to the British islands in the introduction.

Let us look at developments in Cuba, Haiti, and the Dominican Republic in detail. As for Cuba, Major General Leonard Wood built up a notable record of achievements during the three years that he served as governor general (1899–1902). Among other things, he established a system of civil government, reorganized the public school system, improved sanitary conditions, and more or less eradicated yellow fever. In contrast, Charles Magoon encountered more controversy while running the Cuban government between 1906 and 1909; Magoon, though, was an expert on Cuban law. During his three years in office he took a complete census, supervised the passage of a new electoral law, improved sanitation, and turned over a surplus to his successor.

The World War 1 years witnessed American military interventions in both the Dominican Republic and Haiti. Troops remained in the former nation from 1916 to 1924. During their presence internal revenue collections were increased, roads and bridges were constructed, port improvements were made, public health was improved, and school attendance was multiplied. On the other hand, the American military government restricted the civil and political liberties of the Dominicans, even employing torture at times, and occasionally resorted to the censorship of the press. When Dr. Carl Kelsey visited this nation at the beginning of the Harding administration under the auspices of the American Academy of Political and Social Science, he discovered that the Dominicans were not hostile to Americans per se, but they were critical of the U.S. government.

In the case of Haiti, there was an American military presence for nearly two decades: from 1915 to 1934. Rear Admiral Knapp, who made an investigation of the situation there, reported in 1920 that

American officers had abused their power, while General Barnett wrote in another report dating from the same year that the unlawful execution of prisoners had occurred. The corvée also had been introduced into Haiti, but was eventually abandoned. Despite these negative findings, the Reverend Colmore, Bishop of Puerto Rico and Haiti, did observe in 1917 that "the marines have literally taught the Haitians how to live decently." To cite specifics, the U.S. military presence had led to a reduced public debt, improved sanitation, and more hospitals, roads, and irrigation projects.

It is quite obvious from this brief survey of Cuba, the Dominican Republic, and Haiti that the American military impact there was of a different nature from what it was with respect to the six Atlantic outposts featured in this volume. Certainly, in the case of the latter there was no attempt to straighten out tangled finances or to supervise elections; nor did the U.S. military inaugurate a policy of imprisoning the local inhabitants and censoring the local press, since it did not exercise sovereign power there. Improvements in sanitation and public health did not enjoy the high priority which they did in Cuba, the Dominican Republic, and Haiti, while the Americans did not undertake a massive program to educate the inhabitants.

The most obvious parallel which one might cite between the two groups of islands would be that of improved roads and port facilities, thanks to the American military presence. The latter, it will be recalled, helped to bring both Bermuda and Greenland into the age of the automobile. In contrast, though, it was the World War 2 bases which did more to stimulate air traffic; the airplane was less of a factor during the first third of the twentieth century than during the second. And because there were American military bases in these six islands as well as American troops, the economic impact of the U.S. presence was considerably greater there. (This is not to deny that the American base at Guantánamo, Cuba, has stimulated the local economy by providing jobs for workers.) The spreading of American culture in Bermuda, Jamaica, and the Bahamas was of course facilitated by the use of English as the mother tongue there; in contrast, French is spoken in Haiti, and Spanish in Cuba and the Dominican Republic, which factor impedes their "coca-colization." English, moreover, is taught in the public schools of Iceland, along with German, Danish, and Icelandic.

In viewing our six islands from the military standpoint, American interest in the three British possessions goes back to the time of the American Revolution and extends through the War of 1812, the U.S. Civil War, and World Wars 1 and 2. Here Bermuda played perhaps the most important role, Jamaica the least; as for the Bahamas, despite military confrontations there during earlier wars they were only marginally involved in World War 2. Neither Greenland nor Iceland entered the pages of American military history prior to World War 2, but in the Azores the U.S. military was active during the War of 1812, the American Civil War, and World War 1.

Aside from the Azores, American annexationists have cast a covetous eye on these Atlantic islands over the years, but the timing has differed in the case of the British and non-British ones. As early as 1867 Secretary of State William Henry Seward expressed an interest in the United States acquiring Greenland and Iceland, while early in the twentieth century both Senator Henry Cabot Lodge and explorer Robert E. Peary followed suit with respect to the former. On the other hand, despite Lodge's proposed swap of Jamaica and the Bahamas for the Philippines after the Spanish-American War, it was not until the period between the two world wars that various members of Congress began to call for the annexation by the United States of the British-held Atlantic islands. This transfer was to constitute full or partial payment of the war debt which Great Britain owed America.

From the economic standpoint, commercial contacts between the United States and all six island states admittedly have deep roots in the past, but the pattern of trade with each has been somewhat dissimilar. At one time Bermuda marketed such agricultural crops as potatoes and onions in the United States, but these eventually fell victim to the Hawley-Smoot Tariff. Likewise, American demand for Azorean whale oil lessened with the development of the petroleum industry in the United States, while Icelandic fish often has been unwelcome in a nation hostile to the importation of fish from neighboring Canada. On the other hand, America proved to be an eager buyer for Greenlandic cryolite on a limited scale, as well as for pineapples, sponges, and hemp from the Bahamas. Finally, Jamaica has furnished the United States with large quantities of bananas and then bauxite over the last century.

Most of the U.S. investment, however, appears to have been concentrated in the British colonies, although in the case of Bermuda in July 1936 the Legislative Council killed an investment companies bill. In the Bahamas, where there was no income tax, a real estate boom developed during the 1920s as a result of American investment; by 1931 the Munson interests had amassed holdings in the Nassau area totalling approximately $1,500,000. U.S. investors also were active in Jamaica, where by 1927 the bulk of foreign investment was American or Canadian rather than British. United Fruit was one of the most

prominent firms there at this time, while U.S. investors had sunk
$6 million into the Jamaican Consolidated Copper Company. But
it was only in Bermuda—of all six islands—that American tourists
arrived in significant numbers prior to World War 1.

Significantly, evidences of anti-Americanism were far more pronounced in the three British islands than in Iceland, Greenland, and
the Azores. Thus, during the early national period political friction
had developed in the Bahamas between the recently arrived southern
Loyalists and the Conchs, or native Bahamians. It was in these islands,
too, that unpleasant diplomatic episodes occurred in the wake of the
liberation of slaves from the *Comet* in 1831 and the *Encomium* in
1834 following their destruction in the treacherous waters, and a century later over the presence between 1925 and 1927 of U.S. Coast
Guard vessels at Gun Cay without the prior permission of the British
authorities. Of course, the most spectacular of these episodes was
the confrontation between Admiral C. H. Davis and Governor Sir
Alexander Swettenham in Jamaica following the great Kingston earthquake of 1907. Swettenham had previously incurred the wrath of
President Theodore Roosevelt by discouraging the employment of
Jamaican workers in the Panama Canal Zone.

Between the two world wars many islanders in the British possessions were concerned about possible economic domination by
the United States and the growing acceptance of American ideas and
institutions there. As for the former, one might refer to the Bahamian
newspaper editorial published during 1925 in the wake of a threatened
inundation of the islands by U.S. business firms, "Rolyat's" assessment of the Jamaican economic scene which appeared in the Kingston
Daily Gleaner in 1931, and Frederick Lewis Allen's 1938 conclusion
that Bermuda was becoming less and less self-sufficient because of the
growing influx of American vacationers and tourists. The anti-U.S.
reaction in the islands, too, sometimes took the form of attempted
censorship. It is not without significance that the economic fears
and censorship attempts were largely absent from the three non-
British islands; this strongly suggests that the U.S. impact there
possibly was of lesser intensity.

Viewed against this background, the American military presence
in these six nations during World War 2 takes on a somewhat different
aspect, because it demonstrates that the United States was no stranger
there. In the case of both the British and the non-British islands, the
diplomatic negotiations were involved and prolonged; this is rather
surprising, since there was a real and direct German military threat to
Greenland, Iceland, and the Azores. Preserving their sovereignty

was more of a concern in Iceland and Bermuda than elsewhere. Prior to the arrival of American troops, the U.S. government was most critical of local censorship in Bermuda, where the British had instituted the practice of stopping the Pan American Clippers and removing foreign mail. In contrast, claims cases were more of a problem in Iceland than elsewhere; it was here that there was the most friction between the American military and the natives. Social relations also were uneasy at times in Bermuda, but in the case of Greenland Danish authorities were largely successful in their attempt to keep the G.I.s and the indigenous peoples separate from each other.

An economic phenomenon which was a focal point of controversy in both the British and non-British island states was the frequently pronounced differential between the American price and wage levels and the local ones. In the case of Iceland, the inhabitants looked upon petroleum products as being excessively expensive during World War 2. As for the Azores, U.S. authorities were fearful that well paid American military personnel might inflate the economy of the islands beyond control; they thus limited the amount of spending money available to each soldier and encouraged the latter to save. An even greater problem arose when local workers received high American wages at the military bases. Not only was the wage differential a precipitating cause of the June 1942 riot in the Bahamas, it also led to native laborers in Bermuda organizing a union.

From an overall standpoint, there obviously was an American impact on all six nations during World War 2, although in the case of Iceland and the Azores it is not always easy to separate this from the British influence. Harold Sutphen has observed that the existence of the American military bases significantly affected the social and economic life of the British colonies; in this connection we have emphasized the problem of wage and price differentials, the eruption of riots and the formation of unions, and the migration of workers to America. As for the introduction of modern life, perhaps as good an example as any was the employment of the automobile in both Bermuda and Greenland. The American military also left behind as a gift to the Icelanders ten thousand Quonset huts, a taste for ice cream sodas, and words like "guy" and "crew cut." Consequently, one might easily extend Sutphen's generalization that "all the sites acquired some degree of 'Americanization'" to the non-British countries as well.

Nevertheless, since the close of World War 2 each of these six island nations has tended to pursue its own separate destiny, despite the continued presence of the American military to a lesser or greater degree everywhere except Jamaica. Prior to the end of that conflict opposition developed in both Iceland and Greenland to the granting of post-war base rights to the United States; yet there are now American military facilities at both Keflavik and Thule, despite the fact that in the case of Iceland politicians at times have called for their removal or downgrading. The year 1959 seems to have been an especially bad one for the Americans there, featuring several unpleasant episodes. On the other hand, the American military presence in Greenland since World War 2 has not been a continuous irritant in U.S. diplomacy with Denmark

American relations with the Azores have generally remained quite friendly, thanks in part to the activities of U.S. military veterinarians and the efforts to improve the food supply. (Portuguese Prime Minister Salazar did bitterly attack American policy towards Africa on occasion.) As for Bermudian relations with the United States, these as a rule have been harmonious; to cite one goodwill gesture, when drought ravaged the islands in 1969, the navy shipped four million gallons of water there, a quarter of which went to the local government. On the other hand, officials in the Bahamas were hesitant at first to grant the American military base rights on Andros Island for the Atlantic Underwater Test and Evaluation Center at the beginning of that decade. This, however, was eventually built with British assistance.

From the diplomatic standpoint, it is perhaps not surprising that the United States has entered into more treaties and executive agreements with Iceland (independent since 1944) and Jamaica (independent since 1962) than with the other four islands. Iceland and Jamaica have likewise received more varied and extensive financial assistance from the American government. Nevertheless, the latter nation was the scene of what was perhaps the most unpleasant diplomatic episode of the post–World War 2 period involving the United States and these six Atlantic nations, the Ambassador Vincent de Roulet affair in 1973.

A continuing problem during the post–World War 2 period has been the high wages paid to local workers at the U.S. military bases elsewhere. In the case of Iceland, not only did these laborers not want to seek employment off the base, but their high salaries contributed to the inflation of the 1950s. An important legal case dating from the immediate post-war years involved Bermuda, where the U.S. Circuit Court of Appeals ruled in November 1947 that those workers employed at Kindley Air Force Base were to be paid at the same rate as their counterparts in America. Significantly, in the case of the Azores local authorities in recent years have come to welcome U.S. spending.

But when one turns to such areas as commerce, investment, and tourism, one discovers that there is no common pattern among the six islands, just as there was none before World War 2. Since that conflict the leading Icelandic exports to America have been cod liver oil, frozen fish, and herring meal, but the percentage of these going to the United States has fluctuated rapidly over the years. In the case of Greenland, miners had completed their excavation of the cryolite deposits by 1966; a stockpile of the mineral, however, still remained on hand for eventual shipment abroad. Less consequential in terms of dollars has been the marketing in America of such Azorean products as handmade embroideries, canned fish, sperm oil, casein, and dasheens.

Looking at the British islands, we find that exports to the United States originating in the Bahamas increased in value from $2 million in 1955 to $48 million in 1969, in Jamaica from $23 million in 1955 to $245 million in 1970. The most important Bahamian exports to America in recent years have been pulpwood and crawfish; in contrast, Jamaica has shipped to the United States bauxite and bananas. As for Bermuda, its limited export trade with America has been bolstered slightly during the 1970s by a renewal of the shipment of lily flowers and lily bulbs.

Unlike trade, American investment has been largely absent from the non-British island states, although in the case of Iceland both private and public U.S. funds had become a key source of investment loan capital and of short-term financing by 1968. In contrast, since 1945 numerous wealthy Americans have invested in the Bahamas. Both here and in Jamaica there were favorable tax policies towards foreign investment, which was one of the major factors stimulating Reynolds Jamaica Mines and Kaiser to mine bauxite in Jamaica after 1950. By May 1972 150 American companies were active there, with a total investment of $850 million. Then there was Bermuda, where in 1947 a group composed of Pan American Airways and the Hilton Hotels acquired a 40 percent interest in the Mid-Ocean Club and three hotels, while in 1948 R. and T. Electronics bought the Bermuda Railway from the government. U.S. investments there have continued to mount in recent years.

New patterns also have emerged since World War 2 in the area of tourism. Greenland has yet to become a vacationers' haven (even for Danes), and relatively few Americans travel to the Azores for either business or pleasure, aside from those returning home to the islands to visit relatives and friends. Yet there was a nearly five-fold increase in those tourists from the United States visiting Iceland during the 1960s; quite a few of them were returning American servicemen. Recent U.S. visitors to Bermuda have included a growing number of American college and university students on their spring break, while in the case of the Bahamas the growth of Freeport has acted as a lure to prospective tourists. Americans who visit Jamaica no longer confine their pleasure jaunts to the winter months, moreover, as they did at one time; such cities as Kingston, Montego Bay, Ochos Rios, and Port Antonio have become increasingly popular with U.S. vacationers since 1945.

American scientists, however, have gone where the tourists did not go: to icy Greenland, still in many respects a terra incognita. Whether it was a question of crossing the ice, or building tunnels or drilling holes into it, or testing the weather above it, American ingenuity generally found answers to the frequently monumental problems involved in surviving in an environment generally hostile to man.

Of all the six islands, it was perhaps Bermuda—where there were ten thousand American servicemen and their dependents present in 1961—which experienced the greatest U.S. cultural impact over the last three decades. At that time the one television station was presenting canned programs, which were 95 percent American aside from the newscasts. On the other hand, Greenland seemingly was the least affected by U.S. culture, while the most interesting reaction to the American cultural presence was that of Iceland. Despite the widespread furor caused by the beaming of American television programs from the base at Keflavik to the city of Reykjavik, the highly literate Icelanders nevertheless applauded personal appearances by such prominent U.S. culture bearers as William Faulkner, Isaac Stern, E. Power Biggs, the Philadelphia Woodwind Quintet, and the U.S. Air Force Band. Yet these same Icelanders could later show their hostility to America by filming the anti-U.S. movie *Gogo* in the early 1960s.

In conclusion, numerous writings that deal with the American impact on the remainder of the world in modern times make reference to the phenomenon of "coca-colization": in nation after nation the agents of U.S. civilization have imposed an American-oriented uniformity upon the inhabitants of these countries. It is, in fact, obvious that there has been a considerable U.S. impact even on foreign states as large as Japan and Canada; one might logically conclude, therefore, that smaller nations like Greenland, the Bahamas, Jamaica, and the Azores would offer even less resistance to this onrushing tide. Obviously, the American military bases set up during World War 2 and the other relationships of various types which have emerged during the last thirty years have subjected these islands to U.S. cultural influence. Yet there has been no large-scale surrender of individuality on their part, no general movement towards a common U.S.-dominated sameness in an age when there is so much talk of American "imperialism."

This, then, is the one great truth which emerges out of the mass of material presented in this narrative. Diversity instead has triumphed, in the case of Greenland and in that of the Bahamas, in that of Jamaica and in that of the Azores, and especially in that of Iceland. If David had not slain Goliath, he at least has stood up to him and asserted his own uniqueness, dwarfed as he may be by the giant.

What the future may bring remains to be seen, as these six nations move at varying rates from colonial status towards independence, and having achieved it confront the sober responsibilities which accompany sovereignty. Each, therefore, must find the most appropriate solutions for itself to those problems which the Jamaicans came face to face with in a five-year plan released shortly after their nation had become independent. "Can a small country," asked this document, "achieve and maintain at once, parliamentary democracy, economic viability, and social justice?" Should Jamaica or any of the others truly implement all three goals, then perhaps it will be a more humble United States which absorbs influences one day rather than radiates them.

NOTES

1. INTRODUCTION

1. *Congressional Record,* 66th Congress, 2nd Session, vol. 59, pt. 4. March 6, 1920, p. 3948.

2. The London *Morning Post* pointed out in an editorial entitled "Not for Sale" on March 6, 1920, that Senator Kenyon was one of the leaders of the Prohibition movement and may have been vexed that Americans could drink legally in Bermuda, the Bahamas, and Jamaica.

3. "America and the West Indies," in London *Daily Telegraph,* March 8, 1920. The two London newspaper items mentioned here are appended to a letter: John W. Davis to Bainbridge Colby, London, March 9, 1920, Record Group no. 59, decimal file 711.44C14/3, National Archives, Washington D.C., hereafter cited as NARG.

4. "Paying Debts with Men," *New York Times,* February 15, 1921, p. 8.

5. William W. Corcoran to Cordell Hull, Kingston, July 11, 1933. NARG 59, decimal file 844D.014/8. The *Daily Gleaner* editorial is attached to this letter.

6. Ibid.

7. "Sea Bases: Ownership vs. Lease," *U.S. News* 10 (January 24, 1941): 11.

8. Cordell Hull, *Memoirs* 1 (New York: Macmillan Company, 1948): 834.

9. U.S. Department of State, *Foreign Relations of the United States, 1940* 3 (Washington: G.P.O., 1958): 60. Hereafter cited as FRUS.

10. Ibid., pp. 66–67.

11. Ibid., p. 68. It is in this August 22 communication to F.D.R. that the British Prime Minister observed, "I do not think that bad man [Hitler] has yet struck his full blow" (p. 69).

12. Ibid., pp. 70–71.

13. Stetson Conn and Byron Fairchild, *The United States Army in World War 2, The Western Hemisphere: The Framework of Hemispheric Defense* (Washington: Office of the Chief of Military History, 1960), p. 58. Churchill noted that Antigua might be useful as a base for flying boats. Hull, 1: 839.

14. *FRUS, 1940,* 3: 61.

15.   Robert Divine, *Foreign Policy and U.S. Presidential Elections, 1940-1948* (New York: Franklin Watts/New Viewpoints, 1974), p. 53.

16.   Charles Callan Tansill, *Back Door to War: The Roosevelt Foreign Policy 1933-1941* (Chicago: Henry Regnery Company, 1952), p. 599.

17.   Ibid., p. 598. In rebutting this interpretation of the Hague Convention Cordell Hull pointed out that it began with the proposition that "belligerents are bound to respect the sovereign rights of neutral powers" (1: 842).

18.   *FRUS, 1940* 3 (1959): 75

19.   This series of events is examined in the chapter on Bermuda.

20.   *FRUS, 1941* 3: 80.

21.   Ibid., p. 84.

22.   American relations with both Greenland and Denmark during 1941 are described at great length in the chapters of this volume dealing with each country.

23.   Harold John Sutphen, *The Anglo-American Destroyers-Bases Agreement, September 1940*, Ph.D. dissertation, Fletcher School of Law and Diplomacy, Tufts University, 1967, pp. 287-88.

24.   Ibid., pp. 288, iv, and 293. Sutphen notes (p. 1) relative to the destroyers that they were transferred to Great Britain by the end of 1940 and were used to convoy operations the following year, but then were placed in mothballs gradually after having made a significant contribution to the war effort.

25.   *Congressional Record*, 88th Congress, 2nd Session, vol. 110, pt. 10, June 16, 1964, p. 13994.

2. THE BAHAMAS

1.   Described by Edgar Stanton Maclay as "a rugged sailor of the old school" Hopkins was eventually forced out of the navy for using profane language and calling the Naval Committee a "pack of lawyer's clerks who knew nothing about naval affairs." See p. 119 of Maclay's article, "A Neglected Hero of the Revolution," in *Daughters of the American Revolution Magazine* 52 (March 1918): 119-23. Consult pp. 120-21 for the comparison with Washington.

2.   Malcolm Lloyd, Jr., contributor, "The Taking of the Bahamas by the Continental Navy in 1776," in *Pennsylvania Magazine of History* 49 (October 1925); 349-66. This article consists of letters from and to Governor Montfort Browne written during 1776 and early 1777.

3.   Carlos C. Hanks—unlike many writers—tends to downgrade Hopkins's achievement: ". . . the expedition had proved of little value except to show the monumental ignorance of naval tactics and gunnery on the part of the officials of the young American Navy." "A Cruise for Gunpowder," *Proceedings of the U.S. Naval Institute* 45 (March 1939): 327.

4.   John J. McCusker, Jr., "The American Invasion of Nassau in the Bahamas," *American Neptune* 25 (July 1965): 215-16.

5.   Thelma Peterson Peters describes the Conchs as "a dour, hardy, unlettered people who lived largely from the sea—as wreckers, beachcombers, fishermen, turtlers, and salt rakers." There were approximately 4,000 of them in 1783, perhaps half of the total Loyalist immigration during the next two years. The quotation is from the summary to be found in *Dissertation Abstracts* 21: 7 (January 1961): 1924, of Peters's 1960 University of Florida Ph.D. dissertation, *The American Loyalists and the Plantation Period in the Bahamas Islands.*

6.   Some of the Loyalists had moved to Florida as early as 1808, establishing a colony at New Smyrna, but the hostility of the Spanish administration there caused them to resettle again soon thereafter.

7.   It is not clear whether the reference is to Great Abaco Island or Little Abaco Island.

8.   W. Adolphe Roberts, *The Caribbean: The Story of Our Sea of Destiny* (Indianapolis: Bobbs-Merrill Company, 1940), p. 287.

9.   Lord John Russell, "The Trade with the Bahamas," *New York Times* September 5, 1863, p. 5.

10.   Frank Tousley Edwards, *The United States Consular Service in the Bahamas during the American Civil War: A Study of Its Function within a Naval and Diplomatic Context,* Ph.D. dissertation, Catholic University of America, 1968. A summary is to be found in *Dissertation Abstracts* 29: 11 (May 1969): 3933A.

11.   B. M. Wilson, "The Bahama Expedition of the State University of Iowa," *Scientific American* 70 (April 14, 1894): 229–30.

12.   Lorin A. Lathrop to Bainbridge Colby, Nassau, October 8, 1920, NARG 59, decimal file 844E.114/1.

13.   Lorin A. Lathrop, memorandum, "Liquor Smuggling from the Bahama Islands," Nassau, June 6, 1942, NARG 59, decimal file 844E.114/8.

14.   *FRUS, 1926* 2 (1941): 1023. Consult pp. 354–55 for the suggestions dealing with such areas as intelligence, liaison, prosecutions, British and U.S. patrol vessels, entry from the high seas, and diplomatic support.

15.   "Bahamas are Back on Pre-Booze Basis," *New York Times,* October 30, 1932, p. 7.

16.   Harry J. Anslinger, memorandum, "Comment on American Influence in the Bahamas," Nassau, November 13, 1925, NARG 59, decimal file 844E.00/7.

17.   Consult p. 5 of W. K. Ailshie to Cordell Hull, Nassau, September 21 1939, NARG 59, decimal file 844E.50/6.

18.   Roosevelt had rejected the Mayaguana site after a personal inspection tour; his judgment was later reaffirmed by the Coast and Geodetic Survey vessel *Hydrographer*. There also was a waning interest on the part of the army towards a Bahamas base.

19.   Authorities do not always agree on the precise number of deaths and injuries.

20.   Paul Blanshard, *Democracy and Empire in the Caribbean* (New York: Macmillan Company, 1947), p. 144.

21.   "Small in Mind," *Nassau Tribune,* May 8, 1943. A copy of this editorial is to be found with the letter from Henry M. Wolcott to Cordell Hull, Nassau, May 17, 1943, NARG 59, decimal file 844E.00/30.

22.   *Congressional Record,* 80th Congress, 1st Session, vol. 93, pt. 8 July 23, 1947, p. 9851.

23.   At this time a bill authorizing a 3,000-mile test range was before the U.S. Congress.

24.   Jack Raymond, "100-Mile U.S. Range in Bahamas to Test Undersea Weapons," *New York Times,* May 15, 1963, pp. 1 and 6; "Anti-Submarine Centre in the Bahamas," London *Times,* May 15, 1963, p. 12. The *New York Times* article set a completion date in 1968, the London *Times* in 1973.

25.   Another interesting aspect of this project was that the laborers were paid wages equal to those which their counterparts in the southeastern United States were receiving.

26.   U.S. Department of Commerce, Bureau of International Commerce, *Foreign Economic Trends: Bahamas,* June 24, 1971, p. 9.

27.   "Life Goes to Nassau," *Life* 20 (April 29, 1946): 135.

28.   The discussion of this material in no way whatsoever constitutes an endorsement of Mastriana's charges against Roosevelt or McLaney. A further insight into Mastriana's character may be drawn from his admission that he had himself declared criminally insane to gain a transfer from prison to a hospital, but later "quit being insane" after the Social Security Administration had threatened to cut off its payments to him!

29.   "What Robert Vesco is Doing in the Bahamas," *Business Week,* March 30, 1974, p. 80. Again, as with Roosevelt and McLaney, much of the information about Vesco is conjectural, and thus should in no way be construed as proof that the latter is legally guilty of criminal acts.

30.   Vaughn A. Lewis, "The Bahamas in International Politics," *Journal of Interamerican Studies and World Affairs* 16 (May 1974): 147.

31.   Actually, there were twelve scales, ranging from $5,000 to $25,000, for permanent settlers according to occupation.

3. JAMAICA

1.   Alumina is the intermediate stage between bauxite and aluminum.

2.   The conservative rural members had returned home to guard against possible Negro insurrections during the holiday season.

3.   An act passed by the island Assembly at the end of February 1783 was designed to benefit all white refugees.

4.   W. J. Gardner, *A History of Jamaica: From Its Discovery by Christopher Columbus to the Year 1872* (London: T. Fisher Unwin, 1909), p. 213.

5.   James Duncan Phillips, *Salem and the Indies* (Boston: Houghton Mifflin Co., 1947), p. 107.

6.   Not only did Castlereagh himself talk of the New Orleans expedition during the peace negotiations at Ghent, but the temporary commandant of the Jamaican naval station opened a letter dealing with the expedition while in the presence of a merchant with American friends and business connections.

7.   Robert Greenhalgh Albion, *The Rise of New York Port, 1815-1860* (Hamden, Connecticut: Archon Books, 1961), pp. 181, 183.

8.   David R. Bard and William J. Baker, "The American Newspaper Response to the Jamaican Riots of 1865," *Journalism Quarterly* 51 (winter 1974): 659–60.

9.   "The Offerings of Jamaica," *New York Times,* June 22, 1882, p. 2. The Governor also makes reference to the sale of cinchona bark (quinine) in England.

10.   There appears to have been a difference of opinion as to whether the Jamaican groves were free from disease or not.

11.   "Jamaica Would Be Free," *New York Times,* January 6, 1898, p. 7.

12.   The parliamentary maneuverings are too complex to summarize here.

13.   On February 6, 1900, an anti-reciprocity memorial from the legislature on the fruit growing state of California was placed before the U.S. House of Representatives.

14.   Despite these statistics, Governor Musgrave had opined in his previously mentioned 1882 interview that "the Atlas Steamship Line subsidized by the Government, has . . . proved of great value in developing the trade. . . ." "The Offerings of Jamaica," *New York Times,* June 22, 1882, p. 2.

15.   For the year ending September 30, 1888, there were net earnings of $106,000 out of total receipts of $278,000, so that the U. S. buyers were not taking over a money-losing proposition.

16.   "Americans Not Daunted," *New York Times,* January 26, 1891, p. 5.

17.   "Sensitive Mr. Blaine." March 15, 1891, p. 16. One may find a description of the displays in general and the U.S. displays in particular in "The Jamaica Fair," *New York Times,* February 13, 1891, p. 9. Here we learn that the exhibition building on the Plain of Liguenea was in the shape of a gigantic cross topped by a great dome 100 feet high, the cupola being gilded and Moorish decorations reaching to the ground; at night an electric searchlight on the dome would flash out over the harbor a mile and a half distant. With Canada dominating the exhibition, the Singer Manufacturing Company offered one of the few American displays of real interest.

18.   "Jamaica Would Be Free," p. 7.

19.   Phil. Robinson, "The Sale of Jamaica to the United States," in *Harper's Weekly* 43 (January 7, 1899): 23.

20.   *FRUS, 1907* 1 (1910): 558.

21.   Ibid., p. 564. Forgotten today and overlooked at the time was the passage by the U.S. Congress of H.R. 24478, "An Act for the Relief of Citizens of the Island of Jamaica," January 18, 1907, Ch. 154, 34 Stat. 850.

22.   "Anglo-American Relations and the Swettenham Incident," *Harper's Weekly* 51 (February 9, 1907): 187. *Harper's,* though, tended to minimize the incident and observed that it aroused less of a furor in the United States.

23.   "The Earthquake in Jamaica," *Blackwood's* 181 (March 1907): 425–28. *Blackwood's* did admit that "our representative was guilty of outrageous conduct."

24.   "Britain and the United States," *Spectator* 48 (January 26, 1907): 128.

25.   Ian Malcolm, "The 'White Flag' in Jamaica," *Nineteenth Century* 61 (June 1907): 917. Malcolm (p. 911) takes the position that there was no mutiny at the penitentiary.

26.   Swettenham himself had written Davis on January 19 that "I also desire to express my most sincere thanks for the desire you expressed to have done more if my scruples had permitted my acceptance of your squadron's services so generously rendered." *FRUS, 1907:* 566.

27.   Untitled article, *Current Literature* 42 (March 1907): 252.

28.   "Anglo-American Relations and the Swettenham Incident," p. 187.

29.   *FRUS, 1905* (1906): 710. On May 8 Minister Barrett wrote the British consul: "It must be remembered that these men are somewhat difficult to deal with and that they complain, no matter how good provision is made for them" (p. 711). The entire correspondence may be found between pages 709 and 712.

30.   Brooks Adams, *America's Economic Supremacy* (New York: Harper and Brothers, 1947), p. 128.

31.   Because of the termination of the bounty, only 1.9% of Jamaican sugar reached America in 1910.

32.   Chester Lloyd Jones, *Caribbean Interests of the United States* (New York: D. Appleton and Co., 1916), p. 39.

33.   Marcus Garvey is related to the colonization movement in general on pp. 43–45 of Edward W. Chester, *Clash of Titans: Africa and U.S. Foreign Policy* (Maryknoll, New York: Orbis Books, 1974), p. 43.

34.   Charles L. Latham to Bainbridge Colby, Kingston, February 15, 1921. NARG 59, decimal file 844d.911/–. Wilbur J. Carr replied for the secretary of state on March 9 that Latham should not *officially* protest the anti-

American articles, but instead handle them informally. (This letter is found with the first.) Fifteen years later a news survey in Jamaica revealed that the American topics most thoroughly covered in the *Daily Gleaner* were (1) administration policies, (2) commercial and trade trends, (3) crimes, (4) general subjects. See John S. Littell, memorandum, "News Survey, Jamaica," Kingston, July 14, 1936, NARG 59, decimal file 844D.911/7.

35. Paul C. Squire to Henry Stimson, Kingston, April 28, 1931, NARG 59, decimal file 844D/911.3. Included is a clipping of "Rolyat's" column from the *Daily Gleaner* for April 27, 1931, entitled "Jamaica Jottings."

36. Squire to Stimson, Kingston, January 20, 1932, NARG 59 decimal file 844D.911/4. The editorial was entitled "The American Way." To quote it further, ". . . America had been selling war munitions and food to England, France and other countries at an enormous price. . . . America made a fortune out of the war, from a debtor she became a creditor nation, from a country which owed great sums to Europe she became a country to whom money was owed by Europe."

37. Squire to Stimson, Kingston, January 22, 1932, NARG 59, decimal file 844D.911/5. The editorial was entitled "Why 'A Fool'?"

38. Squire to Stimson, Kingston, July 28, 1931, NARG 59, decimal file 711.44D/1.

39. George Alexander Armstrong to Cordell Hull, Kingston, July 27, 1936, NARG 59, decimal file 844D.12/9. At 25 pages this is more of a memorandum than a letter. Of Smith, whom Armstrong describes on p. 16 as a "pure demagogue," the Governor observes (p. 28) that "when he retired, he intended to buy a phonograph and place on it records of Jag Smith's speeches, and then enjoy himself throwing things at the machine."

40. "Gives Up Jamaica Stores," *New York Times,* October 5, 1919, 2: 1.

41. Jamaican coconut exports proliferated during the 1920s.

42. J. L. Wilson-Goode, "The Trade of Jamaica," *Board of Trade Journal* (November 22, 1923): 546.

43. Jamaica was exporting on the average only 12 million oranges per year during the 1920s, compared with 107 million at the turn of the century when the Florida crop experienced a two years' failure.

44. Consult Squire to Stimson, Kingston, July 28, 1931, p. 9, for the withholding of statistics from the Kingston consulate by the Governor, for unspecified reasons.

45. Peter Abrahams, *Jamaica: An Island Mosaic* (London: Her Majesty's Stationery Office, 1957), p. 152.

46. Squire to Stimson, Kingston, July 28, 1931.

47. Paul Blanshard, *Democracy and Empire in the Caribbean* (New York: Macmillan Company, 1947), p. 100.

48. Stetson Conn, Rose C. Engleman, and Byron Fairchild, *The United States Army in World War 2, The Western Hemisphere: Guarding the United States and Its Outposts* (Washington: Office of the Chief of Military History, 1964), pp. 419–20.

49. This 72-page work may be found at Maxwell Air Force Base, Montgomery, Alabama. Consult p. 41.

50. Blanshard, p. 100.

51. The other members of the West Indies Federation were Trinidad, Barbados, Grenada, St. Lucia, St. Vincent, Dominica, Antigua, St. Christopher-Nevis-Anguilla, and Montserrat.

52. The Ras Tafarians took their name from one of Haile Selassie's family names.

53. *Congressional Record,* 87th Congress, 1st Session, vol. 107, pt. 6, May 4, 1961, p. 7306.

54.   "Ten-Year Development Program Proposed for Jamaica," U.S. Department of State *Bulletin* 28 (January 26, 1953): 141.
55.   Consult chapter 7 of Wendell Bell, *Jamaican Political Attitudes in a New Nation* (Berkeley: University of California Press, 1964). The moral rightness poll appears on p. 152, the effectiveness one on p. 161. Bell's highly elaborate analysis of the social characteristics of those interviewees assuming opposite sides on these key questions defies summary here. The 1962 and 1974 statistics come from pages 7 and 8 of the preliminary draft of an unpublished 41-page paper by J. William Gibson, Jr., and Wendell Bell entitled "Jamaica Faces the Outside World at Home and Abroad: The First Twelve Years of Nationhood."
56.   With respect to the Canadian company, it processed bauxite into alumina on the island instead of exporting it.
57.   Thomas Balogh, "A New Deal in Jamaica," *Venture* 9 (June 1957): 5.
58.   See p. 118 of Norman Girvan, *Foreign Capital and Economic Underdevelopment in Jamaica* (Jamaica: Institute of Social and Economic Research, University of the West Indies, 1971). Girvan devotes three entire chapters (2, 3, and 4) to bauxite; it should be noted that Alcoa itself eventually turned to Jamaica for this raw material.
59.   According to Owen Jefferson (p. 140) this agreement "has served to dampen the growth of the Jamaican industry" (Jamaica: Institute of Social and Economic Research, University of the West Indies, 1972]. The bauxite industry is analyzed in depth between pp. 150 and 169.
60.   R. Hart Phillips ties in the presence of slums with the growth of the Ras Tafari movement, stating that the latter has concentrated there.
61.   "Our Man in Kingston," *Time* 102 (August 6, 1973): 39; George Crile, "Our Man in Jamaica," *Harper's*, 249 (October 1974): 87-96. The quotations from the latter article appear on pp. 88, 92, and 94.
62.   Consult pp. 138–39 of Sir Harold Mitchell, *Caribbean Patterns: A Political and Economic Study of the Contemporary Caribbean* (Edinburgh: W. & R. Chambers, Ltd., 1967).
63.   Despite the fact that blacks obviously monopolize high official positions in Jamaica today, this by no means implies that Americans no longer deal with whites there on important matters. This is especially true of the business world. To quote Carol S. Holzberg, "Native Whites are disproportionately represented among the Island's national entrepreneurial elite, and as national entrepreneurs these Whites continue to dominate the organization, direction and finance of the highest productivity sectors and largest local capital interests." See p. 3 of her 27-page unpublished paper "Social Stratification, Cultural Nationalism, and Political Economy in Jamaica: The Role of the National Entrepreneurial Elite." Ms. Holzberg has most kindly furnished me with a copy of this.
64.   Walter N. Tobriner to Edward Chester, Washington, August 11, 1972. Former Ambassador Tobriner's letter—plus a 3-page memorandum—is a very valuable current assessment of the Jamaican situation.

4. BERMUDA

1.   Bergen Evans, compiler, *Dictionary of Quotations* (New York: Bonanza Books, 1968), p. 57.
2.   The Spanish did leave some pigs behind, whose descendants were running wild at the time of the arrival of the English.
3.   Hudson Strode, *The Story of Bermuda* (New York: Harrison Smith and Robert Haas, 1932), pp. 56–57.
4.   David L. White, *The Economic Impacts of America on Bermuda*, senior project, Bard College, 1956, pp. 44–45. To quote the author, "This was especially designed to assure the Continental Congress that goods sent by them

to Bermuda would not be reshipped to loyalist colonies, especially the British West Indies, and it also served to supply Bermuda with provisions from ships detained there enroute to the West Indies."

5. Henry C. Wilkinson, *Bermuda in the Old Empire* (London: Oxford University Press, 1950); Addison E. Verrill, "Relations between Bermuda and the American Colonies during the Revolutionary War," *Transactions of the Connecticut Academy of Arts and Sciences* 13 (1907): 47–64. Verrill here sets the date of Deane's visit in 1776, while Wilkinson places it a year earlier, in 1775.

6. Verrill, p. 62.

7. Walter Hayward Brownell, *Bermuda: Past and Present* (New York: Dodd, Mead and Co., 1935), p. 50.

8. "Bermuda and the American Revolution," *Bermuda Historical Quarterly* 14 (spring 1957): 34–37. The article consists of the letter; the quotation occurs at its beginning.

9. See p. 445 of Isaac J. Greenwood, "Bermuda during the American Revolution," *New England Historical and Genealogical Register* 50 (October 1896).

10. "The Tucker Papers," *Bermuda Historical Quarterly* 7 (January-March 1950): 16–17.

11. Verrill, p. 59.

12. White, p. 55.

13. Thomas Melville Dill, "Bermuda and the War of 1812," *Bermuda Historical Quarterly* 1 (July-September 1944): 143.

14. As one might expect, Randolph's version of the encounter differed somewhat from the one printed in the *Bermuda Journal*.

15. U.S. Congress, *Message from the President of the United States, in compliance with a Resolution of the Senate, with copies of Correspondence in relation to the seizure of slaves on board the brigs "Encomium" and "Enterprise,"* Senate Document no. 174, 27th Congress, 2nd Session, February 14, 1837, p. 35.

16. Among the crops raised were early potatoes, onions, and arrowroot.

17. White, p. 109.

18. Allen once observed, "I have once been attacked in my office and once knocked down in the street within a few days, the general sentiment is 'it's good enough for him, he's a damned Yankee.'" See n. 16, p. 15, of Frank E. Vandiver, ed., *Confederate Blockade Running through Bermuda 1861–1865: Letters and Cargo Manifests* (Austin: University of Texas Press, 1947). Four members of the *Tallahassee* crew once assaulted Allen in his own consulate, while an officer and seamen from the *Florida* attacked him on the street at night and severely beat him.

19. For the biography of one individual who served aboard a blockade runner, see Walter B. Haywood, "Johnny Tabb," *Bermuda Historical Quarterly* 7 (January-March 1958): 44–47. Tabb, the captain's clerk aboard the *Robert L. Lee,* was eventually captured and imprisoned with fellow poet Sidney Lanier; after the war he took a teaching position before becoming a Roman Catholic priest.

20. J. Holland Rose, A. P. Newton, and E. A. Benians, *The Cambridge History of the British Empire 2, The Growth of the New Empire, 1783–1870* (Cambridge: Cambridge University Press, 1940), p. 740.

21. White, p. 79.

22. "Surplus Whiskey," *New York Times,* April 8, 1883, p. 4. Subtitled "How Bermuda Darkies Fatten on the Genuine American Blue Grass," this article accuses local blacks of clandestinely draining whiskey barrels at the Hamilton ship pier with the aid of gimlets and straws.

23. "Bermuda Wants Reciprocity," *New York Times,* July 17, 1893, p. 8. Entitled the same as an earlier article, published on October 3, 1892, on p. 9, this news item revealed that the duty which Bermuda paid the U.S. under the 1890 McKinley Tariff surpassed the entire revenue collected under the Bermuda tariff of 1892.

24. White, pp. 77–8.

25. One Boer prisoner, upon seeing more ocean from a hilltop instead of land, observed of the islands, "But where is the interior?" Frederick Lewis Allen, "Bermuda Base," *Harper's* 187 (September 1943): 344.

26. *Congressional Record,* 57th Congress, 1st Session, vol. 35, pt. 1, January 15, 1902, p. 690.

27. According to White, p. 90, the government of Bermuda paid the Quebec line a subsidy of $22,500 for the first year and $17,500 for the second.

28. Arthur Walworth, *Woodrow Wilson,* 2 vols. (New York: Longmans Green and Co., 1958), 2: 101, n. 2.

29. On February 10, 1917, the Post Office Department informed the State Department that the periodicals on the list would not be accepted for mailing to Bermuda. See NARG 59, decimal file 844h.918/2.

30. Dyer's Island became the temporary home of the biological station.

31. Brownell, pp. 106-7, discusses American military involvement in Bermuda during World War 1. The passage quoted appears on the latter page.

32. These statistics do not include the lily bud and bulb trade.

33. A motion to increase the sum to L2,040 was defeated.

34. In a survey of the Bermudian political scene for this year prepared by the American consul, the latter observed: ". . . it may not be amiss to remark that, wholly from the American side, there is a small but increasing disposition to inquire whether Bermuda may not be made into a place to escape taxation." See p. 9 of Harold L. Williamson, "Annual Political Report for Bermuda," Hamilton, December 8, 1936, NARG 59, decimal file 844H.00/3.

35. *Congressional Record,* 47th Congress, 1st Session, vol. 13, pt. 6, July 22, 1882, p. 6343.

36. Strode, p. 150.

37. Furness had bought out Quebec in 1919.

38. "The whole boom phenomenon in Bermuda during the depression," notes White on p. 93, "is explained by an American circumstance. Americans who were afraid to travel in Europe in the height of a depression and who shied away from expensive jaunts while there were breadlines in America and who also may have been feeling something of a financial pinch, went to closer, less expensive, and still overseas Bermuda."

39. On p. 629 of "A Submerged Beach off Bermuda," *Science,* n. s. 74 (December 18, 1931): 629-30, it is pointed out that ". . . the present dry land of Bermuda is slightly less than the area of Manhattan Island (19.3, as compared with 22 square miles), while the area added by the inclusion seaward of these submerged beaches would increase this to 576 square miles."

40. John R. Tunis, "Bermuda and the American Idea," *Harper's* 160 (March 1930): 453.

41. White, p. 94.

42. Williamson, p. 1.

43. Jim Bishop, "Our $50,000,000 Base at Bermuda," *Colliers* 114 (September 4, 1944): 20.

44. *Congressional Record,* 76th Congress, 3rd Session, vol. 86, pt. 13, February 26, 1940, p. 989.

45. Describing the activities of the censors in 1942, Luis Marden writes: "About a thousand men and women from England live and work in what were formerly the luxury hotels of the water front. They do not like to be photographed, and keep to themselves, even in their hours of relaxation." "Americans in the Caribbean," *National Geographic* 81 (June 1942): 723.

46. Frederick Lewis Allen, "Bermuda Base," *Harper's* 187 (September 1943): 345.

47.   Samuel Eliot Morison, *History of United States Naval Operations in World War 2* 1, *The Battle for the Atlantic: September 1939-May 1943* (Boston: Little, Brown and Co., 1960), pp. 82–3.
48.   Kindley Field was named after Captain Field E. Kindley, a World War 1 ace who shot down twelve German aircraft before dying in a crash at Kelly Field, Texas, in 1920.
49.   John Hall, letter, "The Battle of Bermuda," *New Republic* 105 (August 4, 1941): 157.
50.   Sutphen notes (p. 279) that when the S.S. *Mauretania* announced in September 1942 that it had room on board for the remaining 1,000 contractors' employees, Admiral James's staff turned "handsprings of joy."
51.   Alan Jackson, "Machine Gun in the Hibiscus," *Saturday Evening Post* 215 (July 25, 1942): 16.
52.   "Bermuda Seeks Tourists," *New York Times,* November 7, 1943, p. 53.
53.   Bishop, pp. 70–71.
54.   Consult the chapter on the Bahamas for parallel material.
55.   Bradley condescendingly observes: "The only industry in the Bermuda Islands is that of American tourists. They raise nothing, they have no resources, their only products are a few thousand tons of garden vegetables." *Congressional Record,* 79th Congress, 1st Session, vol. 91, pt. 6, September 5, 1945, pp. 8331–32.
56.   "Envoy of Canada for Self-Interest," *New York Times,* February 4, 1945, p. 21. Lord Burghley spoke at the annual dinner of the Canadian Society of New York.
57.   Allen, p. 348, observes in this connection that ". . . if one were able to get from one end of [Bermuda] to the other in an hour or two tourists and residents would soon feel confined; psychologically, Bermuda would shrink to an islet."
58.   "Bermuda Accepts Offer," *New York Times,* April 19, 1945, p. 3; U.S. Department of the Navy, Naval History Division, *History of Naval Facilities in Bermuda,* 1951, Base Maintenance Files, Navy Yard, Washington. The latter notes the total mileage as 14½, not 18½ as the *New York Times* reports.
59.   Earlier treaties between the United States and Bermuda had included the parcel post agreement of 1906 and the money order agreement of 1907.
60.   It will be recalled that there was now a Labour government in Great Britain, not a Conservative one.
61.   Since the islands prior to World War 2 had been lightly policed, it is perhaps not surprising that a number of Americans felt that the United States— whose military police were quite active there in wartime—should enjoy such a special privilege.
62.   ". . . his Naval Aide, Capt. H. K. Foskett, saw in it an opportunity to enforce every rule in the book of Navy regulations and did." "President Leaves Bermuda for Home," *New York Times,* August 31, 1946, p. 8.
63.   J.H.D., "Our Offshore Campus." *House and Garden* 109 (May 1956), 94–95.
64.   According to Bishop's World War 2 account (p. 71), all the houses in Bermuda caught their own water on the roofs, the latter being built of terraced limestone which cleansed the water. For the American military alone the system of rainwater catchment areas totalled 20 acres.
65.   See respectively "Praise for Tugmen as the Mount Julie Is Pulled-off," in Bermuda *Royal Gazette,* February 22, 1974, and "Customs Changes for U.S. Base," Bermuda *Royal Gazette,* February 7, 1974. The author wishes to thank Sue K. Smith for furnishing him with these clippings.
66.   In 1969 the Department of Tourist and Trade Development of Bermuda distributed a film entitled *Bermuda: The Island Nobody Wanted,* whose script drew heavily on Mark Twain's reports of his visit to the islands.

67.   Kenneth McNaught, "Crown Colony or U.S. Protectorate?" *Saturday Night* 76 (September 30, 1961): 23.

5. ICELAND

1.   The material on Miles and Browne comes from p. 45 of an article by Richard F. Tomasson in *Atlantica and Iceland Review* entitled "Iceland on the Brain," most kindly furnished to the author by George McGrath of Icelandic Loftleider.
2.   Brainerd Dyer, "Notes and Documents: Robert J. Walker on Acquiring Greenland and Iceland," *Mississippi Valley Historical Review* 27 (September 1940): 264.
3.   *Congressional Record*, 71st Congress, 1st Session, vol. 71, pt. 3, June 11, 1929, p. 2684. He also penned an entire book entitled *Iceland and Egypt in the Year 1874.*
4.   Kneeland's observation appears on p. 45 of Vilhjalmur Stefansson. *Iceland: The First American Republic* (Garden City: Doubleday and Co., 1947).
5.   Icelanders are among the most literate people in the world; since medieval times the island has produced more than its share of literary talent and genius.
6.   The resolution passed both houses unanimously after there had been a brief discussion over whether the statue of Ericsson should instead be a memorial; of the $55,000 finally appropriated, a final balance of $3,200 remained unspent. It should be noted that the explorer's name is sometimes found spelled with one s.
7.   Green H. Hackworth, *Digest of International Law,* 8 vols. (Washington: G.P.O., 1940–44), 1: 213.
8.   Between 1928 and 1931 Germany not only surveyed the fjords of Iceland for submarine use, but also designated certain areas of the interior for landing fields and weather stations, while photographing the island thoroughly.
9.   Charles A. Lindbergh, memorandum, "Greenland-Iceland Transatlantic Air Route," New York, May 1934, file EF 22-2, Navy Yard, Washington, p. 9.
10.   "Nye Lauds Iceland for Lack of Army," *New York Times,* June 18, 1939, p. 32.
11.   *Congressional Record*, 76th Congress, 3rd Session, vol. 86, pt. 7, June 6, 1940, pp. 7680–81.
12.   This order was approved by F.D.R.
13.   Richard W. Johnston, *Follow Me! The Story of the Second Marine Division in World War 2* (New York: Random House, 1948), pp. 8–9.
14.   Such an invitation would have required the calling of the Icelandic parliament to approve it.
15.   *FRUS, 1941* 2 (1959): 783.
16.   "The American Occupation of Iceland," *American-Scandinavian Review* 29 (September 1941): 258–59.
17.   Samuel Eliot Morison, *History of United States Naval Operations in World War 2* 1, *The Battle for the Atlantic September 1939–May 1943* p. 74.
18.   "The President Enters the War," *Christian Century* 58 (July 16, 1941): 902.
19.   *Congressional Record*, 77th Congress, 1st Session, vol. 87, pt. 12 (appendix), July 9, 1941, p. A3300. "The only freedom we have left here," observed Osmers, "is to answer 'Ja' to the President's proclamations."

20. Benedikt Gröndal, *Iceland: From Neutrality to NATO Membership* (Oslo: Universitetsforlaget, 1971), p. 33.
21. John L. Zimmerman, "A Note on the Occupation of Iceland by American Forces," *Political Science Quarterly* 62 (March 1947): 106.
22. Morison, p. 78.
23. The marines serving in France during World War 1 had been transferred from navy control by President Woodrow Wilson; F.D.R.'s action here placed the Icelandic Marine Brigade under a different administrative and disciplinary system from the one to which they were accustomed.
24. *FRUS, 1943* 2 (1964): 311.
25. The British approach was to proclaim martial law.
26. The marine figures were as of May 1.
27. *FRUS 1941* 2: 774.
28. As late as 1940 refined sugar was the leading American import into Iceland, followed by iron and steel, various grains and grain products, coconut and soybean oil, electric resistance wire, and automobile parts.
29. Because of the war effort it was proving difficult for Great Britain to supply Iceland with these items; the latter also was experiencing problems in buying goods in the United States with blocked sterling.
30. This 4-page report accompanies Assistant Secretary of State (name illegible) to Frank Knox, Washington, October 30, 1941, file no. EF-22-1, Navy Yard, Washington. It is stated on p. 3 of the report that ". . . the cooperation of the Icelanders in observing a proper attitude towards the troops is dearly to be insisted on. . . ."
31. Lincoln MacVeagh to Cordell Hull, Reykjavik, November 11, 1941, NARG 59, decimal file 859A.20/162. The exception was a rape case; two two-page lists of complaints are attached to this letter.
32. There were reports circulating that the British soldiers had a "very profound" disrespect for the Icelandic police, and that there had been numerous cases of shooting and considerable damage to property involving the former.
33. MacVeagh to Hull, Reykjavik, May 11, 1942, NARG 59, decimal file 859A.20/187. The two categorical statements were "that the Icelanders have committed no acts of sabotage, and that representatives of the Icelandic Government are not afforded an opportunity to be present at investigations conducted by the military."
34. There also were reports to the effect that a number of Icelandic taxicab drivers were concentrating their efforts on making liquor and women available to American soldiers.
35. For Hopkins, see Sólrun D. Jensdóttir Hardarson, "The 'Republic of Iceland,' 1940–44: Anglo-American Attitudes and Influences," *Journal of Contemporary History* (October 1974): 49. For Hull, consult *FRUS, 1942*, 3 (1959): 13. Hardarson's avowed objective was to examine Iceland's last years before independence from the British point of view, using newly opened Foreign Office Archives at the Public Record Office.
36. *FRUS, 1944* 2 (1965): 993.
37. One must not forget that in its early history Iceland was a republic for several centuries.
38. Louis G. Dreyfus to Hull, Reykjavik, June 24, 1944, NARG 59, decimal file 711.59A/6-2444. Two editorials from the Communist newspaper *Thjodviljinn* and the conservative newspaper *Visir* are attached: Dreyfus notes that *Visir* was controlled by Bjorn Olafsson, secretary of commerce and owner of the local Coca Cola factory.
39. "Iceland Demands Return of Bases," *New York Times,* August 27, 1944, p. 5.

40. Gröndal, pp. 36–37. Stalin had taken the position that those countries which declared war on Germany prior to March 1, 1945, should be charter members of the United Nations; during the ensuing discussion F.D.R. declared: "I should like to add one name to the list for the sake of clarity— the newest republic in the world, Iceland."

41. Clifton Lisle, "Hark Back: The Iceland Occupation," *General Magazine and Historical Chronicle* 51 (autumn 1948). According to Lisle, the American Claims Board was afflicted by overly extensive regulations which made no provision for emergencies.

42. *FRUS, 1943* 2: 309.

43. Agnes Rothery, *Iceland: New World Outpost* (New York: Viking Press, 1948), p. 190.

44. John Joseph Hunt, *The United States Occupation of Iceland, 1941–1946.* Ph.D. dissertation, Georgetown University, 1966, p. 375. This summary is found on p. 439A of vol. 27 of *Dissertation Abstracts* for 1966.

45. John B. Ritch, III, "Iceland," *Atlantic* 123 (April 1969): 40.

46. Other nations adhering to the 12-mile limit included the Soviet Union, Communist China, Mexico, and Indonesia.

47. *Iceland and the Law of the Sea* (Reykjavik: Government of Iceland, 1972), p. 22.

48. Gearhart also wanted to purchase Greenland from Denmark.

49. "Wallace Says U.S. Force Should Quit Iceland Base," *New York Times,* March 22, 1946, p. 4.

50. Henry A. Wallace, "Aiding Iceland's Defenses," *New York Times,* May 15, 1951, p. 10. In assessing the situation five years later Wallace observed, "Now when we help her at her own request she will respect and trust us."

51. Pressure from Russia undoubtedly contributed to the turndown.

52. A review of the agreement might be undertaken after five years; if talks remained deadlocked at the end of six months, either government could terminate it, effective a year later.

53. "We Surrender Our Iceland Base," *Christian Century* 63 (October 23, 1946): 1269. Here the *Christian Century* again emphasized Russian protests, as it did in a May 8 article.

54. "U.S. Forces Arrive to Defend Iceland," *New York Times,* May 8, 1951, p. 13.

55. When the base commander at Keflavik offered to build a new road to Reykjavik in place of the poor one currently existing, the Icelandic government rejected this offer, making the counterproposal that the United States give Iceland the money with which it would construct the highway with Icelandic labor. One suspects that the authorities in Reykjavik really did not want a better road built, since it might lead to more American soldiers visiting the capital.

56. Donald E. Nuechterlein, *Iceland: Reluctant Ally* (Ithaca: Cornell University Press, 1961), p. 192.

57. According to Porter McKeever, Jonasson "flushed with anger" when he was confronted with the charge that he was anti-American.

58. "Why Iceland Wants U.S. Troops To Go Home," *U.S. News and World Report* 41 (July 20, 1956): 38.

59. "North Atlantic Council Recommends Continuation of U.S. Icelandic Defense Agreement," U.S. Department of State *Bulletin* 25 (August 20, 1956): 307.

60. At this time there were around 4,000 U.S. troops and pilots at Keflavik.

61. The Tariff Commission's recommendation had been made two months earlier, on October 12.

62. Nixon also extended Christmas greetings from "Ike" to the people over the radio.
63. This loan was channelled through the Iceland Bank of Development.
64. This was to be financed out of the proceeds from the sale of surplus property to the Icelandic government since World War 2; there previously had been educational exchange on a limited scale between the United States and Iceland under the Smith-Mundt Act (1948).
65. The items involved here were wheat flour, barley, corn, rice, cottonseed and soybean oil, linseed oil, tobacco, fruit, and cotton.
66. Funds for this project were obtained from the sale of surplus agricultural commodities to Iceland under Public Law 480; this loan was to be administered for the International Cooperation Administration by the Export-Import Bank.
67. "U.S. Grants Iceland $6 Million for Monetary Stabilization," U.S. Department of State *Bulletin* 44 (January 16, 1961): 84–85. According to this article, the grant "will be used to pay for the importation of various commodities in the same manner as for loans which in past years have been obtained from the International Cooperation Administration."
68. These funds, made possible under a special provision of Public Law 480, were to be used to help develop four technical institutes in the areas of mathematics, physics, chemistry, and geophysics.
69. According to Johnson, in 1953 the Army Department had notified the State Department that it lacked the funds under existing claims statutes to finance a settlement.
70. Thingvellir, of course, had long been a favorite sightseeing spot for foreign tourists.
71. According to Nuechterlein (p. 197n), "a report on the incident by the Defense force asserted that there was no water or 'mud' on the ground at the time, contrary to the reports which appeared in the Icelandic papers."
72. "Departure in a Dispute," *Newsweek* 54 (September 28, 1959): 54; "End of an Incident," *Time* 74 (September 28, 1959): 16–17. *Time* reported that Pritchard, who was not even in Iceland at that moment, had done a good job during the few months that he had been there; afterwards he was placed in charge of the New York Air Defense Sector, "a juicy new assignment."
73. Among the signers of the petition were writers, professors, artists, scientists, doctors, and labor union leaders; none of them, however, was a known Communist.
74. *Congressional Record,* 88th Congress, 1st Session, vol. 109, pt. 5, April 24, 1963, pp. 7045–46. According to *Variety*'s reviewer, one "Denk," "The best thing said about Americans is a remark by a local taxi driver: 'He is not like the other Americans.'"
75. The author is indebted to Mr. Zinkoff, who has furnished him with issues of the *White Falcon, Jr.,* for the years since 1971.
76. Gröndal, p. 69.
77. Ritch, p. 43.
78. Robert Ross, "Yanks, Go Home," *Commonweal* 65 (November 16, 1956): 174.

6. THE AZORES

1. Samuel Eliot Morison, *The Maritime History of Massachusetts, 1783-1860* (Boston: Houghton Mifflin Co., 1921), pp. 193, 293, for material on the Dabneys.
2. The congressional action of 1882, together with various U.S.-Portugal diplomatic maneuverings in 1850, will be examined at the appropriate chronological points in the narrative.

3.   "Portugal," *New York Times,* May 21, 1874, p. 1. For Tripoli during the 1870s, see p. 121 of Edward W. Chester, *Clash of Titans: Africa and U.S. Foreign Policy* (Maryknoll, New York: Orbis Books, 1974).

4.   Emily Hahn, "A Reporter at Large: The Azores," part 2, "The Longest Distance between Two Islands," *New Yorker* 35 (November 21, 1959): 143.

5.   U.S. Department of Commerce and Labor, *Commercial Relations of the United States with Foreign Countries during the Year 1908,* 2 vols. (Washington: G.P.O., 1909). Consul E. A. Creevey's report appears in 1: 313–16, while this 592-page volume is also available as Serial Set 5499.

6.   Clemens's visit to Bermuda is described in that chapter.

7.   Francis M. Rogers, *The Portuguese Heritage of John Dos Passos* (Boston: Portuguese Continental Union of the United States of America, 1976), p. 24. The author is indebted to the P.C.U. for sending him, unsolicited, this fascinating document.

8.   James H. Guill, "Nine Keys to Atlantic Defense," *Proceedings of the United States Naval Institute* 79 (October 1953): 1077.

9.   "Denies Naval Base Report," *New York Times,* April 13, 1918, p. 2.

10.   Seward W. Livermore, "The Azores in American Strategy-Diplomacy, 1917–1919," *Journal of Modern History* 20 (September 1948): 201. To date the Livermore article remains the only scholarly treatment of any aspect of Azorean-American diplomacy, except for Professor J. K. Sweeney's recent work on the World War 2 period.

11.   Herbert C. Pell to Cordell Hull, Lisbon, July 2, 1940, NARG 59, decimal file 853B.00/34.

12.   At least twice during World War 2, in 1941 and 1943, F.D.R. referred to these visits in his correspondence with Portuguese Prime Minister Salazar.

13.   Dasheens, or taros, are described in the second edition of Webster's *New International Dictionary* are being "grown throughout the tropics for [their] edible starchy tuberous roots."

14.   Pell to Hull, Lisbon, July 2, 1940. Also see the enclosed memorandum from Jose Maria Bensaude, Ponta Delgada, May 17, 1940.

15.   *FRUS, 1941* 2 (1959): 839.

16.   "Get Tough, Pepper Urges Senate," *New York Times,* May 7, 1941, p. 12.

17.   Admiral Stark testified before the Pearl Harbor investigating committee in 1946 to this effect.

18.   William L. Langer and S. Everett Gleason, *The Undeclared War, 1940–1941* (New York: Harper and Brothers, 1953), (published for the Council on Foreign Relations), pp. 516–17. Given a free hand by F.D.R., Undersecretary of State Sumner Welles drafted a message for possible submission to Congress on May 20 opposing the transfer of the Atlantic islands to the Axis Powers, which the President later rejected at the insistence of Hull.

19.   Curiously, F.D.R. was apparently not informed about the original Portuguese protest, or Hull's reply, until after the exchange of messages had taken place; at least, that is the impression which he gave at a contemporary press conference.

20.   *FRUS, 1941* 2.

21.   Charles A. Beard, *President Roosevelt and the Coming of the War, 1941: A Study in Appearances and Realities* (New Haven: Yale University Press, 1948), p. 453. Beard here offers the first scholarly indictment of F.D.R.'s foreign policy on a day-by-day basis from the isolationist standpoint. Undersecretary of State Sumner Welles's memorandum of the proceedings of this conference were brought to the attention of the Pearl Harbor investigating committee in 1946. See "Roosevelt Urged Anglo-U.S. Police," *New York Times,* December 19, 1946, p. 12.

22. *FRUS, 1942* 3 (1959): 869.
23. *FRUS, 1943* 2 (1964): 553.
24. Ibid., p. 559.
25. Ibid., p. 566.
26. Samuel Eliot Morison, *History of United States Naval Operations in World War 2* 10, *The Atlantic Battle Won: May 1943-May 1945* (Boston: Little, Brown and Co., 1960), p. 45.
27. *FRUS, 1944* 4 (1966): 14. The 49-year-old Norweb had just concluded a successful tour of duty in Peru; J. K. Sweeney attributes the eventual construction of air facilities in the Azores by the American military to his efforts. See p. 3 of the unpublished paper by Sweeney, "Genesis of an Airbase: The United States, Portugal, and Santa Maria."
28. *FRUS, 1944* 4: 44. The legation in Portugal had been raised to the status of an embassy on June 20.
29. Ibid., p. 52.
30. Ibid., p. 64.
31. Ibid., pp. 82-83.
32. According to Sweeney ("Genesis of an Airbase," p. 14), the U.S. Joint Chiefs of Staff were far from satisfied with the Santa Maria agreement.
33. Commander, U.S. Naval Forces, Azores, *Report on Establishing U.S. Naval Activities in the Azores, January to August 1944,* p. 3, command file, World War 2, Navy Yard, Washington.
34. Ibid., p. 10.
35. "Azores Agreement Cements U.S. Relations with Lisbon," *New York Times,* November 22, 1948, p. 7.
36. "The Strategic Azores," *New York Times,* December 31, 1961, 4: 8.
37. Jack Raymond, "U.S. and Portugal Uneasy on Bases," *New York Times,* October 25, 1964, p. 35.
38. This and much additional material dealing with the period may be found in *Historical Annex to 1605th Air Base Wing History, 1 July 1964-31 December 1964,* 3 vols., Maxwell Air Force Base, Montgomery, Ala. Supporting documents here complement a basic narrative.
39. *Congressional Record,* 91st Congress, 1st Session, vol. 115, pt. 11, June 5, 1969, p. 14875.
40. Among the development projects in Portugal to be financed by the Export-Import Bank loan were "airport construction, railway modernization, bridge-building, electric power generation, mechanization of agriculture, harbor construction and town planning, and the supplying of equipment for schools and hospitals." "The Azores Agreement," *Current History* 64 (April 1973): 178.
41. Republican Senator Clifford P. Case of New Jersey demanded that the United States suspend economic aid to Portugal until the two nations signed a treaty.
42. Hyman Bloom to Edward Chester, Ponta Delgada, November 22, 1972. American Consul Bloom's letter is a goldmine of current information on the Azores and is cited several times in the narrative.
43. "Department Discusses Agreements on Azores and Bahrain Facilities," Department of State *Bulletin* 66 (February 28, 1972): 280. Earlier Johnson had pointed out: "the agreement contains no new defense commitment to Portugal—in fact, the grant to the United States of base rights in the Azores involves no defense or security commitments by the United States at all. We are not required to station troops at Lajes. We could, without violating this agreement, bring them home tomorrow."
44. Angelo J. Cerchione, "The Island and the Smile," manuscript, p. 2. Captain Cerchione personally furnished the author with a copy of this important study of U.S. military veterinarians assisting the people of the Azores; his work helps explain why American-Azorean relations have remained harmonious since World War 2.

45.   Ibid., p. 20.

46.   Casein is described in the second edition of Webster's *New International Dictionary* as "a protein produced when milk is curdled by rennet."

47.   "U.S. Base's Future Disturbs Azores," *New York Times,* May 10, 1968, p. 5; Tad Szulc, "Letter from the Azores," *New Yorker* 47 (January 1, 1972): 56.

48.   *Congressional Record,* 85th Congress, 2nd Session, vol. 104, pt. 13, August 6, 1958, p. 16931.

49.   This episode is discussed at length in the chapter on Jamaica.

7. GREENLAND

1.   Brainerd Dyer, "Notes and Documents: Robert J. Walker on Acquiring Greenland and Iceland," *Mississippi Valley Historical Review* 28 (September 1940): 266. Francis Lieber wrote Charles Sumner three years later that the report had been suppressed, but Dyer discounts this charge.

2.   It was rumored in Canadian circles in 1897 that the American government had approached its Danish counterpart about the purchase of Greenland ("Rumor about Greenland," *New York Times,* September 30, 1897, p. 7). The latter editorialized that Denmark's "almost useless possession" "could be assimilated without filling good politicians with apprehension or bad ones with delight." (October 2, 1897, p. 6).

3.   *FRUS, 1917* (1926): 561–62. To quote Egan, "Greenland is looked on by the Danes very much as our people formerly looked upon Alaska. The Government here is so much occupied with internal economic and political differences in Denmark that it gives very little attention to the development of the resources of Greenland, which is practically terra incognita."

4.   Marie Peary, "Peary's Predictions on Greenland's Value," *Current History* 52 (November 26, 1940): 27. This article was condensed from an earlier, longer one in the *Christian Science Monitor.*

5.   This article places the total imports in 1910 at 86 tons, not zero.

6.   A good map of Greenland showing the routes of explorers is to be found in William Herbert Hobbs, "The University of Michigan Greenland Expedition of 1926–1927," *Geographical Review* 16 (April 1926): 257.

7.   Jeannette Mirsky, *To the Arctic* (London: Allan Wingate, 1949), p. 230.

8.   Hugh J. Lee, "Peary's Transections of North Greenland, 1892–1895," *Proceedings of the American Philosophical Society* 82 (June 1940): 929.

9.   Peary's comment upon reaching Cape Morris Jesup was: "I felt my eyes rested at last upon the Arctic Ultima Thule" (Mirsky, p. 232).

10.   Mirsky, p. 230. In 1913 Rasmussen and Freuchen pointed out that Peary Land is a part of Greenland, not an island.

11.   According to Minister to Denmark John E. Risley, he had a conversation with Danish Foreign Minister Vedel in which the latter observed (p. 203) that "the inhabitants of Greenland [Eskimos] were not sufficiently advanced in civilization to make it safe to be brought into contact with people or excursions from other lands." See *FRUS, 1894* (1895).

12.   Philip E. Mosely, "Iceland and Greenland: An American Problem," *Foreign Affairs* 18 (July 1940): 744.

13.   The 1931 Cramer-Paquette flight was sponsored by Transamerican Airlines.

14.   Lt. Col. Joseph Bush, *Strategic Value of Greenland to the Army Air Forces,* thesis, Air University, May 1947, Maxwell Air Force Base, Montgomery, Ala., p. 13.

15.   Russell Owen, "Antarctic Radio 'Speaks' Greenland," *New York Times,* May 8, 1929, p. 2. This article points out that ". . . it is one of the peculiarities of radio that at a point nearly half way around the world from us the signals concentrate or come together as they travel on many paths around the globe and, as they meet, they become stronger."

16.   *Congressional Record,* 76th Congress, 3rd Session, vol. 86, pt. 15, May 27 (legislative day of Wednesday, April 24), 1940, p. 3255.

17.   Basil Rauch, *Roosevelt: From Munich to Pearl Harbor* (New York: Creative Age Press, 1950), p. 196.

18.   The U.S. Coast Guard cutter which carried Penfield to his port also brought along supplies for the inhabitants.

19.   Yet Henrik de Kauffmann had informed Undersecretary of State Sumner Welles on April 15 that "the people in Greenland had stacks of food supplies sufficient to last for at least 2 years." *FRUS, 1940* 2 (1957): 355.

20.   William L. Langer and S. Everett Gleason, *The Challenge to Isolation, 1937-1940* (New York: Harper and Brothers, 1952), published for the Council on Foreign Relations, p. 687.

21.   At this time there was formal censorship of mail in Bermuda, leading to friction between American and British authorities.

22.   Charles A. Beard, *President Roosevelt and the Coming of the War, 1941* (New Haven: Yale University Press, 1948), p. 16.

23.   John B. Ocheltree, report, "Relations of the United States Armed Forces in Greenland with the Native Population," Godthaab, November 2, 1943, NARG 59, decimal file 859B.20/149, p. 6.

24.   John A. Logan summarizes the agreement as giving ". . . the United States the right to construct, maintain, and operate such landing fields, seaplane facilities, and radio and meteorological installations as were necessary to protect Danish sovereignty and to prevent the strategic lodgment of a non-American aggressor in Greenland. . ." (*No Transfer: An American Security Principle* [New Haven: Yale University Press, 1961], p. 350).

25.   At the time of the signing of the agreement, the Nazis were attempting to control the Danish government through their diplomatic representative Dr. Cecil von Renthe-Fink.

26.   Herbert W. Briggs, "The Validity of the Greenland Agreement," *American Journal of International Law* 25 (July 1941): 510-11.

27.   This was no far-fetched analogy. The Japanese ambassador himself raised the parallel with Hull in a conversation which took place during this period.

28.   Cordell Hull to Frank Knox, Washington, April 28, 1941, file no. EF22-2, Navy Yard, Washington. Hull added: "You will be interested to know that the German propaganda has already made much of the assertion that the contact of Greenlanders with Americans will result in the enslavement, miscegenation, and ultimate extinction of the native population."

29.   William L. Langer and S. Everett Gleason, *The Undeclared War, 1940-1941* (New York: Harper and Brothers, 1953), published for the Council on Foreign Relations, p. 430.

30.   One official had charged that U.S. authorities had refused to pay funds cabled from Denmark to America unless he and other Danish officials received orders to leave the U.S.

31.   "The Greenland Ice Plateau," *Air University Quarterly Review* 7 (spring 1955): 80-83. This staff brief concluded that "the trials of the Ice Cap Detachment were sufficient to indicate that no stable inland sites could be organized, supplied, and maintained if their connecting link with the coast was to be on the surface and over the rough ice area" (p. 82).

32.   Most of these "incidents" were of minor significance compared to some which occurred in Iceland during World War 2, but one must remember that under normal circumstances Greenland did not employ a large police force.

33. Randolph also recommended that the United States acquire the Atlantic and Pacific islands of England and France.

34. The Sabine Island base had been set up by the Germans in August 1942.

35. Unlike Fabyanic, Morison tends to emphasize the importance of the airfields.

36. Bernt Balchen and Corey Ford, "War below Zero," *Reader's Digest* 44 (May 1944): 66.

37. Arvid G. Holm, "Transmitting Translation of Article on American Activities in Greenland," Godthaab, January 18, 1946, cover letter plus p. 5, NARG 59, decimal file 711.59B/1-1846, p. 4.

38. James K. Penfield, "Greenland Turns to America," *National Geographic* 82 (September 1942): 383.

39. Another agreement dating from the same year established a consultative committee on Greenland defense projects.

40. Curiously, much of the area around Cape Morris Jesup is free from ice.

41. Charles J. Hubbard, "Should Greenland Be American?" *Collier's* 116 (November 10, 1945): 16f.

42. That fall Rasmussen denied the existence of any Communist pressure, pointing out that the Reds held only 18 of the 149 seats in the lower house of the Danish parliament, and 1 out of 78 seats in the upper house.

43. Cecil R. Roseberry, "Men against the Icecap," *Saturday Evening Post* 228 (April 7, 1956): 82.

44. The first U.S. weather station had been established at Thule in September 1946.

45. Bill Brinkley, "$1,500 a Month, No Place to Go," *Life* 33 (September 22, 1952): 140–51. Thus far civilian casualties had been limited to 2 deaths and 92 injuries, most of them minor; a doctor at the Thule hospital observed in this connection that Thule was "the healthiest place in the world."

46. Roseberry, pp. 82–84. There is a map of the route taken by members of Operation Southwind on p. 39.

47. "Fist Clench under Ice," *Time* 70 (September 16, 1957): 70–72. In this article the possibility of icecap missile bases is suggested.

48. Roseberry, p. 84.

49. It theoretically could have been shipped by air.

50. The deeper holes had to be filled with diesel oil, since otherwise the ice core samples would explode when the pressure existing at great depths was removed, and the ice sheet would flow together and close the hole.

51. Annual layering, however, is visible only down to 300 feet; below that level it is necessary to employ such devices as the carbon-14 test.

52. It would have been possible to raise the roof at Camp Century again but it also would have been necessary to undertake a costly overhaul of the reactor's nuclear fuel elements. From the overall standpoint, however, such bases were not as necessary now that Polaris submarines could operate beneath the polar icecap.

53. Austin Kovacs, *Camp Century Revisited: A Pictorial View, June 1969* (Hanover, N.H.: U.S. Army Cold Regions Research and Engineering Laboratory, 1970). To quote the abstract, "The effects of trench closure are dramatically shown" by the 96 photographs.

54. In contrast, at Palomares, Spain, hundreds of people were examined and tons of soil were removed in the aftermath of a similar incident.

55. William McC. Blair, Jr., to Edward Chester, Washington, May 3, 1972.

56. The Danish government is to receive no less than 80 percent of the profits in taxes and royalties from the 20 oil companies making up the 6 consortiums involved.

BIBLIOGRAPHICAL ESSAY

The 965 separate items on which this manuscript is based may be divided into five main categories: books and pamphlets, magazine and journal articles, newspapers, governmental publications, and archival materials. Of these five major groupings, the newspapers proved the most fruitful source of information, especially the *New York Times*. *The Times* of London was consulted for only the three British islands. But even in the case of Bermuda, Jamaica, and the Bahamas articles on U.S. relations appeared more frequently in the *New York Times;* nor were the stories which did reach publication in the London *Times* as comprehensive, generally speaking.

A wide variety of governmental publications were also consulted, including some rare items from the three British islands. As for the United States, there is a considerable amount of pertinent data in the State Department's *Foreign Relations of the United States* series, especially for the World War 2 years, and in the Commerce Department's *Foreign Economic Trends and Their Implications for the United States* series for the post-war era; but the *Congressional Record* is more valuable for the twentieth century as a whole. The most useful archival collection proved to be that at the National Archives in Washington, although the author also examined the collections at the Navy Yard there, at the Naval Aviation Office (Arlington, Virginia), and at the Air Force Historical Research Center (Montgomery, Alabama).

General works such as the several *Digest of International Law* series, *Treaties and Other International Agreements of the United States of America, 1776-1949,* the several *Treaties in Force* volumes, and

Historical Statistics of the United States: Colonial Times to 1957
proved of only limited value as points of departure. From the military standpoint, more has been written with respect to the United
States and these six islands for the eras of the American Revolution
and the Civil War than for those of the War of 1812 and World War
1. More material is available overall for the three British islands (especially Jamaica) than for the three non-British ones, with the data on
the Azores being the most fragmentary. Aside from the military aspects,
the economic factor has been the one most frequently analyzed.

Since it is the focal point of this volume, it is quite appropriate
that there are a number of works which examine various phases of
the establishment by the United States of military bases on these six
islands during World War 2. These include Samuel Eliot Morison's
multi-volume *History of United States Naval Operations in World
War 2* and Harold John Sutphen's 1967 Fletcher School of Law and
Diplomacy thesis, *The Anglo-American Destroyers-Bases Agreement,
September 1940,* as well as such comprehensive multi-author series
(all of which carry the imprint of the Government Printing Office
in Washington) as *The United States Army in World War 2; Pearl
Harbor to Guadalcanal: History of U.S. Marine Corps Operations
in World War 2;* and *Building the Navy's Bases in World War 2.*
Another multi-author series of importance (this one published by
the University of Chicago Press)—especially for Iceland and Greenland—
is *The Army Air Forces in World War 2.* Those seeking the diplomatic
background might turn to Cordell Hull's *Memoirs;* Charles Callan
Tansill's *Back Door to War: The Roosevelt Foreign Policy, 1933-
1941;* William L. Langer and S. Everett Gleason's *The Challenge to
Isolation, 1937-1940* and *The Undeclared War, 1940-1941;* and
Basil Rauch's *Roosevelt from Munich to Pearl Harbor.*

A wide variety of books and articles have been written dealing
with the British West Indies as a unit, or the Caribbean in general.
While such works as Paul Blanshard's *Democracy and Empire in the
Caribbean* have pertinent material on the World War 2 era, Chester
Lloyd Jones's *Caribbean Interests of the United States* is valuable
for the World War 1 period. For earlier decades, one might consult
J. Holland Rose, A. P. Newton, and E. A. Benians, *The Growth of
the New Empire, 1783-1870* for the years between the War of 1812
and the American Civil War; Wilbur H. Siebert, *The Legacy of the
American Revolution to the British West Indies and Bahamas* on
the activities of the Loyalists; and the multi-volume series by Lawrence

Henry Gipson, *The British Empire before the American Revolution*. Also of value are such commercial studies as Robert Greenhalgh Albion's *The Rise of New York Port, 1815–1860* and Bernard Bailyn's *The New England Merchants in the Seventeenth Century*.

More newspaper articles have been published by the *New York Times* on American relations with Jamaica than on any of the other five islands covered in this monograph, while *The Times* of London has carried as many stories on Jamaica as it has on Bermuda and the Bahamas combined. The *New York Times* coverage is as strong for the Gilded Age as it is for the twentieth century. In addition, the author has been furnished with a series of newspaper clippings from the Kingston *Daily Gleaner* for the years 1953–65. There also are some newspaper clippings from this publication in the diplomatic correspondence found in Record Group no. 59 at the National Archives; one likewise finds newspaper clippings there for the other five islands as well.

With respect to articles in magazines and journals, a number of items appeared at the time of the Swettenham incident of 1907, while many of the other articles have an economic focus. The leading historical and scholarly pieces include: David R. Bard and William J. Baker, "The American Newspaper Response to the Jamaican Riots of 1865" (*Journalism Quarterly,* winter 1974); Cedric L. Joseph, "The Strategic Importance of the British West Indies, 1882–1932" (*Journal of Caribbean History,* November 1973); Ransford W. Palmer, "A Decade of West Indian Migration to the United States, 1962–1972" (*Social and Economic Studies,* December 1974); James Duncan Phillips, "British Depredations in the West Indies" (Essex Institute *Historical Collections,* July 1942); George S. Sadler, "Wartime Utilization of Jamaicans in United States Industrial Establishments" (*Monthly Labor Review,* November 1945); and Mary Elizabeth Thomas, "Jamaica and the U.S. Civil War" (*Americas,* January 1972). There also is a contemporary article by George Crile on the controversial ambassador Vincent de Roulet in *Harper's* for October 1974.

One of the leading writers on present-day Jamaica is Wendell Bell of the sociology department of Yale University; along with various other studies he has written *Jamaican Leaders: Political Attitudes in a New Nation*. Economic studies of consequence include Gisela Eisner, *Jamaica, 1830–1930: A Study in Economic Growth,* and Lowell Joseph Ragatz, *The Fall of the Planter Class in the British Caribbean, 1763–1833*. More specialized is Charles Morrow Wilson, *Empire in Green and Gold: The Story of the American Banana Trade*. A general treatment is Peter Abrahams, *Jamaica: An Island Mosaic*. There are a number of references to Jamaica during its early years of independence in the

Congressional Record, with Adam Clayton Powell as that nation's leading spokesman. Diplomatic correspondence for the inter-war years in Record Group no. 59 at the National Archives periodically reports the anti-American sentiment in certain quarters. There also is published material in the *Foreign Relations* series for 1905 and 1907.

Aside from a few items for the late Gilded Age, the *New York Times*'s systematic coverage of American-Bermudian relations did not begin until after World War 1, with the articles since World War 2 focusing on the military base. While the magazine and journal articles quite frequently emphasize military topics, there also are some on oceanography as well. One might single out as outstanding among the historical and scholarly pieces: William Beebe, "Bermuda Oceanographic Expeditions" (*Zoologica,* April 1931); Thomas Melville Dill, "Bermuda and the War of 1812" (*Bermuda Historical Quarterly,* July-September 1944); S. W. Jackman, "Admiral Wilkes Visits Bermuda during the Civil War" (*American Neptune,* July 1964); A. E. Verrill, "Relations between Bermuda and the American Colonies during the Revolutionary War" (*Transactions of the Connecticut Academy of Arts and Science,* July 1907). Another interesting essay is John R. Tunis, "Bermuda and the American Idea" (*Harper's,* March 1930); a contemporary assessment is Frederick Lewis Allen, "Bermuda Base" (*Harper's,* September 1943).

There is a scattering of references to Bermuda in the *Congressional Record*, all but one of them from the twentieth century. Walter Hayward Brownell has written a general study of the island, *Bermuda: Past and Present,* as has Hudson Strode in his *The Story of Bermuda.* For the early years, see Henry C. Wilkinson, *Bermuda in the Old Empire.* More specialized military studies include Wilfred Brenton Kerr, *Bermuda and the American Revolution,* and Frank Vandiver, *Confederate Blockade Running through Bermuda, 1861–1865: Letters and Cargo Manifests.* A key unpublished monograph is David L. White's 1956 senior project at Bard College, *The Economic Impacts of America on Bermuda.* The inter-war years items in Record Group no. 59 at the National Archives cover a wide variety of topics, while the *Foreign Relations* volumes for 1862, 1863, 1864, 1865, and 1936 are especially pertinent.

The *New York Times* did not begin to publish articles regularly on American relations with the Bahamas—apart from several isolated pieces —before the end of World War 1. Over the years the majority of these items have had an economic orientation, with the military ones largely confined to the decade of the 1940s. There have been a number of magazine and journal articles since World War 2 focusing on the recent economic boom, which has been partly based on gambling. Among the more important historical and scholarly articles have been Vaughn A.

Lewis, "The Bahamas in International Politics" (*Journal of Interamerican Studies and World Affairs*, May 1974); Malcolm Lloyd, "The Taking of the Bahamas by the Continental Army in 1776" (*Pennsylvania Magazine of History*, October 1925); John J. McCusker, "The American Invasion of Nassau in the Bahamas" (*American Neptune*, July 1965). With an occasional isolated exception, references to the United States and the Bahamas did not begin to appear in the *Congressional Record* until the decade of the 1960s.

At least two of the most useful books on the islands are not readily accessible: A. Talbot Bethell's *The Early Settlers of the Bahama Islands with a Brief Account of the American Revolution,* and Zoé C. Durrell's *The Innocent Island: Abaco in the Bahamas.* Two pertinent doctoral dissertations are Frank Tousley Edwards, *The United States Consular Service in the Bahamas during the American Civil War* (Catholic University of America, 1968) and Thelma Peterson Peters, *The American Loyalists and the Plantation Period in the Bahamas Islands* (University of Florida, 1960). Of unusual interest is a series of letters for the decade of the 1920s in Record Group no. 59 at the National Archives dealing with the lucrative illegal traffic in alcoholic beverages which went on between the Bahamas and the United States. The *Foreign Relations* volumes for 1926 and 1932 also contain material of significance.

Perhaps the best starting place for those interested in Greenland and Iceland is Franklin Scott, *The United States and Scandinavia.* Two significant articles, both dating from 1940, are Brainerd Dyer, "Robert J. Walker on Acquiring Greenland and Iceland" (*Mississippi Valley Historical Review*, September) and Philip E. Mosely, "Iceland and Greenland: An American Problem" (*Foreign Affairs*, July). Then three years later the Smithsonian Institute published Austin H. Clark's monograph *Iceland and Greenland.*

As for Iceland alone, magazine and journal articles dealing with this country break down into three main categories: military, economic, and immigration. One might cite as being of especial interest Lyman Burbank, "Problems of NATO Diplomacy: Fish and an Air Base in Iceland," (*South Atlantic Quarterly*, spring 1959); Sólrun B. Jensdóttir, "The 'Republic of Iceland,' 1940–44: Anglo-American Attitudes and Influences" (*Journal of Contemporary History*, October 1974); Clifton Lisle, "Hark Back: The Iceland Occupation" (*General Magazine and Historical Chronicle*, autumn 1948); and John L. Zimmerman, "A Note on the Occupation of Iceland by American Forces" (*Political Science Quarterly*, March 1947). A unique perspective is provided by the murdered Nazi leader George Lincoln Rockwell in his "No Wonder Iceland

Hates Us" (*American Mercury,* January 1957). Aside from a few earlier items, references to Iceland did not begin to appear in the *Congressional Record* until the Hoover administration.

The bulk of the archival material on Iceland in Record Group no. 59 at the National Archives deals with the World War 2 period, and features a long list of complaints about the behavior of American soldiers there. There also is a great deal of information in the *Foreign Relations* volumes for the years 1940 through 1944. Unquestionably, the best book in English on American relations with Iceland is Donald E. Nuechterlein's *Iceland: Reluctant Ally,* which ties these in with the complex multi-party system and coalition government of the island. Other key monographs include William Charles Chamberlain, *Economic Development of Iceland through World War 2;* Agnes Rothery, *Iceland: New World Outpost;* Vilhjalmur Stefansson, *Iceland: The First American Republic;* and Thorstina Walters, *Modern Sagas: The Story of the Icelanders in North America.*

Magazine and journal articles published on Greenland prior to World War 2 almost invariably stressed the scientific exploration of the island, while those dealing with military activities from World War 2 on also frequently touch upon this topic. Some of the leading pieces on Greenland are: Robert A. Bartlett, "Greenland from 1898 to Now" (*National Geographic Magazine,* July 1940); Herbert W. Briggs, "The Validity of the Greenland Agreement" (*American Journal of International Law,* July 1941); Erik J. Friis, "Standing Guard in Greenland" (*American Scandinavian Review,* September 1960); William Herbert Hobbs, "The Early Attempted Flights to Europe over Greenland" (*Proceedings of the U.S. Naval Institute,* January 1949); Hugh J. Lee, "Peary's Transections of North Greenland, 1892-1895" (*Proceedings of the American Philosophical Society,* June 1940); and Hans W. Weigert, "Iceland, Greenland and the United States" (*Foreign Affairs,* October 1944). The handful of articles on Greenland published in the *New York Times* prior to World War 2 focused on cryolite, while the bulk of the items from 1941 on dealt either with the military bases or the scientific activities of the American military.

Greenland has fared poorly in the *Congressional Record* from the standpoint of citation, with the handful of items concentrated around the time of the outbreak of World War 2. Prior to that conflict the Smithsonian Institution published a series of articles by Robert A. Bartlett on his expeditions to Greenland in its annual *Explorations and Field-Work* series. Several post-war reports on the scientific activities of the U.S. Army there are quite worthwhile, but were not distributed widely. Books in English on Greenland are not common, and Knud

Hertling's *Greenland: Past and Present* was published in Copenhagen. Thomas A. Fabyanic did produce a M.A. thesis at St. Louis University in 1966 entitled *Shield against Aggression: Greenland, 1940-1945.* There are a few items in Record Group no. 59 at the National Archives dealing with contacts (which were of course discouraged) between the American military and the local inhabitants, while the *Foreign Relations* series has material, not only for the wartime years 1940, 1941, and 1945, but for 1894, 1895, and 1917 as well.

Regular coverage of the Azores in the *New York Times* dates from World War 2, although there also are several items from the World War 1 period. The bulk of these articles focus on the military bases there. Surprisingly, one finds little, if anything, on the Azores in the *Congressional Record* until the years 1958-64, at which time such New England senators as Edward Kennedy and John Pastore began to call for American assistance to the victims of the Azorean earthquakes and volcanic disturbances, and for their entry into the United States. As for magazine and journal articles, these cover a variety of topics in addition to the military. Among the key historical and scholarly pieces are Robert Clarke, "Open Boat Whaling in the Azores" (*Discovery Reports,* February 1954); Arminius T. Haeberle, "The Azores: Picturesque Half-way House of American Transatlantic Navigators" (*National Geographic Magazine,* May 1919); Augustus E. Ingram, "Early Consular Days in the Azores" (*Foreign Service Journal,* 1936); Seward W. Livermore, "The Azores in American Strategy-Diplomacy, 1917-1919" (*Journal of Modern History,* September 1948); C. M. Robinett, "Guns, Diplomacy, and Litigation" (*Proceedings of the U.S. Naval Institute,* November 1950), and T. W. Sheridan, "The American Marine Thermopylae" (*Proceedings of the U.S. Naval Institute,* April 1937). Emily Hahn also wrote a three-part series on the Azores for the *New Yorker* in 1959, but these pieces tend to be fragmentary and impressionistic.

The historical scholar today who probably is the most interested in the Azores—especially for the World War 2 period—is Professor J. K. Sweeney of South Dakota State University, who during the decade of the 1970s began to produce a series of convention papers and scholarly articles on this topic. Unfortunately, one does not find many books on the United States and the Azores, although there are such highly specialized monographs as Leo Pap's *Portuguese-American Speech* and Francis M. Rogers's *The Portuguese Heritage of John Dos Passos.* Record Group no. 59 at the National Archives yields almost nothing of value on the Azores, although there is an assessment by W. G. Tomlinson of American military activities in the islands during 1944 in the Command File World War 2 at the Navy Yard. Nevertheless, the *Foreign Relations* volumes for the years 1941 through 1947 do have a considerable amount of data on the United States and the Azores, as do those for the years 1876 and 1901.

Those readers seeking a complete bibliography of the 965 items employed in the preparation of this manuscript—not all of which have been discussed above, may obtain these from the author. But as has been pointed out several times in this discussion, a number of these items are not readily accessible, should the reader care to inspect them personally himself or herself. This is especially true of those items which were published abroad, but this generalization also applies to some of the American items as well.

INDEX

A. & P., 39
ABC-1 Staff Agreement, 128,167
Acheson, Dean, 177
Adams, Charles Francis, 21, 96
Adderly, Abraham, 18
Admiralty Court, 90
A.F.L.-C.I.O., 75
Agency for International Development,
    77, 78
Agriculture Department, 80
Air Jamaica, 83
Air Transport Agreement of 1969
    (Jamaica), 83
Air Transport Command, 111, 171
Alabama, 53, 158
Allen, Charles, 95, 97, 234, 236
Allies, 31, 132, 138, 171
Alumina Jamaica, 74
Aluminum Corporation of America
    75, 80, 84
American Airlines, 173
American Claims Board 239
American Overseas Airlines, 145
American Red Cross, 194
"American Red Cross Society
    Resolve", 104
Anaconda Company, 80
Anslinger, Harry, 25
ARCO, 214
Armed Forces Radio and Television
    Service, 152
Armstrong, George, 232
Army Audit Bureau, 210
Army Corps of Engineers, 210, 212

Army Transarctic Group, 211
Army Transportation Arctic Group
    211, 212
Army Transportation Corps, 211
Army Transportation Environmental
    Operations Group, 211
Army War Plans Division, 166
Asgeirsson, Asgeir, 140, 141, 147, 149,
    150, 152
Atlantic Fleet, 5
Atlantic Fruit Company, 63, 68
Atlantic Underwater Test and
    Evaluation Center, 36, 223
Atlas Steamship Lines, 230
Axis, 111, 112, 131, 138, 241
Azores Common Defense Pact, 176, 177

Bahamas Agricultural Industries, 41
Bahamas Development Board, 31
Bahamas Government Indus. Estates, 42
Bahamian Club, 41
Baker, Captain, 92
Balchen, Bernt, 200, 202, 204, 209
Ballistic Missile Early Warning System,
    214
BARTAD, 46
Base Lease Agreement, 12, 13
Base Lease Commission, 11
Bay Street Oligarchy, 33, 34, 41, 46
Bayley, C. J., 21
Beaverbrook, Lord, 9
Belmont Manor Hotel, 106
Benediktsson, Bjarni, 152
Benguet, 38

Berle, Adolf A., 127, 197, 203
Bermuda Chamber of Commerce, 107, 112
Bermuda Clipper, 106
Bermuda Labor Board, 112
Bermuda Railway 116, 224
Bermudian Hotel, 116
Bernbaum, Maurice, 78
Bethlehem Steel Corporation, 38
Björnsson, Sveinn, 137, 138, 139, 140
Blackburn, Luke, 97
Blair, William McC., 213
Bluie East 2, 201, 207
Bluie West 1, 200
Bluie West 8, 200, 208
Board of Trade, 105
Bonbright, James, 176
Bonesteel, C. H., 132, 135
Boston Fruit Company, 55, 57, 58, 59, 63
Boston Trust Company, 59
Bourne, Colonial Secretary, 60
Bowles, Chester, 76
Braisted, Frank A., 113
British Overseas Airways, 42
Brown, William, 91
Browne, Montfort, 16, 17, 228
Brownson, L. E., 111
Bruere, George, 87, 88, 89, 91
Brun, Carl, 203
Brun, Eske, 195, 196, 198, 201, 203, 204, 205, 206, 208
Burgley, Lord, 113, 236
Bustamente, Alexander, 67, 72, 76, 78
Butler, Chargé, 11
Byrd, Richard, 191, 200
Byrnes, James, 145, 207

Camp Century, 212, 213, 245
Camp Knox, 132
Camp Lloyd, 192
Camp Scott, 192
Camp Tuto, 212
Canadian-American Trade Agreement, 105
Canaris, Wilhelm, 126
CARE, 182
Caribbean Airways, 65
Carneiro, Costa, 170
Castle Harbour Hotel, 116
Censorship Board, 163
Central Intelligence Agency, 83, 183
Century Group, 8
Cerchione, Angelo, 180, 242
Cessna Skywagon Aircraft, 77
Chamberlain, Joseph, 57, 99
Chevrolet, 143

Chevron, 214
Christiansen, Laurence, 26
Churchill, Winston, 7, 8, 9, 116, 127, 129, 131, 153, 167, 168, 169, 171 227
Citizens and Southern (Atlanta), 82
Clay, James, 157
Clayton, John 157
Coast and Geodetic Survey, 229
Coca Cola, 238
"Coca-colization", 219, 225
Colasurdo, Lewis, 40
Commerce Department, 125
Committee on Military Affairs (Senate), 106
Committee on Naval Affairs (House), 113
Committee to Defend America by Aiding the Allies, 8, 167
Commonwealth Sugar Agreement, 75
Communists, ix, 73, 131, 137, 138, 140, 141, 146, 147, 149, 151, 182, 207, 217, 238, 240, 245
ComNavZor, 173, 175
Confederacy, 20, 21, 22, 53, 95, 96, 97, 158
Continental Congress, 49, 88, 89, 90, 233
Continental Illinois, 82
Coote, Eyre, 51
Corcoran, William, 6
Countinho, Governor, 183
Creevey, E. A., 160, 164, 241
Crescent Corporation, 40
Crosby Brothers, 37, 40
Crucible Steel Company, 38
Cruft, Edward, 122
Cumming, Hugh, 195
Cunard, Samuel, 28
Cunha, Paulo, 176

Dabney, Charles, 157, 158
Dabney, John Bass, 155, 156, 159
Dabney, Samuel, 159
Dabneys, 240
Daniels, Josephus, 161
Danish-American Agreement of 1951, 209
Darling, Charles, 53
Davis, C.H., 60, 61, 221, 231
D-Day invasion, 204
DD-DE Shakedown Task Force, 111, 113
Deane, Silas, 89, 234
Debs, Eugene, 106
Decatur, Stephen, 93, 94
Defense Areas Agreement, 13
Delafield Industries, 41

Delta Air Lines, 83
Denham, Edward, 66
Department of Tourist and Trade Development, 236
Destroyers-for-bases deal, 8, 13, 31, 110
Deveaux, Andrew, 18
Development Finance Corporation (Jamaican), 77
Dewey, Thomas, 107
Dill, Thomas, 93
Dingley Tariff, 57, 99
Distant Early Warning Line, 214
Division of Western European Affairs, 124, 126, 195
Doherty, William, 76, 77, 79
Dreyfus, Louis, 137, 238
Duke of Windsor, 31, 32, 33, 34
Dulles, John Foster, 149
Dunn, Herbert, 162, 163
Dunn, James Clement, 194
Dye, John, 31

Eanes, Ramalho, 183
Eastern Airlines, 42
Eckford, Q. O., 56
Economic Investigation Committee, 34
Edward VII, 61
Egan, Maurice, 186, 243
Eisenhower, Dwight, 116, 142, 146, 149, 150, 176, 180, 204, 240
Elder-Dempster Combine, 57
Erickson, A. W. 28, 38
Esso, 81, 82
Ewert, Colonel, 70
Export-Import Bank, 42, 77, 78, 79, 240, 242
Eyre, Edward, 53, 54

Fair Labor Standards Act, 115
Farquharson, C. F., 56
Federal Loan Administration, 127
Finletter, Thomas, 209
First National Bank (Chicago), 82
First National City Bank (New York), 38, 82
Fish, Bert, 170, 172
Fisher, Fred, 27
"Fist Clench", 211
Flagler, Henry, 28
Florida East Coast Hotel Company, 24, 28
Florida East Coast Railway, 28
Ford, 143
Foreign Claims Act, 150
Foreign Relations Committee

(Senate) 166, 179
Foreign Relations Subcommittee on Multinational Corporations (Senate), 79
Foreign Service, 79
Forrestal, James, 145
Fort Bell, 110, 113
Fort Cunningham, 96
Fort Fisher, 97
Fort Montagu Hotel, 29
Fort Simonds, 70, 71
"Forty Thieves", 108
Foskett, H. K., 236
Francis, Carlton, 44
Frazier, Raymond, 123
Fruit Trading Association, 57
Fulbright Act, 150
Furness-Bermuda Line, 106, 235

G.I.'s 138, 222
Gallery, Daniel, 139
General Armstrong, 156, 157, 159
General Board, 5
General Cigar, 82
General Electric, 82
General Foods, 34, 35
Gibbons, Morris, 112
Glaze, Thomas, 136
Goldberg, Arthur, 76, 81
Goodrich, Mr., 91
Goodwin, David, 33
Goodyear Company, 82
Göring, Herman, 128
Gould, James, 16
Grand Bahama Port Authority, 37
Great Abaco Highway, 41
Great Depression of 1929, 68, 103, 217
Greeley, Horace, 53
Greene, W. Maxwell, 101
Greenslade, John, 10, 110
Grey, Edward, 61
Groth, Edward, 125
Groves, Wallace, 37, 38, 39, 41
Gulf Oil, 38, 214

Hackworth, Green, 8, 9
Halifax, Lord, 129, 168
Hamburg-American Steamship Company, 63
Harris, Captain, 22
Hartford, Huntington, 37, 39, 40, 41
Hawley, Seth, 21
Hawley-Smoot Act, 103, 108, 220
Hickling, Thomas, 155, 159, 160, 163
Hickling, Jr., Thomas, 158
Hilton Hotel Corporation, 116, 224

Hitler, Adolf, 8, 166, 168, 193, 198, 203, 227
Hocking, H. H., 56
Hoover, Admiral, 70
Hoover, Herbert, 104, 124
Hopkins, Esek, 16, 17, 228
Hopkins, Harry, 128, 129, 136, 197, 238
Howard, Esmé, 60
Huff Enterprises, 43
Huggins, E. V., 210
Hughes, Admiral, 103
Hughes, Charles Evans, 106, 190
Hughes, Howard, 45
Hull, Cordell, 9, 11, 31, 126, 127, 128, 129, 132, 133, 134, 167, 168, 169 170, 172, 173, 174, 194, 195, 199, 228, 238, 241, 244

Iceland Bank of Development, 240
Iceland Defense Force, 146
Iceland Purchasing Commission, 134
Icelandic Steamship Company, 123
Ikateq Air Base, 207
Independent Norwegian Company, 132
Industrial Encouragement Act, 38
Inter-American Treaty of Reciprocal Assistance, 146, 207
International Bank for Reconstruction and Development, 72
International Bauxite Association, 81
International Business Machines, 82
International Center for Settlement of Investment Disputes, 81
International Telephone and Telegraph, 82
Ivens, Thomas, 158
Ivigtut Mine Company, 196

Jackson, Robert, 9, 10, 47, 115
Jamaica Banana Producers' Association 68, 69
Jamaica Development Bank, 78
Jamaica Public Service Corporation, 82
Jamaican Consolidated Copper Company, 68, 221
James, Commandant, 111, 236
Jewell, John, 160
Jóhannesson, Olafur, 152
Johnson and Johnson, 82
Johnson, Lyndon, 76, 78, 141, 150, 152, 210, 240
Johnson, U. Alexis, 179, 242
Joint Chiefs of Staff, 168, 172, 242
Jonásson, Herman, 129, 130, 135, 136, 148, 149, 239
Jones, Arthur, 115

Jones, Jesse, 127
Justice Department, 45, 115

Kaiser Aluminum and Chemical Corporation, 74, 80, 224
Kaiser Bauxite Company, 81
Kammerlocker, Anton, 180
Kasson, John, 57
Kauffman, Henrik de, 194, 195, 197, 198, 199, 244
Keith, Minor, 54, 57, 58
Kennan, George, 172
Kennedy, John, 37, 76, 78, 150, 182
Kilgarif, Lt. Colonel, 135
Kindley Field, 110, 114, 117, 223, 236
King, Ernest, 128, 129, 173
King, Henry, 93
King, Jr., Martin Luther, 78
Knollys, Lord, 111
Knox, Frank, 111, 129, 199
Kryolith Mine-og Handelsselskabet, 187
Kuhn, Loeb and Company, 73
Kuniholm, Bartel, 128

Lafayette, Marquis de, 90
Lajes Field, 171, 172, 173, 174, 176, 177, 178, 179, 180, 181, 242
Lansing, Robert, 163, 190
Latham, Charles, 231
Lathrop, Loren, 24, 25
L. D. Baker Company, 55
Lee, Robert E., 97
Livingston, Robert, 91
Lodge, Henry Cabot, 4, 5, 23, 59, 186, 220
"Log Conference", 103
Lopez, Aaron, 49
"Loran", 77
Lothian, Lord, 8, 11, 194
Loyalists, 17, 18, 19, 20, 23, 46, 49, 50, 90, 91, 221, 228, 229
Ludwig, Daniel, 38
Lyons, Lord, 21

Mac Donald, Ramsay, 103
Macmillan, Harold, 36, 37, 116
MacVeagh, Lincoln, 128, 132, 135, 136
Malcolm, Michael, 18
Manley, Norman, 67, 69, 71, 72, 73, 75, 76, 79
Mary Carter Paint, 41
Mason, James, 96
Mastriana, Louis, 44, 45, 230
Maxwell Air Force Base, 232

McAdoo, William Gibbs, 6, 106
McClellan, George, 5
McDonough Construction Company, 114
McKinley Tariff, 55, 56, 98, 99, 234
McLaney, Mike, 44, 45, 230
Meeks, Field, 133
Merritt-Chapman and Scott
  Corporation, 114
Mid-Ocean Club, 116, 224
Military Airlift Command, 111
Mint Julep, 201
Mitchell, John, 45
Moffat, Jay, 124, 126
Monroe Doctrine, 3, 5, 127, 131, 186,
  194, 197, 216
Morton Salt Company, 38
Munson Interests, 29, 220
Murphy Oil, 214
Murray, George, 92
Mutual Security Agency, 144

National Defense Act, 8
National Workers Union, 75
Navy Department, 22, 70, 112, 161
  162, 195
New York West India Improvement
  Company, 59
Niblack, A.P., 5
96th Construction Batallion, 173
9th Construction Batallion, 133
Nixon, Richard, 45, 78, 149, 179, 240
North Atlantic Council, 149
North Atlantic Treaty Organization,
  146, 149, 176, 177, 209
Northeast Airlines, 42
Norweb, Raymond, 173, 174, 242
Nugent, Lieutenant Governor, 51

Oakes, Field, 35
Oakes, Harry, 27
Ocheltree, John, 201
Olafsson, Bjorn, 238
Old Colonial Hotel, 28
Oliver, George, 159
Operation Blue Jay, 209, 210
Operation King Dog, 212
Operation Lead Dog, 211
Operation Nord, 209
Operation Parkway, 209
Operation Southwind, 211, 245
Order in Council (1812), 50, 93
Outboard Marine Corporation, 38
Owens-Illinois Glass Company, 37, 38,
  41, 43, 46

P-3 Orion aircraft, 117

Pacific Mail Steam Ship Company, 58
Pan American Airways, 11, 29, 40, 42,
  65, 66, 83, 109, 116, 125, 154, 171,
  173, 174, 175, 222, 224
Patricio, Rui, 179
Patterson Field, 132, 133
Paulsen, Carl C. von, 202
Payne-Aldrich Tariff, 99
Peace Corps, 76, 77, 79
Pell, Herbert, 165
Penfield, James, 195, 196, 198, 205
Peninsular Life Insurance Company, 38
Pennsylvania Salt Manufacturing
  Company, 187
"People-to-People" program, 180
Perkins, Chargé, 198, 200
Pick, Lewis, 210
Pinder, George, 26
Pindling, Lynden, 39, 40, 41, 43, 44, 45,
  46, 47
Pittman-Bloom Joint Resolution, 197
Polaris Submarines, 245
Polk, Frank, 190
Popple, William, 87
Port Authority, 38
Powell, Adam Clayton, 43, 76, 152
Precision Valve Corporation, 42
Preparedness Investigating Committee
  (Senate), 210
Preston, Andrew, 54, 55
Prince of Wales, 6, 30, 103
Princess Hotel, 105
Pritchard, Albert, 151, 240
Pritchard, William, 18
Prohibition, 24, 27, 227
Project Eastwind, 211
Project Mint Julep, 211
Project Snowman, 201, 208, 211
Public Law 480 (Title IV), 143, 240

Quebec Steamship Company, 98, 100,
  101, 235

R. & T. Electronics Corporation, 116,
  224
Raeder, Erich, 128, 166
Randolph, Midshipman, 94, 234
Rasmussen, Gustav, 207, 208, 245
Reed, Harry, 210
Reed, Samuel, 156, 159
Reid, William, 95
Resorts International, 40, 41
Reuter, General von, 162
Reynolds Jamaica Mines, 74, 81, 224
Reynolds Metal Company 80

Risley, John, 243
Rockefeller, Laurance, 39
Rogers, William, 152, 179
"Rolyat", 65, 221, 232
Roosevelt, Elliot, 44, 45, 200, 230
Roosevelt, Franklin, 7, 8, 10, 32, 33, 71,
   110, 128, 129, 130, 131, 132, 136, 161,
   162, 164, 165, 166, 168, 169, 170, 171,
   172, 174, 194, 196, 197, 198, 200, 202,
   227, 229, 237, 238, 239, 241
Roosevelt, Theodore, 4, 5, 61, 122, 156,
   186, 221
Roulet, Vincent de, 79, 80, 84, 223,
Royal Air Force, 36, 174
Royal Greenland Trading Company, 206
Royal Mail Steam Packet Company, 63,
   101
Royal Victoria Hotel, 20, 28
Rusk, Dean, 178
Russell, John, 21

St. George Hotel, 116
Salazar, António de Oliveira, 166, 167,
   168, 169, 171, 172, 173, 174, 178,
   182, 183, 223, 241
Scavenius, Eric, 198
Seabees, 32, 133, 173
Seabulk International, 42
Seaverns and Company, 54
Securities and Exchange Commission 40,
   45, 73
Sedwick, Robert, 49
Semnes, Rafael, 53
Seward, William Henry, 3, 21, 122, 185,
   220
Silva, Samuel, 159
Sims, William, 162
Singer Manufacturing Company, 231
Sinton, William, 197
Six M's, 40
Sixth Cavalry Regiment, 33
Slidell, John, 96
Slocum, Joshua, 159
Smale, William, 25
Smith, A. D., 202
Smith, Edward (Bermuda), 89
Smith, Edward (Greenland), 202
Snyder, Nicholas, 60
Sondestrom Air Base, 208, 209
South Greenland Survey Party, 197
Sowell, Ingram, 112
Squire, Paul, 65, 69
Standard Oil Company of California, 38
Standard Oil Company of New Jersey, 1
   123
Stark, Harold, 129, 131, 168, 241

State Department, 8, 9, 22, 101, 104,
   115, 117, 127, 145, 153, 156, 157,
   162, 163, 165, 177, 183, 186, 190,
   194, 195, 196, 217, 235, 240
Stefánsson, Stefán, 128, 131
Stennett, Martinius, 138
Stimson, Henry, 104, 129, 131, 169,
   172
Storr, John, 19
Street, John, 155
Strong, Alden, 112
Svane, Askel, 195, 196, 198, 199
Swan, 97
Swettenham, Alexander, 60, 61, 62,
   221, 231
Sykes, Robert, 208

Tabb, Johnny, 234
Tariff Amendment Act, 25
Tariff Commission, 142, 149, 239
Tariff Conference Committee, 64
Task Force 4998-A, 201
Taylor, Allan, 65
Taylor, Myron, 169
Texaco, 82
Thor, Vilhjalmur, 127
Thórs, Olafur, 136, 137, 145
Thórs, Thór, 128, 133, 134
Tobriner, Walter, 83, 233
"Tommies", 138
Tourist Bureau, 68
Tower, Chargé, 57
Townsend, Captain, 51
Trade and Development Board, 112
Trade Centre, 70
Trades Union Council, 71
Trans World Airlines, 173, 181
Transamerican Airlines, 243
Transportes Aeroes Portugueses, 181
Trenchard, S. D., 21
Truman, Harry, 116, 145
Tucker, Henry (18th Century), 88, 89
Tucker, St. George, 91

Underwood-Simmons Tariff, 99
Union Carbide, 143
United Fruit Company, 28, 58, 63, 64,
   67, 68, 69, 80, 220
U. S. Steel Corporation, 38, 41
United Steel Workers of America, 75

V-E Day, 113
Vargas, Getúlio, 171
Vaudreuil, Admiral, 91
Vaughn, Jack, 77

Vedel, Foreign Minister, 243
Vernam Naval Air Station, 70
Vesco, Robert, 45, 46, 230
Virginia Company, 85

Walker, Norman, 95
Walker, Robert, 122, 185
Wallace, Henry, 145, 239
War Department, 4, 70, 71, 100, 132
War Shipping Administration, 134
Ward Steamship Line, 28
Warner, Chargé, 136
Washington, George, 45, 88, 89, 91, 93, 228
Waterloo Hotel Company, 29
Webster, Daniel, 157
Wedderburn, Deputy Inspector General, 60

Welles, Sumner, 11, 129, 168, 194, 241, 244
Wenner-Gren, Axel, 34, 39
West, George, 195
Whirlpool Corporation, 38
White, Ivan, 76
Wilde, John de, 73
Wilkes, Charles, 96
Williamson, Harold, 108
Wilson-Goode, J. L., 67, 68
Wilson-Gorman Tariff, 56, 99
Wilson, Woodrow, 64, 101, 102, 106, 190, 238
Winant, John, 11, 12, 167, 173
Woodring, Harry, 193

Xanadu Princess Hotel, 45